The Future of the Past

THE FUTURE OF THE PAST

ARCHAEOLOGISTS, NATIVE AMERICANS, AND REPATRIATION

edited by

TAMARA L. BRAY

Garland Publishing
New York & London

Published in 2001 by
Garland Publishing, Inc.
29 West 35th Street
New York, NY 10001

Published in Great Britain by
Garland Publishing, Inc.
11 New Fetter Lane
London EC4P 4EE

Garland is an imprint of the Taylor & Francis Group.

Printed in the United States of America on acid-free paper.

10 9 8 7 6 5 4 3 2 1

*Library of Congress Cataloging-in-Publication Data is available from the
Library of Congress.*

Bray, Tamara L.
The future of the past : archaeologists, Native Americans,
          and repatriation / edited by Tamara L. Bray
ISBN: 0-8153-3834-1
Includes bibliography and references.

This book is dedicated to Ed Ladd, whose gentle approach to the work of repatriation helped build bridges of understanding.

Contents

Contributors

Lisa M. Anderson is the coordinator for compliance with the Native American Graves Protection and Repatriation Act at the New York State Museum. She is also a Ph.D. candidate in Anthropology at the State University of New York at Albany.

Brenda J. Baker is Assistant Professor of Anthropology at Arizona State University. She received her Ph.D. from the University of Massachusetts, Amherst in 1992 and directed the NAGPRA program at the New York State Museum from 1994 to 1998. Her research interests focus on bioarchaeology, human osteology and paleopathology in North America and Egypt.

Tamara L. Bray is Assistant Professor of Anthropology at Wayne State University. She received her Ph.D. from the State University of New York at Binghamton. Between 1991 and 1995, she worked in the Office of Repatriation at the Smithsonian Institution's National Museum of Natural History. She is co-editor of the volume *Reckoning With the Dead* (1994) and author of several articles on the subject of repatriation.

Phillip E. Cash Cash (Cayuse, Nez Perce) has had extensive experience working in the Native community in the areas of anthropology, repatriation and cultural linguistics. He recently earned his M.A. from the American Indian Studies program at the University of Arizona and plans to continue his graduate studies in the area of linguistics, focusing on the endangered languages of the Columbia Plateau region.

Walter R. Echo-Hawk, is a Senior Staff Attorney for the Native American Rights Fund in Boulder, Colorado. He holds a political science degree from Oklahoma State University and a law degree from the University of New Mexico. He helped to lead the campaign to obtain passage of the Native American Graves Protection and Repatriation Act. Among his publications is the award-winning book *Battlefields and Burial Grounds* (1994).

Christina E. Garza obtained her M.A. in Anthropology with a Concentration in Applied Archaeology from Northern Arizona University. She is currently an Applications Specialist in the Computer Support section of Arizona State Parks.

Ronald L. Grimes is Professor of Religion and Culture at Wilfrid Laurier University in Waterloo, Ontario, Canada. He is a founding editor of the *Journal of Ritual Studies* and the *Ritual Studies Group of the American Academy of Religion*. He is also the author of several books including *Marrying & Burying: Rites of Passage in a Man's Life*; *Readings in Ritual Studies*; and *Deeply into the Bone: Re-Inventing Rites of Passage*.

Jonathan Haas is Curator of North American Archaeology at the Field Museum in Chicago. He received his B.A. from the University of Arizona in 1970, and his doctorate from Columbia University in 1979. He has conducted over 30 years of archaeological field work in both North and South America. He served on the initial NAGPRA Review Committee and has written extensively about repatriation matters in a museum context. Among his recent publications are *"The Origins of War and Ethnic Violence"* and *"Power, Objects, and a Voice for Anthropology."*

Richard W. Hill, Sr., is the former Director of the North American Indian Museum Association and has been involved with repatriation issues for nearly three decades. He previously served as Assistant Director of Public Programs at the National Museum of the American Indian in Washington, D.C. and Director of the Institute of American Indian Arts Museum in Santa Fe, New Mexico. He has also taught Native American Studies at the State University of New York at Buffalo for twenty years. He resides at the Tuscarora Nation near Niagara Falls, New York.

Thomas W. Killion is Director of the Repatriation Program at the National Museum of Natural History, Smithsonian Institution. He received his doctorate from the University of New Mexico in 1987 and has conducted extensive archaeological research in both Latin America and the U.S. Since 1991, he has worked closely with Native American groups in this hemisphere on issues of repatriation, museum anthropology, and archaeological fieldwork.

Edmund J. Ladd, was a member of the Coyote Clan of the Zuni Pueblo. He received his M.S. in Anthropology from the University of New Mexico in 1964. He worked for the National Park Service for 30 years and was Chief Archaeologist of the Pacific Region when he retired in 1984. Following his retirement, he joined the staff of the Museum of New Mexico's Laboratory of Anthropology as Curator of Ethnology and was instrumental in program and exhibit development at the Indian Arts and Culture Center. He had a long history of involvement with Zuni repatriation efforts and has a number of publications on this topic. He died on November 15, 1999, in Santa Barbara, California.

Maria A. Liston is an Associate Professor in the Department of Anthropology and Classical Studies at the University of Waterloo in Ontario. She received her Ph.D. from the University of Tennessee in 1993. Her research interests are focused on the prehistoric archaeology of Greece and historic military sites in North America.

Stephen Loring is a Museum Anthropologist in the Arctic Studies Center of the National Museum of Natural History, Smithsonian Institution. He earned his Ph.D. in 1992 from the University of Massachusetts at Amherst. He conducts archaeological, ethnohistorical, and ethnological research in Labrador, Alaska, and the Aleutian Islands and has been a pioneer in the areas of community archaeology and repatriation in the North.

Shirley Powell is a former professor in the Department of Anthropology and former Director of the Anthropology Laboratories of Northern Arizona University where she helped to implement cooperative agreements for student training and research with the Navajo and the Hopi. From 1978 to 1987, she was the Director of the Peabody Coal Company/Southern Illinois University Black Mesa Archaeological Project. She is the author of numerous books and articles on the archaeology of Black Mesa and the northern Southwest, including *Mobility and Adaptation* and *People of the Mesa*. She currently lives and work in Dolores, Colorado, where she is town Mayor.

Janet D. Spector is Professor Emerita at the University of Minnesota. She currently lives in Albuquerque, New Mexico. She received her B.S. (1966), M.A. (1970), and Ph.D. (1974) degrees in Anthropology from the University of Wisconsin at Madison. Her research and teaching interests focus on feminist anthropology and archaeology and the archaeology of colonialism in the Upper Great Lakes. Her book, entitled *What This Awl Means: Feminist Archaeology at a Wahpeton (Dakota) Village* (1993), was nominated for the Minnesota Book Award in the category of History.

Jack F. Trope is the Director of the Western Area Office for the Save the Children Federation. Prior to serving in this position, he was a partner in the law firm of Sant'Angelo and Trope, P.C. and Senior Staff Attorney at the Association on American Indian Affairs. He was involved in the negotiations that culminated in the passage of the Native American Graves Protection and Repatriation Act and has represented clients seeking repatriation under NAGPRA. He is also currently a member of the Board of Directors for the American Indian Ritual Object Foundation.

Tamara L. Varney received her B.S. from Trent University and her M.S. from the University of Guelph in Ontario, Canada. She is currently a Ph.D. candidate in the Department of Archaeology at the University of Calgary. Her research interests include human osteology, paleopathology, taphonomy, and mortuary patterns with a focus on prehistoric and historic populations of Northeastern North America and the West Indies.

Joe Watkins (part Choctaw Indian) received his B.A. from the University of Oklahoma and his Ph.D. from Southern Methodist University. He is Agency Archaeologist for the Bureau of Indian Affairs in Oklahoma, acting as liaison between local, state, federal and private agencies on Native American issues. His primary interests are in ethics in archaeology and relations between archaeologists and Native peoples. He is currently a member of the Ethics Committee of both the Society for American Archaeology (SAA) and the American Anthropological Association (AAA), as well as Chair of the Native American Scholarships Committee for the SAA.

Richard G. Wilkinson is a Professor of Anthropology at the State University of New York at Albany. He received his Ph.D. from the University of Michigan. His research interest focuses primarily on bioarchaeology. His recent publications in this area are concerned with health, population dynamics, and mortality among ancient peoples of the Great Lakes region and Oaxaca.

Larry J. Zimmerman received his Ph.D. from the University of Kansas. He is Department Executive Officer for American Indian and Native Studies at the University of Iowa and Research Associate in the Office of the State Archaeologist of Iowa. He has served as editor of *Plains Anthropologist* and the *World Archaeological Bulletin*, and as associate editor of *American Antiquity*. His publications focus on Plains archaeology, computer applications and Native American issues.

Acknowledgments

Initial work on this book project began while I was working in the Repatriation Office at the Smithsonian's National Museum of Natural History. I had been hired together with two colleagues in 1991 to operationalize the Smithsonian's repatriation mandate as given in the National Museum of the American Indian Act (*see* Appendix 1). These were the early days of repatriation at the Smithsonian, a time filled with mixed senses of anticipation, embattlement, experimentation and possibility. Many colleagues participated in constructing the repatriation process at the Museum and in shaping a collective understanding of this phenomenon. Among these I would like to especially acknowledge the contributions of Tom Killion, Tim Baugh, Don Ortner, Melinda Zeder, Stephen Loring, Gary Aronsen, Stephanie Makseyn-Kelley, Stuart Speaker, Phillip Minthorn, Javier Urcid, Beverly Byrd, Johanna Humphrey, Dave Hunt, Carol Butler, Lauren Grant, and Pablita Abeyta.

While working for the Smithsonian, I had the opportunity to meet with Native peoples from many different parts of the country. Over the course of four years, through lengthy discussions and frank exchange, I learned much about the meaning and significance of repatriation for Native peoples. In particular, I would like to thank Greg Arnold, Eddie Ayau, Larry Dick, Roger Echo-Hawk, Walter Echo-Hawk, Adeline Fredlin, Hank Gobin, Rick Hill, Merle Holmes, Peter Jemison, Ed Ladd, Johnson Meninick, Vera Metcalf, Tessie Naranjo, Jim Noteboom, Louie Pitt, Gordon Pullar, Bobby A?yit Rose, Rory Snowbird, Henry Sockbeson, Minerva Soucie, Nelson Wallulatum, Rosita Worl, Bonnie Wuttunee-Wadsworth, and Bill Yallup for their conversation and insights.

The cover design for this volume was created by the artist Lucille Davis Grimm. Stephen Loring helped devise the title for this volume in a moment of inspiration late into a dinner party one evening. Curt Grimm has shown continuing interest and much patience through the long history of this project.

CHAPTER ONE

American Archaeologists and Native Americans
A Relationship Under Construction

Tamara L. Bray

At the dawn of the new millennium, American archaeology finds itself at the threshold of a new, more humanistic orientation toward the past. At the core of this transformation is a redefinition of the relationship between archaeologists and Indian peoples. Over the past twenty years, the discipline of archaeology has suffered the loss of a unified vision of its purpose and goals. This general experience of disciplinary fragmentation is best understood within the context of the post-positivist, anti-colonialist, and post-modernist movements that have swept through many sectors of late twentieth-century academia. In the case of American archaeology, the somewhat reluctant turn toward a more self-conscious, inclusive and humanistic approach to the construction of knowledge about the past has been accelerated by the passage of repatriation legislation.

THE REPATRIATION WATERSHED

The term repatriation, as used in this book, refers to the federally prescribed return of human remains and specific categories of objects to culturally affiliated Indian tribes. The force of this directive has had a profound effect on the way both archaeologists and physical anthropologists conceive of and conduct research in the United States. The issue of repatriation has also become a focal point for many within the Native American community due to deeply held convictions about the need to rectify past injustices and prevent further transgressions. No less profound is the impact repatriation has had on the museum world with regard to collections management, curation practices, and public exhibits. Embedded within the repatriation mandate are a number of issues that fundamentally challenge the archaeological profession's views and treatment of Native American peoples, call into question the "absolute" values of science, and force critical rethinking of the role of archaeology, anthropology, and museums in contemporary society.

Repatriation has often been formulated as a highly polarized debate with museums, archaeologists, and anthropologists on one side, and Native Americans on the other (Echo Hawk 1986; Goldstein and Kintigh 1990; Jones and Harris 1997; Meighan 1992; Preston 1989; Riding In 1992; Zimmerman 1992). One of

the central points of contention is whether Native American interests in reburying the skeletal remains of ancestral populations should take precedence over the
interests of archaeologists and physical anthropologists in studying and preserving them. As a result, the divide over repatriation has often been glossed as one
of religion versus science (Clark 1998; Meighan 1992). Characterizing the issue in
this way has the effect of casting Native peoples as anti-science or anti-intellectu-
al, playing upon and reinforcing existing stereotypes of Native Americans as
non-progressive and backward-looking. Locating repatriation within its specific
historic and sociopolitical context, however, brings into relief the asymmetrical
power relations that have actually given rise to and helped shape the contours of
this debate (Bray 1996; McGuire 1989; Zimmerman 1989).

The idea of recovering ancestral remains for reburial began to acquire widespread support during the civil rights movements of the 1960s (Hill, this volume;
Trope and Echo-Hawk 1992, reprinted this volume). During this period, Native
Americans, like other minority groups in the United States, gained increased
political influence and recognition. It was within the activist climate of this era
that Native peoples began to express their long-felt resentment towards archaeological excavations, the public display of Indian skeletons, and the permanent
curation of Native American remains in museums. The fact that Native American
dead were accorded different treatment than Whites, and the seeming disregard
with which archaeologists treated the sensibilities of modern tribes became powerful symbols of oppression and the pervasiveness of racist attitudes for the
Native community.

In 1974, the activist group American Indians Against Desecration was formed
with the explicit intent of bringing political pressure to bear on the question of the
return and reburial of Native American remains. Through the efforts of this group
and the media attention they were able to attract, the repatriation issue percolat-
ed into the public consciousness and eventually captured the attention of several
sympathetic law-makers. The first federal legislation to treat the issue of repatriation was the National Museum of the American Indian Act (P.L. 101-185). Passed
in 1989, it required the Smithsonian Institution to return all culturally identifiable
Native American remains and associated funerary objects to culturally affiliated
tribal groups. The subsequent year saw passage of the Native American Graves
Protection and Repatriation Act (NAGPRA) (P.L. 101-601). In addition to afford-
ing protection to unmarked Native burials, this law also expanded the repatriation mandate to cover additional categories of cultural items, specifically sacred
objects and items of cultural patrimony, and all other federally funded museums,
institutions, and agencies (*see* Appendices 1 and 2).

Since passage of NAGPRA, museums have scrambled to meet collection
inventory deadlines imposed by the law. The National Park Service, charged with
implementation of the act, has held countless instructional meetings to clarify
legal intent, requirements, and procedures. Tribes have formed standing commit-
tees or appointed `NAGPRA coordinators' to sift through the mountains of inven-
tory data transmitted by museums. Mandatory consultations between tribal
representatives and museum personnel have been undertaken with varying
degrees of cooperation. Innumerable articles and news stories have been written

on the subject; considerable quantities of human remains and associated funerary items have been repatriated to tribes; and archaeologists still find themselves divided over the issue.

Repatriation has created what might usefully be understood as a federally mandated 'zone of contact' between Native people, archaeologists, and museums. The notion of a 'contact zone,' borrowed from Pratt's work on nineteenth-century Western travel, is defined as the "space of colonial encounters . . . in which peoples geographically and historically separated come into contact with each other and establish relations. . . ." Such a "contact perspective," which stands in opposition to a "frontier mentality" with its unidirectional implications, emphasizes how subjects are constituted in and by their relations to each other, stressing co-presence, interaction, and interlocking understandings and practices (ibid.; see also Clifford 1997).

Repatriation may be usefully understood as a 'contact process,' one that occurs within a new kind of intercultural space essentially decreed by federal mandate. Within this conceptual framework, the human remains and cultural objects that are the focal point of repatriation become the fundamental physical elements of a contact history, sites of political negotiation and occasions for ongoing interaction. Rather than being containers of a fixed or singular meaning, the significance of these items may be seen as contingent and emergent. Formulated within the discourse of repatriation, the remains and objects in question have become crucial press in the politics of identity and recognition.

A contact perspective also permits the difficulties that often characterize repatriation-related encounters to be understood as problems of cross-cultural communication, translation, and inequality. As Jacknis (1996:284) observes, the interlocutors in these encounters often develop "a shared code, like a pidgin or creole... that allows speakers of different languages to communicate without necessarily reaching full agreement or even full comprehension." Archaeologists, most of whom are trained first and foremost as anthropologists, presumably have the skills to work at this cultural interface.

REINVENTING ARCHAEOLOGY AS A DEMOCRATIC ENTERPRISE

The hesitancy some archaeologists may feel about engaging a 'contact perspective' stems from a deep commitment to Western science and the ideals of objectivity and comprehensive truth embedded within this tradition. The long-standing preoccupation with the practices and goals of the natural versus the social sciences hinges on the issue of objectivity. The idea that core sciences like physics perform their operations upon a separate, empirical world in a value-free context, is typically contrasted with the way social sciences like history and anthropology constitute the objects of their study intersubjectively and without the benefit of neutral detachment. Archaeology has traditionally occupied the borderlands between science and history, periodically leaning more toward one side, then swinging back toward the other.

It has been generally recognized since the 1960s, however, that scientific theories of any stripe are under-determined by the evidence, that data are theory-laden and recognized only within specific conceptual frameworks, and that facts

are mediated through an array of auxiliary hypotheses (see Wylie 1995). Post-positivist philosophers of science have extended these observations, noting that even
the core sciences must be understood to incorporate an interpretive, hermeneutic
dimension (Kuhn 1970; Hesse 1960; Salmon 1984; Wylie 1995). It has also been
amply demonstrated that the study of the past is always a political undertaking
(Leone 1984; Rubertone 1989; Schmidt and Patterson 1995; Sued Badillo 1992). A
parallel argument is made by feminist scholars and historians of science that even
core scientific disciplines are cultural and political enterprises, whatever commitment their practioners may have to a stance of detached neutrality (Code 1991;
Haraway 1988, 1991; Harding 1986, 1991). Even though these points are by now
accepted by most in the academic community, they still continue to be contentious within some circles (see Wylie 2000).

The `moralization of objectivity' (Conkey and Gero 1997:427; Daston and Gal-
ison 1992) is one of the key aspects of mainstream archaeology to be confronted
if we hope to redefine the field as a more inclusive and democratic endeavor
(after Leone and Preucel 1992). One domain of critical inquiry that has tried to
come to terms with the concept of objectivity is feminist theory. As Haraway
(1991:183-188) notes, we often seem trapped between two poles of a tempting
dichotomy with regard to objectivity. We recognize, on the one hand, that there
have been very strong arguments made for the social construction of all knowledge claims, especially scientific ones. Yet unmasking the doctrine of objectivity
cuts out everyone's claims to even partial truths about the world, giving all pro-
nouncements essentially equal status.

The dilemma has become how to simultaneously have an account of radical
historical contingency for all knowledge claims *and* a commitment to faithful
accounts of a "real" world that science strives to deliver. Recognizing the need for
a usable doctrine of objectivity that could accommodate these paradoxical
requirements, feminist theorists have developed the notion of "embodied objectivity" (Haraway 1991:185-196). This concept incorporates the ideas of situated
knowledge and partial perspective. Fundamental building blocks of feminist science, these ideas lead to a notion of objectivity that is, as Haraway (ibid.) puts it,
usable but not innocent.

Engaging a critical science perspective is not about the myth of being beyond
human agency and responsibility in a neutral realm above the fray. "The science
question in feminism is about objectivity as positioned rationality; its images are
not the products of escape and transcendence ... i.e. `the view from above,' but the
joining of partial views and halting voices into a collective subject position, . . .
i.e., of views from somewhere" (Haraway 1991:196). Feminist science argues for
politics and epistemologies of location, positioning and situating, where partiali-
ty—not universality—is the prerequisite to being heard to make rational knowledge claims (Ibid.:195). I would suggest that such an approach to science holds
much promise for the theory and practice of a responsible and inclusive archaeology in the twenty-first century.

These comments on the impossibility of political neutrality and objectivity in
any human endeavor are intended as prologue to the papers that follow which
collectively point to the need for American archaeology to reinvent itself. Many

scholars have written about the fact that science in general, and archaeology in particular, are not disinterested undertakings (cf. Kohl and Fawcett 1995; Layton 1989; Leone et al. 1987; Leone and Preucel 1992; Miller and Tilley 1984; Schmidt and Patterson 1995; Trigger 1989). Whether or not the practitioner is aware of the uses to which his or her research and theories are put, social theory serves some purpose if it has any relevance at all. Following the suggestions of Leone and Preucel (1992), archaeology needs to become a more inclusive, responsive and democratic activity. Various labels have been suggested for this endeavor, including 'covenantal archaeology' (Powell et al. 1993; Wood and Powell 1993), 'ethno-critical archaeology' (Zimmerman 1996), 'ancient Indian history' (Echo-Hawk 1993, 1997), and `indigenous archaeology' (Nicholas and Andrews 1997). Regardless of how it is to be known, such a course is being charted for the discipline by virtue of the repatriation mandate. The papers presented in this volume offer some markers for the road that lies ahead.

REFERENCES CITED

Bray, Tamara L. 1996. "Repatriation, power relations, and the politics of the past." *Antiqui-ty* 70:440–444.

Clark, Geoffrey. 1998. "NAGPRA, religion, and science." *Anthropology Newsletter*, April, pp.24–25.

Clifford, James. 1997. "Museums as contact zones." In *Routes: Travel and Translation in the Late Twentieth Century*, ed. J. Clifford, pp. 188–219. Cambridge: Harvard University Press.

Code, L. 1991. *What Can She Know? Feminist Theory and the Construction of Knowledge*. New York: Cornell University Press.

Conkey, Margaret and Joan Gero. 1997. "Programme to practice: Gender and feminism in archaeology." *Annual Review of Anthropology* 26:411–437.

Daston, L. and P. Galison. 1992. "The image of objectivity." *Representations* 40:81–128.

Echo-Hawk, Roger. 1993. "Exploring ancient worlds." *Society for American Archaeology Bulletin* 11(4):5–6.

——— 1997. "Forging a new ancient history for Native America." In *Native Americans and Archaeologists*, ed. Nina Swidler et al., pp. 88–102. Walnut Creek, California: Altamira Press.

Echo-Hawk, Walter. 1986. "Museum rights vs. Indian rights: Guidelines for assessing competing legal interests in Native cultural resources." *New York University Review of Law* 14(2):237–253.

Goldstein, Lynne and Keith Kintigh. 1990. "Ethics and the reburial controversy." *American Antiquity* 55:585–591.

Handsman, Russell and Trudi Lamb Richmond. 1995. "Confronting colonialism: The Mahican and Schaghticoke peoples and us." In *Making Alternative Histories*, ed. P. Schmidt and T. Patterson, pp. 87–118. Santa Fe, New Mexico: School of American Research Series.

Haraway, Donna. 1991. "Situated knowledges: The science question in feminism and the privilege of partial perspective." In *Simians, Cyborgs and Women*, ed. D. Haraway, pp. 183–201. New York: Routledge.

Harding, Sandra. 1986. *The Science Question in Feminism*. Ithaca: Cornell University Press.

——— 1991. *Whose Science? Whose Knowledge?* Ithaca: Cornell University Press.

Hesse, Mary. 1960. *Models and Analogies in Science*. Notre Dame, Indiana: University of Notre Dame Press.

Jacknis, Ira. 1996. "Repatriation as social drama: The Kwakiutl Indians of British Columbia, 1922–1980." *American Indian Quarterly* 20(2):274–286.

Jones, Gareth and Robyn Harris. 1997. "Contending for the dead." *Nature* 356:15–16.

Kelly, Robert. 1998. "Native Americans and archaeology: A vital partnership." *Society for American Archaeology Bulletin* 16(4):24–26.

Kohl, Philip and Claire Fawcett (eds.) 1995. *Nationalism, Politics and the Practice of Archaeology*. Cambridge: Cambridge University Press.

Kuhn, Thomas. 1970. *The Structure of Scientific Revolutions*. Chicago: University of Chicago Press.

Landers, Robert. 1991. "Is America allowing its past to be stolen?" *Congressional Quarterly's Editorial Research Reports* (January 18) 3:34–46.

Layton, Robert. 1989. "Introduction: Conflict in the Archaeology of Living Traditions." In *Conflict in the Archaeology of Living Traditions*, ed. R. Layton, pp. 1–21. London: Unwin-Hyman.

Leone, Mark. 1984. "Interpreting ideology in historical archaeology: Using the rules of perspective in the William Paca garden." In *Ideology, Prehistory, and Power*, eds. C. Tilley and D. Miller, pp. 25–36. Cambridge: Cambridge University Press.

Leone, Mark, Parker Potter, and Paul Shackel. 1987. "Toward a critical archaeology." *Current Anthropology* 28(3):283–302.

Leone, Mark and Robert Preucel. 1992. "Archaeology in a democratic society: A critical theory perspective." In *Quandaries and Quests: Visions of Archaeology's Future*, ed. L. Wandsnider, pp. 115–135. Southern Illinois University, Occasional Papers, No. 20.

McGuire, Randall. 1989. "The sanctity of the grave: White concepts and American Indian burials." In *Conflict in the Archaeology of Living Traditions*, ed. R. Layton, pp. 167–184. London: Unwin-Hyman.

Meighan, Clement. 1992. "Another View on Repatriation: Lost to the Public, Lost to History." *The Public Historian* 14(3):39–50.

Mihesuah, Devon. 1996. "American Indians, anthropologists, pothunters, and repatriation: Ethical, religious, and political differences."*American Indian Quarterly* 20(2):229–237.

Miller, Daniel and Christopher Tilley (eds.). 1984. *"Ideology, Power, and Prehistory."* Cambridge: Cambridge University Press.

Nicholas, George and Thomas Andrews. 1997. "Indigenous Archaeology in the postmodern world." In *At a Crossroads: Archaeology and First Peoples in Canada*, eds. G. Nicholas and T. Andrews, pp. 1–18. Vancouver, B.C.: Archaeology Press.

Powell, Shirley, Christine Garza, and A. Hendricks. 1993. "Ethics and ownership of the past: The reburial and repatriation controversy." In *Archaeological Method and Theory, Volume 5*, edited by M. Schiffer, pp. 1–42. Tucson: University of Arizona Press.

Preston, Douglas. 1989. "Skeletons in our museum's closets." *Harper's Magazine* (February) pp. 66–75.

Pratt, Mary Louise. 1992. *Imperial Eyes: Travel Writing and Transculturation.* London: Routledge.

Rubertone, Patricia. 1989. "Archaeology, colonialism, and 17th century Native America: Towards an alternative explanation." In *Conflict in the Archaeology of Living Traditions*, ed. R. Layton, pp. 32–45. London: Unwin-Hyman.

Salmon, Wesley. 1984. *Scientific Explanation and the Causal Structure of the World.* Princeton: Princeton University Press.

Schmidt, Peter and Thomas Patterson (eds.). 1995. *Making Alternative Histories.* School of American Research Series, Santa Fe, New Mexico.

Stoffle, Richard and Michael Evans. 1994. "To bury the ancestors: A view of NAGPRA." *Practicing Anthropology* 16(3):29–33.

Sued Badillo, Jalil. 1992. "Facing up to Caribbean history." *American Antiquity* 57:599–607.

Trigger, Bruce. 1989. *A History of Archaeological Thought.* Cambridge: Cambridge University Press.

Trope, Jack and Walter Echo-Hawk. 1992. "The Native American Graves Protection and Repatriation Act: Background and legislative history." *Arizona State Law Journal* 24(1):35–77.

White Deer, Gary. 1998. "From specimens to SAA speakers: Evolution by federal mandate." *Society for American Archaeology Bulletin* 16(3):6–8.

Wood, John and Shirley Powell. 1993. "An ethos for archaeological practice." *Human Organization* 52(4):405–413.

Wylie, Alison. 1995. "Alternative histories: Epistemic disunity and political integrity." In *Making Alternative Histories*, edited by P. Schmidt and T. Patterson, pp. 255–272. School of American Research Series, Santa Fe, New Mexico.

——— 2000. Questions of evidence, legitimacy, and the (dis)unity of science. *American Antiquity* 65(2): 227–237.

Zimmerman, Larry. 1989. "Human bones as symbols of power: Aboriginal American belief systems towards bones and 'grave-robbing' archaeologists." In *Conflict in the Archaeology of Living Traditions*, ed. R. Layton, pp. 211–216. London: Unwin-Hyman.

——— 1992. "Archaeology, reburial, and a discipline's self-delusion." *American Indian Culture and Research Journal* 16(2):37–56.

——— 1996. "Epilogue: A new and different archaeology?" *American Indian Quarterly* 20(2):297–307.

The Native American Graves Protection and Repatriation Act
Background and Legislative History[1]

JACK F. TROPE AND WALTER R. ECHO-HAWK

INTRODUCTION

On November 23, 1990, President George Bush signed into law important human rights legislation: the Native American Graves Protection and Repatriation Act ("NAGPRA") (*see* Appendix 2). This legislation culminates decades of struggle by Native American tribal governments and people to protect against grave desecration, to repatriate thousands of dead relatives or ancestors, and to return stolen or improperly acquired religious and cultural property to Native owners.

In many ways, NAGPRA is historic, landmark legislation for Native Americans. It represents fundamental changes in basic social attitudes toward Native peoples by the museum and scientific communities and the public at large. NAGPRA provides nationwide repatriation standards and procedures for the return of Native remains and certain protected materials from federal agencies and federally funded institutions. Because of the massive scope of the repatriation problem, however, a lengthy implementation period can be expected for this human rights legislation.[2] This article seeks to facilitate implementation of the new national policy by providing attorneys, Indian tribes, museums, and scientists with (1) background on the repatriation issue; and (2) an informed analysis of the provisions of NAGPRA and their interaction.

The Native American repatriation topic involves a wide array of complex, and sometimes competing, social interests, including human rights, race relations, religion, science, education, ethics, and law. Much has been written on the topic from the perspective of these social interests (see, for example, Green and Mitchell 1990). Admittedly, the law has played a relatively minor role in considering these often conflicting interests. It is appropriate, however, that the law play a significant role because it should embody the highest values and ethics of the society that it is intended to serve.

Across the nation, society has vigorously debated these issues in recent years. Museums and scientists have argued that Native human remains have scientific and educational value and, therefore, should be preserved for these important purposes. Tribes have argued that protection of the sepulchre of the dead is an important attribute in our society. This protection includes fundamental legal rights that everyone—except Natives—can take for granted. Unfortunately, the law and policy that protects the sanctity of the dead and the sensibilities of the living has failed to protect Native Americans. This article suggests that American laws have indeed failed to accord Equal Protection. Moreover, the resulting disparate racial treatment has caused painful human rights violations in tribal communities. As the repatriation struggle became protracted and reached the federal level, it became a test for our country's commitment to the underlying values of the Bill of Rights and to our American sense of social justice.

Much of the national debate culminated in the passage of NAGPRA, though implementation of that law and its national policy remain. NAGPRA is the primary subject of this article, which will cover four areas: 1) the historical origins, nature, and scope of the controversy from a Native American perspective; 2) a summary of legal and political rights that are at stake when Indian tribes seek to repatriate their dead relatives; 3) legal and legislative activities in this area of rapid social change; and 4) a description of the background, legislative history, and provisions of NAGPRA.

THE ORIGINS, SCOPE, AND NATURE OF THE REPATRIATION ISSUE

HUMAN REMAINS AND FUNERARY OBJECTS

In all ages, humankind has protected the sanctity of the dead. Indeed, respect for the dead is a mark of humanity and is as old as religion itself. British Prime Minister William Ewart Gladstone once wrote:

> Show me the manner in which a nation or a community cares for its dead, and I will measure with mathematical exactness the tender sympathies of its people, their respect for the laws of the land, and their loyalty to high ideals (quoted in Wooley 1990:1).

Like most other nations, respect for the dead is deeply ingrained in American social fabric and jurisprudence. One legal commentator noted:

> After a lifetime of investigation of the Origin of religious structure, the great Sir James G. Frazier concluded that awe toward the dead was probably the most powerful force in forming primitive systems for grappling with the supernatural. The sepulture of the dead has, in all ages of the world, been regarded as a religious rite. The place where the dead are deposited, all civilized nations, and many barbarous ones, regard, in some measure at least, as consecrated ground. In the old Saxon tongue the burial ground of the dead was "God's Acre." [American cases] all agree in principle: The normal treatment of a corpse, once it is decently buried, is to let it lie. This idea is so deeply woven into our legal and cultural fabric that it is commonplace to hear it spoken of as a "right" of the dead and a charge on the quick. [No] system of jurisprudence permits exhumation for less than what are considered weighty, and sometimes compelling, reasons.[3]

These basic values are strictly protected in all fifty states, and the District of Columbia, by statutes that comprehensively regulate cemeteries and protect graves from vandalism and desecration (Yalung and Wala 1992). Criminal laws prohibit grave robbing and mutilation of the dead and ensure that human remains are not mistreated. Statutes in most states guarantee that all persons, including paupers, indigents, prisoners, strangers, and other unclaimed dead, are entitled to a decent burial.

Disinterment of the dead is strongly disfavored under American common law except under the most compelling circumstances, and then only under close judicial supervision or under carefully prescribed permit requirements, which may include judicial consent.[4] Common law goes to great lengths to protect the sanctity of the dead (Jackson 1950).

Unfortunately, the above legal protections, which most citizens take for granted, have failed to protect the graves and the dead of Native people. Massive numbers of Indian dead have been dug up from their graves and carried away. National estimates are that between 100,000 and two million deceased Native people have been dug up from their graves for storage or display by government agencies, museums, universities and tourist attractions. The practice is so widespread that virtually every Indian tribe or Native group in the country has been affected by non-Indian grave looting.

The dark and troubling circumstances of how these Native dead were obtained has been thoroughly documented by historians. Human remains were obtained by soldiers, government agents, pothunters, private citizens, museum collecting crews, and scientists in the name of profit, entertainment, science, or development (Bieder 1986, 1990, 1992; Cole 1985; Riding In 1992).

The problem that the law seeks to remedy is one that has characterized Indian/White relations since the Pilgrims landed at Plymouth Rock in 1620. The first Pilgrim exploring party returned to the Mayflower with corn taken from Indian storage pits and items removed from a grave: "We brought sundry of the prettiest things away with us, and covered up the corpse again" (Heath 1963[1622]:28).

Early interest in systematically collecting Indian body parts began before the Civil War. Dr. Samuel Morton, the father of American physical anthropology, collected large numbers of Indian crania in the 1840s. His goal was to scientifically prove, through skull measurements, that the American Indian was a racially inferior "savage" who was naturally doomed to extinction (Bieder 1986). Morton's findings established the "Vanishing Red Man" theory, which was embraced by government policy-makers as "scientific justification" for relocating Indian tribes, taking tribal land, and conducting genocide—in certain instances—against American Indians (Bieder 1986; Thornton 1987).

Later, the search for Indian body parts became official federal policy with the Surgeon General's Order of 1868. The policy directed army personnel to procure Indian crania and other body parts for the Army Medical Museum (Bieder 1990:36–37). In ensuing decades, over 4,000 heads were taken from battlefields, burial grounds, POW camps, hospitals, fresh graves, and burial scaffolds across the country. Government headhunters decapitated Natives who had never been buried, such as slain Pawnee warriors from a western Kansas battleground, Cheyenne and Arapaho victims of Colorado's Sand Creek Massacre, and defeated Modoc leaders who were hanged and then shipped to the Army Medical Museum.

One 1892 account of rainy night grave robbing of fifteen Blackfeet Indian graves is chilling:

> I collected them in a way somewhat unusual: the burial place is in plain sight of many Indian houses and very near frequent roads. I had to visit the country at night when not even the dogs were stirring after securing one [skull] I had to pass the Indian sentry at the stockade gate which I never attempted with more than one [skull], for fear of detection. On one occasion I was followed by an Indian who did not comprehend my movements, and I made a circuitous route away from the place intended and threw him off his suspicions. On stormy nights— rain, snow or wind & bitter cold, I think I was never observed going or coming, by either Indians or dogs, but on pleasant nights—I was always seen but of course no one knew what I had in my coat . . . the greatest fear I had was that some Indian would miss the heads, see my tracks & ambush me, but they didn't. I regret the lower maxillae are not on each skull, I got all I could find, and they are all detached save one. There is in the box a left radius & ulna of a woman, with the identical bracelets on that were buried with her. The bones of themselves are nothing, but the combination with the ornaments make them a little noticeable (Bieder 1990:45–46).

During this period, collecting crews from America's newly founded museums engaged in competitive expeditions to obtain Indian skeletons. As Franz Boas, the famous American anthropologist, observed in the 1880s, "it is most unpleasant work to steal bones from graves, but what is the use, someone has to do it" (Bieder 1990:30). Scientific means were not always used by museum collecting expedition during this period, which can better be described, in some instances, as "fervid rip-and-run operations" (Cole 1985:175). Some museums employed outright deception in order to obtain skeletons. New York's American Museum of Natural History, for example, literally staged a fake funeral for a deceased Eskimo to prevent his son from discovering that the museum had stolen the remains (Harper 1986). In 1990, one Sioux leader decried these museum activities in testimony before the United States Senate:

> [T]his [Bieder Report] is a very difficult report for an Indian to read. Earlier I talked about meeting with many of the traditional people. They constantly tell us that the white man won't believe you unless it's written in black and white. It's got to be written in black and white . . . So today we have something written in black and white. It's a very sad account of the atrocities. It's a shameful account of how museums—some of the museums that were here today actually competed with each other and hired people to rob graves of Native American people (Jerry Flute, U.S. Senate Hearings on s. 1021 and 1980, p. 76).

At the turn of the century, Congress continued its deplorable federal policy with the passage of the Antiquities Act of 1906. That Act, which was intended to protect "archaeological resources" located on federal lands from looters, defined dead Indians interred on federal lands as "archaeological resources" and, contrary to long standing common-law principles, converted these dead persons into "federal property." The Antiquities Act allowed these dead persons to be dug up pursuant to a federal permit "for the permanent preservation [of the remains] in public museums." Since then, thousands of Indian dead have been classified as "archaeological resources" and exhumed as "federal property."

In summary, American social policy has historically treated Indian dead differently than the dead of other races. Unfortunately, it has been commonplace for public agencies to treat Native American dead as *archaeological resources, property, pathological material, data, specimens,* or *library books* but not as *human beings.* Many contemporary examples of mistreatment of Native graves and dead bodies occurred in recent years under this rubric, which shocked the Nation's conscience as social ethics have changed and society has become more sensitive to this Equal Protection problem.

SACRED OBJECTS AND CULTURAL PATRIMONY

One pattern that defines Indian-White relations in the United States is the one-way transfer of Indian property to non-Indian ownership. By the 1870s, after most tribes were placed on small reservations, the Government's acquisition of Indian lands had in large part been accomplished. Thereafter, the pattern shifted from real estate to personalty and continued until most of the material culture of Native people had been transferred to White hands. That massive property transfer invariably included some stolen or improperly acquired Native sacred objects and cultural patrimony. Native owners who sought the return of their property, as it turned up in museums, experienced inordinate difficulty in securing its return.[5]

One historian commented on the enormous transfer of cultural property that occurred in a short, fifty-year period:

> During the half-century or so after 1875, a staggering quantity of material, both secular and sacred—from spindle whorls to soul-catchers—left the hands of their native creators and users for the private and public collections of the European world. The scramble . . . was pursued sometimes with respect, occasionally with rapacity, often with avarice. By the time it ended there was more Kwakiutal material in Milwaukee than in Mamalillikulla, more Salish pieces in Cambridge than in Comox. The City of Washington contained more Northwest Coast material than the state of Washington and New York City probably housed more British Columbia material than British Columbia itself (Cole 1985:286).

Though some of that property transfer was through legitimate trade and intercourse, a significant amount of Native property was acquired through illegitimate means. This problem was brought to the attention of Congress by the Carter Administration in 1979, following a one-year study mandated by the American Indian Religious Freedom Act. The report noted the following:

> Museum records show that some sacred objects were sold by their original Native owner or owners. In many instances, however, the chain of title does not lead to the original owners. Some property left the original ownership during military confrontations, was included in the spoils of war and eventually fell to the control of museums. Also in times past, sacred objects were lost by Native owners as a result of less violent pressures exerted by federally-sponsored missionaries and Indian agents.

Most sacred objects were stolen from their original owners. In other cases, religious property was converted and sold by Native people who did not have ownership or title to the sacred object. Today in may parts of the country, it is common for "pothunters" to enter Indian and public lands for the purpose of illegally expropriating sacred objects. Interstate trafficking in and exporting of such property flourishes, with some of these sacred objects eventually entering into the possession of museums.[6]

The adverse impacts that a refusal to return stolen or improperly acquired sacred material has upon First Amendment rights of tribal religious practitioners, and upon basic property rights, has been noted by scholars and other commentators (Blair 1979a, 1979b; Echo-Hawk 1986; Horse Capture 1989). This issue has increasingly become of great concern among tribes and traditional religious practitioners. NAGPRA establishes a national standard and procedure for the return of this property to Native owners.

LEGAL RIGHTS TO REPATRIATE THE DEAD

THE FAILURE OF THE LEGAL SYSTEM TO PROTECT NATIVE BURIAL SITES

1. Common Law

The legal system also contributed to the disparate treatment of Native American human remains and funerary objects by failing to incorporate indigenous needs and values into the common law as it developed in the United States. The jurisprudence that protects the sanctity of the dead and the sensibilities of the living is the common law, which we inherited from England. Common law is judge-made law that is supposed to safeguard considerations of justice and equity; it evolves and changes over time to meet society's changing needs. Unfortunately, during its development in this country, the common law failed to take into account unique indigenous burial practices and mortuary traditions. As explained by one legal scholar:

> At a sensitive point in time when American courts were developing a foundation of experience-based common law and legislators were enacting specific statutes for cemeteries and burials reflecting the American condition and requirements, the courts and law-makers were deprived of the benefit of consideration of practical issues of appropriate disposition of prehistoric aboriginal remains and grave goods and the property rights of Indians to these items. Thus, when issues later surfaced in the courts, the judicial system was forced to attempt to apply an established body of statutes and experience-based common law to situations that law had not previously considered and with which it was ill-suited to deal (Price 1991:22).

The lack of access to courts by Native Americans during this formative period is understandable. Disputes between Native people and American citizens were usually settled on the battlefield instead of in courtrooms. Furthermore, in light of prevailing racial views of the time, Indians had little realistic hope of a fair hearing in American courts. Just as racial oppression against African-Americans was justified by United States Supreme Court decisions such as *Plessy v. Ferguson,*[7] similar decisions branded Indian Nations as ignorant and uncivilized.[8] Supreme Court decisions characterized Indians "as an inferior race of people, without the privileges of citizens."[9] It was not until 1879 that a federal court ruled that an Indian was a "person" within the meaning of federal law.[10] Moreover, Indians were not granted citizenship until 1924.

Hence, American legal protections for the dead did not take into account unique Native mortuary practices such as scaffold, canoe, or tree burials. The law did not protect unmarked Native graves like it protected marked European graves. Nor did the law recognize that Native people maintain close religious connections with ancient dead; instead, the right to protect the dead was limited to the descendent's immediate next of kin. The law also failed to take into account relevant historical circumstances such as government removal of tribes away from their burial grounds, and the need to accord legal protection for the graves and cemeteries that were involuntarily left behind.

Native people were faced with highly ethnocentric decisions in some common-law cases. For example, in *Wana the Bear v. Community Construction, Inc.* (1982), the court held that a historic Indian cemetery was not a "cemetery" within the meaning of state cemetery-protection laws.[11] In *State v. Glass*, the court held that older human skeletal remains are not considered "human" for purposes of an Ohio grave-robbing statute, which leaves only aboriginal remains in an unprotected status in that state.[12] The decision in *Carter v. City of Zanesville* held that a cemetery may be considered "abandoned" if no further interments are done.[13] The abandonment doctrine might make sense if applied to European communities that voluntarily abandon local cemeteries, but it becomes highly ethnocentric when applied to cemeteries of relocated Indian tribes.

2. State Statutory Law

Loopholes in state statutory law, which universally supplement common law protections, contributed to the failure to protect Native graves (Yalung and Wala 1992). State grave and cemetery protection statutes typically regulated and protected marked graves, but not unmarked graves. Because in many instances Indian graves are unmarked, they received no statutory protection. As such, many unmarked Indian graves were discovered, disturbed, or dug up through construction, natural causes, or pothunting—and the remains were never reburied. For example, Illinois, despite comprehensive grave-protection laws, allowed an entire Indian cemetery containing 234 men, women, and children to be uncovered for public display at the Dixon Mounds Museum (Dellios 1991)

LEGAL THEORIES SUPPORTING PROTECTION AND REPATRIATION OF NATIVE DEAD

Despite the failure of law and social policy to protect Native American graves in the past, a proper non-discriminatory application of the law provides a strong legal basis for tribal grave protection and repatriation efforts. In addition to new statutory rights, five sources of law exist that can provide the underpinning for tribal grave protection efforts and repatriation claims: 1) the common law; 2) the Equal Protection clauses of the Fifth and Fourteenth Amendments; 3) the First

Amendment; 4) the sovereign right of Indian tribal governments to govern internal domestic affairs; and 5) Indian treaties.

1. Common Law

If applied equally, common law offers a variety of protections for Native Americans. Although the area of common law that protects the dead is voluminous and sometimes obscure, it dispels many popular myths and legal fictions that have been injurious to Native Americans. First, no "property interest" exists in a dead body in the eyes of the common law. This rule makes it impossible to own the remains of a Native American; the dead of any race are simply not chattels to be bought or sold in the marketplace.

Second, the popular fiction that a landowner may own and sell the contents of Indian graves located on his land is legally erroneous. A landowner only has *technical possession* of graves located on his land and is required to hold them *in trust* for the relatives of the deceased. Therefore, no institution may have title to dead Indians obtained from landowners because landowners have no title to convey.

Another harmful myth that is popular among pothunters and private collectors is that objects *found* in Indian graves belong to the finder under a *finders–keepers, losers–weepers* rule. This myth runs afoul of the rule that personal possessions interred with the dead are not abandoned property. To the contrary, whenever funerary objects are removed from graves, they belong to the person who furnished the grave or to his known descendants. Thus, the title that pothunters and collectors have to objects that were removed from Indian graves may be invalid under the common law.

In summary, common law protections should apply to Indian graves and Indian dead with the same force that the courts have applied them to the dead of other races. In fact, some courts have applied the common law to protect Indian dead.[14]

2. Equal Protection

Disparate racial treatment in matters affecting Indian dead may run afoul of the Equal Protection Clauses of the Fifth and Fourteenth Amendments. An Equal Protection claim may arise if government agencies treat Indian graves or remains differently than the dead of other races. Laws and policies that treat Indian dead as archaeological resources, property, or historic property are suspect when compared to laws that ordinarily protect the dead of other races. Overt discrimination, such as the 1868 Surgeon General's Order, could not pass muster today under the Equal Protection Clause.

3. The First Amendment

First Amendment Free Exercise rights are implicated if the government withholds Indian dead from next of kin or tribes of origin. humankind has always buried the dead with religion, and Native Americans are no different. Therefore, it is not surprising that Native religious beliefs and practices may be infringed upon when tribal dead are desecrated, disturbed, or withheld from burial by the government. In 1855, Chief Seattle told United States treaty negotiators, "To us the ashes of our ancestors are sacred and their resting place is hallowed ground."

Indeed, Indian Tribes, Native Alaskans, and Native Hawaiians commonly believe that if the dead are disturbed or robbed, the spirit is disturbed and wanders—a spiritual trauma for the deceased that can also bring ill upon the living. The adverse impacts of such interference on tribal religion was described by the Carter Administration to Congress in 1979, as follows:

> Native American religions, along with most other religions, provide standards for the care and treatment of cemeteries and human remains. Tribal customary laws generally include standards of conduct for the care and treatment of all cemeteries encountered and human remains uncovered, as well as for the burial sites and bodies of their own ancestors. Grounded in Native American religious beliefs, these laws may, for example, require the performance of certain types of rituals at the burial site, specify who may visit the site or prescribe the proper disposition of burial offerings.
>
> The prevalent view in the society of applicable disciplines is that Native American remains are public property and artifacts for study, display, and cultural investment. It is understandable that this view is in conflict with and repugnant to those Native people whose ancestors and near relatives are considered the property at issue. Most Native American religious beliefs dictate that burial sites once completed are not to be disturbed or displaced, except by natural occurrence.[15]

State interference with religious-based mortuary beliefs and practices has given rise to a Free Exercise cause of action when other citizens are concerned. The continuing strength of First Amendment protection, however, must be reassessed in light of a recent United States Supreme Court decision. In *Employment Division of Oregon v. Smith*, the Supreme Court seriously weakened religious liberty for all citizens.[16]

4. Sovereign Rights

Political rights of Indian Nations as sovereigns can provide another legal basis to repatriate dead tribal members and ancestors. One basic attribute of tribal sovereignty that has been repeatedly recognized by the Supreme Court is the right of Indian tribes to govern domestic internal affairs of their members. In *United States v. Quiver*,[17] the Court said that "the relations of the Indians among themselves—the conduct of one toward another—is to be controlled by the customs and laws of the tribe, save when Congress expressly or clearly directs otherwise."

One internal domestic matter that falls squarely within this zone of tribal sovereignty is the relationship between the living and the dead. Therefore, domestic relationships involving the dead may not be interfered with by federal or state government except "when Congress expressly or clearly directs otherwise." In *Mexican v. Circle Bear*,[18] the court applied these principles and granted comity to a tribal court order that provided for the disposal of the body of an Indian who had died within state jurisdiction, even though tribal and state law differed. Thus, Indian tribal governments, acting in their *in parens patriae* capacity, may act to repatriate tribal dead in the same way that the United States acts for its citizenry to repatriate MIA's from Southeast Asia.

5. Treaties

Indian treaty rights may also provide a legal theory for tribes to repatriate members or ancestors who have been exhumed from lands ceded by treaty. A treaty is "not a grant of rights to the Indians, but a grant of rights from them—a reservation of those not granted."[19] Simply stated, if a treaty does not expressly delineate the reserved tribal powers or rights, it does not mean that they have been divested. To the contrary, "when a tribe and the Government negotiate a treaty, the tribe retains all rights not expressly ceded to the Government in the treaty so long as the rights retained are consistent with the tribe's sovereign dependent status."[20]

Therefore, no treaty expressly granted the United States a right to disturb Indian graves, expropriate Indian dead from ceded lands, or divest a tribe of its pre-existing power to protect those dead. If burials are removed from lands ceded by treaty, a strong argument exists that the signatory tribe implicitly retained or reserved the right to repatriate and rebury the remains.

An implied treaty right becomes apparent when applicable canons of Indian treaty construction are applied to most land cession treaties. The canons require a court to interpret the treaties as understood by the Indians, given their practices and customs as of the date that the treaty was consummated. Thus, even though treaties ceded tribal lands to the United States, it cannot be implied that signatory tribes also relinquished their right to protect tribal dead buried in the ceded lands. Grave robbing was abhorrent to tribal religion. Therefore, the intent to allow desecration cannot fairly be imputed to the Chiefs who signed the treaties.

Similarly, it cannot be presumed that the United States intended to obtain Indian lands in order to desecrate Indian graves and obtain dead bodies, at least not until the 1868 Surgeon General's Order. This type of activity was a common-law felony and the canons of treaty construction preclude imputing an illegal intent to the United States as the fiduciary for Indian tribes.

Although a bundle of legal rights is clearly secured to Indian tribes by the Bill of Rights, treaties, common law, and Federal Indian law, the court system is too costly, time consuming, uncertain, and erratic to adequately redress massive repatriation problems. This is especially true for small, impoverished tribes faced with the problem of having to repatriate large numbers of tribal dead from many different states. Instead, remedial human rights legislation is the superior alternative.

PRE-NAGPRA LEGISLATION

STATE LEGISLATION

There are two types of relevant state legislation: (1) protection for unmarked graves; and (2) actual repatriation legislation.

1. Protection for Unmarked Graves

Thirty-four states have passed unmarked burial-protection laws in recent years, and there is a definite national trend towards the passage of such legislation. These laws typically prohibit intentional disturbance of unmarked graves, provide guidelines to protect the graves, and mandate disposition of human remains from the graves in a way that guarantees reburial after a study period. The constitutionality of these laws has been uniformly upheld in recent cases.

2. Repatriation Legislation

Five states have passed repatriation statutes since 1989. Three statutes were passed in response to specific repatriation and reburial matters, and three are general repatriation laws. The five states are California, Hawaii, Kansas, Nebraska, and Arizona.

In 1989, Hawaii appropriated $5 million from its Land Banking Law to purchase a Native Hawaiian burial ground owned by a private developer who had dug up over 900 remains in order to build a hotel—$500,000 of those funds were used to rebury the dead.

Similarly, in 1989, Kansas passed implementing legislation concerning a reburial agreement between state officials; the owner of a tourist attraction, which displayed 165 Indians from an Indian burial ground; and three Indian tribes that provided that the dead would be reburied by the descendent tribes. In addition, in 1991, the Kansas State Historical Society obtained legislation to allow it to deaccession and repatriate Pawnee Indian remains in its collection. The remains had been obtained from vandalized graves.

In 1989, Nebraska enacted a general repatriation statute entitled the "Unmarked Human Burial Sites and Skeletal Remains Protection Act" (see Peregoy 1992). This landmark legislation requires all state-recognized museums to repatriate "reasonably identifiable" remains and grave goods to tribes of origin on request. Under Nebraska's law, the Pawnee Tribe repatriated over 400 Pawnee dead from the Nebraska State Historical Society (Reeves 1990). The Pawnee Tribe reburied the dead in 1990—despite continued resistance by the Nebraska State Historical Society (see Echo-Hawk and Echo-Hawk 1991).

In 1990, Arizona passed a sweeping repatriation statute to repatriate human remains, funerary objects, sacred objects, and objects of tribal patrimony. Under this law, culturally or religiously affiliated remains held by state agencies are repatriated to tribes of origin. Moreover, remains that are not culturally affiliated with a tribe still must be reburied within one year nearest to the place where the remains were discovered.

During the same period that individual states started to enact legislation designated to ensure appropriate treatment of Indian human remains and funerary objects, the Federal Government, at the urging of Indian tribes and national organizations, also began to seriously consider the need for uniform, national legislation addressing this issue. That process culminated in the enactment of the Native American Graves Protection and Repatriation Act in 1990.

FEDERAL LEGISLATION

In 1986, a number of Northern Cheyenne leaders discovered that almost 18,500 human remains were warehoused in the Smithsonian Institution (Preston 1989). This discovery served as a catalyst for a concerted national effort by Indian tribes and organizations to obtain legislation to repatriate human remains and cultural artifacts to Indian tribes and descendants of the deceased. Between 1986 and 1990, a number of bills were introduced in the 99th, 100th, and 101st Congresses to address this issue.

In the 99th and 100th Congresses, Senator John Melcher, a Democrat from Montana, introduced two bills that would have provided for the creation of a Native American Museum Claims Commission.[21] The Commission was intended to provide a mechanism for the resolution of disputes between museums and Native Americans regarding the repatriation of "skeletal remains, cultural artifacts, and other items of religious or cultural significance." The bill's purpose was "to demonstrate basic human respect to Native Americans on these issues which are fundamentally important to them." In its final form, the Commission would have been empowered to mediate disputes, and, if such efforts failed, to issue orders following an evidentiary hearing. The legislation was vigorously opposed by, *inter alia*, the Smithsonian Institution, the American Association of Museums, and the Society for American Archeology. Consequently, the bill was not enacted.

In the 101st Congress, the Commission approach was abandoned in favor of legislation that would directly require repatriation of human remains and cultural artifacts, and protect burial sites. Senator John McCain, a Republican from Arizona; Senator Daniel Inouye, a Democrat from Hawaii; Representative Morris Udall, a Democrat from Arizona; and Representative Charles Bennett, a Democrat from Florida, each introduced bills dealing with different aspects of the repatriation issue.[22]

Each of the bills attempted to protect against the future illegal excavation of burial sites, albeit in a different manner. The McCain, Inouye, and Udall bills provided for an inventory, notice, and repatriation process for human remains and certain cultural artifacts in the possession of federal agencies, and also provided for a repatriation process applicable to federally-funded museums. The Inouye and Udall bills extended the inventory and notice requirement to federally-funded museums. The McCain, Udall, and Bennett bills included criminal penalties for illegal trafficking in protected remains or objects. The Inouye and one of the Udall bills created a Review Committee to oversee implementation of the legislation. These bills were each considered at the congressional hearings that preceded the enactment of NAGPRA. The provisions in these bills were subsumed in or superseded by the final enacted legislation.

Two other activities that would have a critical impact upon the effort to obtain general repatriation and grave protection legislation also occurred during this period. The first event occurred on November 28, 1989, when the National Museum of the American Indian (NMAI) Act was enacted into law (*see* Appendix 1). This Act created a National Museum of the American Indian within the Smithsonian Institution. Of significance for this article, the legislation also addresses the issue of human remains and funerary objects in the possession of the Smithsonian.

The NMAI Act requires the Smithsonian, in consultation with Indian tribes and traditional Indian religious leaders, to inventory human remains and funerary objects in its possession or control. The purpose of the inventory is to identify the origins of such remains based upon the best available scientific and historical documentation. If the tribal origin of remains or objects are identified by a preponderance of the evidence, the Indian tribe must be promptly notified. Upon request of a lineal descendant or culturally affiliated tribe, human remains and funerary objects associated with those remains are required to be expeditiously returned. Associated funerary objects include both those objects found with the remains and objects "removed from a specific burial site of an individual cultur-ally affiliated with a particular Indian tribe." The NMAI Act establishes a special committee to monitor and review the "inventory, identification, and return of Indian human remains and Indian funerary objects," including assistance in the resolution of disputes concerning repatriation.

The repatriation provisions in the National Museum of the American Indian Act were the result of an agreement between the Smithsonian Institution and Indian leaders. The NMAI Act's repatriation provisions were aimed at rectifying "some of the injustices done to Indian people over the years" and providing the promise that "one day their ancestors will finally be given the resting place that they so deserve." In his statement during debate, Senator John McCain, Republi-can from Arizona, specifically noted that this bill "is an important first step ... [that] sends a clear signal to those in the museum community who have dis-missed repatriation as a transitory issue that they would be wise to carefully con-sider the bills [pertaining to museums and federal agencies other than the Smith-sonian] currently before the Congress."[23]

The National Museum of the American Indian Act set an important precedent later cited by supporters of the Native American Graves Protection and Repatri-ation Act during the floor debate preceding the passage of NAGPRA.

The second event involved the creation of a year-long dialogue, which was suggested by the American Association of Museums and sponsored by the Heard Museum in Arizona. The participants in the dialogue were museums, scientists, and Native Americans. The dialogue centered around the appropriate treatment of human remains and cultural artifacts. In early 1990, the *Report of the Panel for a National Dialogue on Museum/Native American Relations* was issued. As summa-rized in the report of the Senate Select Committee on Indian Affairs pertaining to NAGPRA, the major conclusions of the Panel were as follows:

> The Panel found that the process for determining the appropriate disposition and treatment of Native American human remains, funerary objects, sacred objects, and objects of cultural patrimony should be governed by respect for Native human rights. The Panel report states that human remains must at all times be accorded dignity and respect. The Panel report indicated the need for Federal leg-islation to implement the recommendations of the Panel.
>
> The Panel also recommended the development of judicially-enforceable stan-dards for repatriation of Native American human remains and objects. The report recommended that museums consult with Indian tribes to the fullest extent pos-sible regarding the right of possession and treatment of remains and objects prior to acquiring sensitive materials. Additional recommendations of the Panel included requiring regular consultation and dialogue between Indian tribes and museums; providing Indian tribes with access to information regarding remains and objects in museum collections; providing that Indian tribes should have the

right to determine the appropriate disposition of remains and funerary objects and that reasonable accommodations should be made to allow valid and respectful scientific use of materials when it is compatible with tribal religious and cultural practices.[24]

As the legislative history indicates, the Panel report "provided a framework" for NAGPRA.

THE NATIVE AMERICAN GRAVES PROTECTION
AND REPATRIATION ACT

On November 16, 1990, the Native American Graves Protection and Repatriation Act was signed into law. NAGPRA is a complex law that sets out detailed procedures and legal standards governing the repatriation of human remains, funerary objects, sacred objects, and objects of cultural patrimony, and provides for the protection and ownership of materials unearthed on federal and tribal lands.

LEGISLATIVE INTENT

NAGPRA is, first and foremost, human rights legislation. It is designed to address the flagrant violation of the "civil rights of America's first citizens."[25] When NAGPRA was passed by the Senate, Senator Daniel Inouye stated that:

> When the Army Surgeon General ordered the collection of Indian osteological remains during the second half of the 19th Century, his demands were enthusiastically met not only by Army medical personnel, but by collectors who made money from selling Indian skulls to the Army Medical Museum. The desires of Indians to bury their dead were ignored. In fact, correspondence from individuals engaged in robbing graves often speaks of the dangers these collectors faced when Indians caught them digging up burial grounds.

> When human remains are displayed in museums or historical societies, it is never the bones of white soldiers or the first European settlers that came to this continent that are lying in glass cases. It is Indian remains. The message that this sends to the rest of the world is that Indians are culturally and physically different from and inferior to non-Indians. This is racism.

> In light of the important role that death and burial rites play in Native American cultures, it is all the more offensive that the civil rights of America's first citizens have been so flagrantly violated for the past century. Even today, when supposedly great strides have been made to recognize the rights of Indians to recover the skeletal remains of their ancestors and to repossess items of sacred value or cultural patrimony, the wishes of Native Americans are often ignored by the scientific community. In cases where Native Americans have attempted to regain items that were inappropriately alienated from the tribe, they have often met with resistance from museums. . . .

> [T]he bill before us is not about the validity of museums or the value of scientific inquiry. Rather, it is about human rights. . . . For museums that have dealt honestly and in good faith with Native Americans, this legislation will have little effect. For museums and institutions which have consistently ignored the

requests of Native Americans, this legislation will give Native Americans greater ability to negotiate.

Other parts of the legislative history also emphasize the "human rights" genesis of NAGPRA. The antecedents and progenitors of NAGPRA were repatriation provisions of the National Museum of the American Indian Act and the Report of the Panel for a National Dialogue on Museum/Native American Relations—both of which placed a major emphasis upon "human rights."

Congress viewed NAGPRA as a part of its trust responsibility to Indian tribes and people, specifically stating that it "reflects the unique relationship between the Federal Government and Indian tribes and Native Hawaiian organizations." The trust responsibility of the Federal Government to Indian tribes and people is a judicially-created concept that requires the United States to "adhere strictly to fiduciary standards in its dealings with Indians." The trust doctrine has given rise to the principle that enactments dealing with Indian affairs are to be liberally construed for the benefit of Indian people and tribes—a canon of construction similar to that applicable to remedial civil rights legislation.

The bill that was enacted reflected a compromise forged by representatives of the museum, scientific, and Indian communities. NAGPRA was designed to create a process that would reflect both the needs of museums as repositories of the nation's cultural heritage and the rights of Indian people. Most importantly, NAGPRA was intended to "establish a process that provides the dignity and respect that our Nation's first citizens deserve." Congress believed that NAGPRA would "encourage a continuing dialogue between museums and Indian tribes and Native Hawaiian organizations and . . . promote greater understanding between the groups." The primary features of the Native American Graves Protection and Repatriation Act of 1990 are summarized below.

REPATRIATION: HUMAN REMAINS AND ASSOCIATED FUNERARY OBJECTS

NAGPRA requires federal agencies (excluding the Smithsonian Institution) and museums (including state and local governments and educational institutions) to return human remains and associated funerary objects upon request of a lineal descendent, Indian tribe, or Native Hawaiian organization where the museum or agency itself identifies the cultural affiliation of the items through the required inventory process. In addition, if a museum or agency inventory does not establish the affiliation of the human remains or associated funerary objects, the Indian tribe or Native Hawaiian organization may still obtain the return of the remains or objects if it can prove, by a preponderance of the evidence, that it has a cultural affiliation with the item. In seeking to prove cultural affiliation, a claimant may utilize "geographical, kinship, biological, archaeological, anthropological, linguistic, folkloric, oral traditional, historical, or other relevant information or expert opinion."

Upon request, Indian tribes and Native Hawaiian organizations must be provided with available documentation by agencies and museums. NAGPRA indicates that such documentation shall be made available to Indian tribes or Native Hawaiian organizations that receive or should have received notice pursuant to 25 U.S.C.A. § 3003(d)—namely, those tribes that are believed to be culturally affiliated with specific items. The legislative history recognizes that § 3003(d) is to be liberally construed to include all tribes that have "a potential cultural affiliation (regardless of whether the showing of such affiliation would be based upon museum records or non-museum sources)." Available documentation includes "a summary of existing museum or Federal agency records, including inventories or catalogues, relevant studies, or other pertinent data." This requirement, however, is not an authorization for the initiation of new scientific studies—although it does not preclude further scientific study either.

"Cultural affiliation" is defined as "a relationship of shared group identity which can be reasonably traced historically or prehistorically between a present day Indian tribe or Native Hawaiian organization and an identifiable earlier group." The House committee explained that this requirement "is intended to ensure that the claimant has a reasonable connection with the materials." Congress recognized, however, that:

> [I]t may be extremely difficult, in many instances, for claimants to trace an item from modern Indian tribes to prehistoric remains without some reasonable gaps in the historic or prehistoric record. In such instances, a finding of cultural affiliation should be based upon an overall evaluation of the totality of the circumstances and evidence pertaining to the connection between the claimant and the material being claimed and should not be precluded solely because of some gaps in the record.[26]

Therefore, claimants need not establish cultural affiliation with "scientific certainty."

"Associated funerary objects" includes two categories of objects. First, it includes objects "reasonably believed to have been placed with individual human remains either at the time of death or later . . . as part of the death rite or ceremony" where both the human remains or objects are presently in the possession or control of a federal agency or museum. The remains and objects need not be in the possession or control of the same agency or museum, only in the possession or control of a museum or agency so that a connection between the objects and remains is possible. Moreover, the "possession or control" language indicates congressional intent to include objects consigned to individuals or museums not covered under NAGPRA if the ultimate determination as to the disposition of those objects is reposed in a federal agency or museum covered by NAGPRA. Second, "associated funerary objects" includes objects "exclusively made for burial purposes or to contain human remains."

Two exceptions exist to the requirement that human remains and associated funerary objects be "expeditiously returned" after cultural affiliation has been determined. The first exception is in those circumstances where the item is "indispensable for completion of a specific scientific study, the outcome of which would be of major benefit to the United States." If this exception applies, the items must be returned within 90 days after the completion of the study. There is no prohibition, however, against voluntary agreements between claimants and agencies or museums that would permit additional studies or other arrangements in regard to cultural items.

The second exception applies if multiple requests for a cultural item are made, and the federal agency or museum "cannot clearly determine which requesting party is the most appropriate claimant." In such a case, the federal agency or museum may retain the item until the parties agree upon disposition (with the Review Committee available for a mediating role) or the dispute is resolved by a court of competent jurisdiction.

As for human remains and associated funerary objects whose cultural affiliation cannot be determined, NAGPRA provides that the statutorily-created Review Committee compile an inventory of culturally unidentifiable human remains and recommend "specific actions for developing a process for disposition of such remains." The Review Committee's recommendations are to be made "in consultation with Indian tribes and Native Hawaiian organizations and appropriate scientific and museum groups." This issue was referred to the Review Committee because there was general disagreement on the proper disposition of such unidentifiable remains. Some believed that they should be left solely to science while others contended that, since they are not identifiable, they would be of little use to science and should be buried and laid to rest.

REPATRIATION: UNASSOCIATED FUNERARY OBJECTS, SACRED OBJECTS, AND ITEMS OF CULTURAL PATRIMONY

NAGPRA requires museums and federal agencies to repatriate unassociated funerary objects, sacred objects, and items of cultural patrimony pursuant to a four-step process.

1. Identification of the Item

First, the claimant must show that the item claimed is an unassociated funerary object, sacred object, or item of cultural patrimony. "Unassociated funerary object" is defined as an object "reasonably believed to have been placed with individual human remains either at the time of death or later . . . as part of a death rite or ceremony" where the human remains are *not* presently "in the possession or control of" a federal agency or museum, but the object can be related to specific individuals, families, or known human remains, or to a specific burial site of a culturally affiliated individual.

"Sacred objects" are defined as "specific ceremonial objects which are needed by traditional Native American religious leaders for the practice of traditional Native American religions by their present day adherents." As the House report explains,

> [T]he definition of "sacred objects" is intended to include both the objects needed for ceremonies currently practiced by traditional Native American religious practitioners and objects needed to renew ceremonies that are part of traditional religions. The operative part of the definition is that there must be "present day adherents" in either instance.

In explaining its legislative intent "to permit traditional Native American religious leaders to obtain such objects as are needed for the renewal of ceremonies," the House Interior Committee recognized that "the practice of some ceremonies has been interrupted because of governmental coercion, adverse societal conditions or the loss of certain objects through means beyond the control of the tribe at the time." Significantly, the definition recognizes that the ultimate determination of continuing sacredness must be made by the Native American religious leaders themselves because they must determine the current ceremonial need for the object. Thus, the term *sacred* is not defined explicitly in the legislative definition. Rather the definition will vary according to the traditions of the tribe or community. Of course, a religious leader's "determination" of sacredness could be challenged on the basis of its "sincerity" just as a First Amendment claim might be similarly challenged. Moreover, the leader cannot simply proclaim that an object is sacred—the object must meet the statutory criteria of having traditional religious significance and future use in a religious ceremony before it can be classified as a "sacred object."

"Cultural patrimony" is defined as "an object having ongoing historical, traditional, or cultural importance central to the Native American group or culture itself." Further, the object must have been considered inalienable by the Native American group when the object was separated from such group, rather than property that was owned and transferrable by an individual Native American; thus, tribal law or custom is determinative of the legal question of alienability at the time that the item was transferred. The Senate Committee report, explaining a similar cultural patrimony provision in an earlier version of the NAGPRA bill, indicated that cultural patrimony refers to items of "great importance" such as Zuni war gods or the Wampum belts of the Iroquois.

2. Cultural Affiliation and Prior Ownership or Control

Once it has been shown that an item is an unassociated funerary object, sacred object, or item of cultural patrimony, either the cultural affiliation must be determined or, in the case of sacred objects and items of cultural patrimony, the requesting tribe or Native Hawaiian organization must show that the object was previously owned or controlled by the tribe, organization, or a member thereof. A direct lineal descendant may also request repatriation of a sacred object owned by an ancestor. If a tribe or Native Hawaiian organization is making a claim based upon prior ownership or control by a tribal member, as opposed to the tribe, the claimant must show that no identifiable lineal descendants exist or that the lineal descendants have been notified and have failed to make a claim.

3. Right of Possession: Claimant's Prima Facie Case

The third step in the process requires a claimant to present "evidence which, if standing alone before the introduction of evidence to the contrary, would support a finding that the Federal agency or museum did not have the right of possession" of the items. Because the original "transfer" of many of these objects occurred when recordkeeping of such transactions was virtually nonexistent— and because of the near impossibility of proving that a legal document does not exist—evidence, by necessity, may include oral traditional and historical evidence, as well as documentary evidence. In making its prima facie case, the claimant is entitled access to "records, catalogues, relevant studies or other pertinent data" possessed by the federal agency or museum that relate to "basic facts surrounding acquisition and accession" of the items being claimed.

"Right of possession" means "possession obtained with the voluntary consent of an individual or group that had authority of alienation." This term was intended "to provide a legal framework in which to determine the circumstances by which a museum or agency came into possession of these . . . objects." Right of possession is based upon the general property law principle that "an individual may only acquire the title to property that is held by the transferor."

4. Right of Possession: Burden of Proof

If the claimant surmounts these three hurdles, the fourth step places a burden upon the museum or agency to prove that it has a right of possession in regard to the items in question. If the museum or agency cannot prove right of possession, the unassociated funerary object, sacred object, or item of cultural patrimony must be returned—unless the scientific study or competing claims exceptions apply.

NAGPRA makes clear that these provisions, as well as those pertaining to human remains and associated funerary objects, are not meant to limit the general repatriation authority of federal agencies and museums. Further, NAGPRA does not preclude agencies or museums from entering into agreements with tribes and organizations regarding any Native American objects owned or controlled by museums or agencies.

INVENTORY: HUMAN REMAINS AND ASSOCIATED FUNERARY OBJECTS

NAGPRA requires museums and federal agencies to complete an item-by-item inventory of human remains and associated funerary objects. "Inventory" is defined as a "simple itemized list that summarizes the information called for by this section." As part of the inventory, the museum or agency is required to "identify the geographical and cultural affiliation of each item," to the extent possible, based upon information within its possession. This provision does not "require museums . . . to conduct exhaustive studies and additional scientific research to conclusively determine . . . cultural affiliation." In fact, NAGPRA specifically states that it "shall not be construed to be an authorization for the initiation of new scientific studies of such remains and associated funerary objects or other means of acquiring or preserving additional scientific information from such remains and objects." Rather, NAGPRA's intent is merely to require a good faith effort to identify cultural affiliation based upon presently available evidence.

The inventory is to be conducted in consultation with Native American governmental and traditional leaders and the Review Committee. These inventories were to have been completed by November 16, 1995. Extensions may be granted by the Secretary of Interior for good cause. Interaction between tribes and museums is expected to occur during the inventory process. The intent of the process is to "allow for the cooperative exchange of information between Indian tribes or Native Hawaiian organizations and museums regarding objects in museum collections." Moreover, the inventory process is not intended to delay any pending actions on repatriation requests. Notice of culturally affiliated objects identified in the inventory is to be provided "throughout the process"—not merely after completion of the entire inventory. Within six months after the completion of the inventory, final notice must be sent to all tribes that are reasonably believed to be culturally affiliated with human remains or associated funerary objects in the possession or control of the museum or agency.

The notice shall include information about the circumstances surrounding the acquisition of each identified item and information about cultural affiliation. NAGPRA broadly intends that all potential tribal claimants, including Native Hawaiian organizations, receive notice. A tribe or Native Hawaiian organization that receives, or should have received, notice may request additional background information from the museum or agency relevant to the "geographical origin, cultural affiliation and basic facts surrounding [the item's] acquisition and accession." The requirement to perform the inventory is not made contingent upon a museum receiving federal funds.

SUMMARIES: UNASSOCIATED FUNERARY OBJECTS, SACRED OBJECTS, AND ITEMS OF CULTURAL PATRIMONY

NAGPRA requires that federal agencies and museums summarize their collections of unassociated funerary objects, sacred objects, and items of cultural patrimony. The summary is "in lieu of an object-by-object inventory" and requires the museum or agency to "describe the scope of the collection, kinds of objects included, reference to geographical location, means and period of acquisition and cultural affiliation, where readily ascertainable."

The museum or agency has three years to compile the summary. After the summary is completed—and presumably during its compilation—a consultation process with Native American governmental and traditional leaders is to occur. As with the inventory process, the summary process is not meant to delay action on pending repatriation requests. The House committee expressed its hope and expectation that the summary would lead to "open discussions" between tribes, museums, and federal agencies. Upon request, all tribes and Native Hawaiian organizations are entitled to obtain data pertaining to geographical origin, cultural affiliation, acquisition, and accession of these objects.

TRIBAL OWNERSHIP AND CONTROL: EMBEDDED CULTURAL ITEMS

NAGPRA expressly provides rules that address ownership or control of cultural items that are discovered in the future on federal and tribal land. In the case of human remains and associated funerary objects, any lineal descendants have the initial right of ownership or control. If lineal descendants of the human remains and associated funerary objects cannot be ascertained or when unassociated funerary objects, sacred objects, and items of cultural patrimony are involved, ownership or control is determined in the following statutory order of priority:

1. The tribe or Native Hawaiian organization owns or controls the disposition of all cultural items discovered on tribal land. Tribal land is defined to include all lands within the exterior boundaries of a reservation, all dependent Indian communities, and any lands administered for Native

Hawaiians pursuant to the Hawaiian Homes Commission Act of 1920, as amended, and the Hawaii Statehood Bill.

2. In the case of federal land, the tribe or Native Hawaiian organization with the closest cultural affiliation to the items has ownership or control. If there is a dispute between tribes, NAGPRA contemplates that the statutorily-created Review Committee may serve as a mediator of the dispute, and that agreements between tribes regarding disputed items could occur.

3. If cultural affiliation of the items cannot be established, but the objects are discovered on aboriginal land that has been the subject of a final judicial determination by the Indian Claims Commission or United States Court of Claims, the tribe that has obtained the judgment has the right of ownership and control over the items, unless another tribe can show a stronger cultural relationship.

The Secretary of the Interior is authorized to promulgate regulations pertaining to the disposition of cultural items unclaimed under this section in consultation with the Review Committee, Native American groups, museums, and scientists.

Whenever a party intends to intentionally excavate cultural items for any purpose, that party must obtain a permit pursuant to the Archeological Resources Protection Act of 1979. If tribal lands are involved, the items may be excavated only after notice to and consent of the tribe or Native Hawaiian organization. If federal lands are involved, the items may be excavated only after notice and consultation with the appropriate tribe or Native Hawaiian organization. As described previously, the tribe or Native Hawaiian organization retains ownership or control over remains and objects unearthed on lands covered by this provision.

If embedded cultural items have been inadvertently discovered as part of another activity, such as construction, mining, logging, or agriculture, the person who has discovered the items must temporarily cease activity and notify the responsible federal agency in the case of federal land or the appropriate tribe or Native Hawaiian organization in the case of tribal land. When notice is provided to the federal agency, that agency has the responsibility to promptly notify the appropriate tribe or Native Hawaiian organization. The intent of this provision is to "provide a process whereby Indian tribes and Native Hawaiian organizations have an opportunity to intervene in development activity on Federal or tribal lands to safeguard Native American human remains, funerary objects, sacred objects or objects of cultural patrimony."

If there is inadvertent discovery, Indian tribes or Native Hawaiian organizations are afforded thirty days to make a determination as to the appropriate disposition of the human remains and objects. Activity may resume thirty days after the Secretary of the appropriate federal department or the Indian tribe or the Native Hawaiian organization certifies that notice has been received. Federal department secretaries may delegate their responsibilities under this provision to the Secretary of Interior. Ownership and control of items inadvertently discovered are governed by the provisions described previously.

PROHIBITIONS AGAINST TRAFFICKING

NAGPRA prohibits all trafficking in Native American human remains for sale or profit except for remains that have been "excavated, exhumed or otherwise obtained with full knowledge and consent of the next of kin or the official governing body of the appropriate culturally affiliated Indian tribe or Native Hawaiian organization." The prohibition is intended to prevent trafficking in human remains that were wrongfully acquired, regardless of when and where obtained, including those removed prior to the enactment of NAGPRA. Violators are subject to a fine of up to $100,000 and face up to a one year jail sentence for a first offense; subsequent violations subject the offender to a fine of up to $250,000 and a maximum of five years in jail.

NAGPRA also prohibits trafficking in other cultural items obtained in violation of the act. Penalties for violation of this prohibition are the same as for trafficking in human remains. The anti-trafficking provision, as it applies to funerary objects, sacred objects, and items of cultural patrimony is for prospective acquisitions only. The prospective limitation however, does not prevent the application of existing state or federal law involving theft or stolen property if relevant to the possession or sale of Indian cultural items.

REVIEW COMMITTEE

NAGPRA creates a Review Committee, appointed by the Secretary of Interior, to monitor and review the implementation of NAGPRA. The Review Committee consists of seven members—three appointed by the Secretary from nominations submitted by Indian tribes, Native Hawaiian organizations, and traditional Native American religious leaders (at least two of the three must be traditional Native America religious leaders); three appointed from nominations submitted by national museum and scientific organizations; and one person chosen from a list compiled by the other six members. Federal officers and employees may not serve on the Review Committee.

The Review Committee composition and nomination process differ from that of the National Museum of the American Indian Act special review committee, which has been heavily criticized as being biased in favor of archaeological interests. NAGPRA seeks to secure a more diverse composition. The Review Committee's function is to:

(1) monitor the inventory and identification process;

(2) upon request, make findings related to the cultural affiliation and return of cultural items, and facilitate the resolution of disputes between interested parties; these findings are non-binding, but are admissible in any court proceeding filed pursuit to NAGPRA;

(3) compile an inventory of culturally unidentifiable human remains and make recommendations as to an appropriate process for their disposition;

(4) consult with the Secretary of the Interior in the development of regulations to implement NAGPRA;

(5) make recommendations as to the future care of repatriated cultural items; and

(6) submit an annual report to Congress.

ENFORCEMENT AND IMPLEMENTATION OF NAGPRA

NAGPRA provides for the Secretary of Interior to assess civil penalties against museums that do not comply with NAGPRA. The amount of the penalties are determined by (1) the archaeological, historical, or commercial value of the item involved; (2) economic and non-economic damages suffered by an aggrieved party; and (3) the number of violations.

The penalty provision is not meant to be an exclusive remedy for violations of NAGPRA. NAGPRA specifically provides that an aggrieved party can allege a violation of NAGPRA through a legal cause of action to enforce NAGPRA's provisions. Federal courts have authority to issue any necessary orders. This action is in addition to any existing procedural or substantive legal rights secured to tribes or Native Hawaiian organizations. If a museum repatriates an item in good faith, however, it is not liable for claims against it predicated upon a claim of wrongful repatriation, breach of fiduciary duty, public trust, or violations of state law.

To facilitate implementation, NAGPRA authorizes the Secretary of Interior to make grants to museums to undertake the inventory and the summary. Tribes and Native Hawaiian organizations may also receive grants to assist them in repatriating cultural items. Unfortunately, Congress failed to appropriate any funding under these provisions in 1991. Because sufficient funding is critical to completely fulfill the promise of NAGPRA, funds hopefully will be made available for these purposes in future fiscal years. Finally, the Secretary of the Interior is authorized to issue regulations by November 16, 1991, to carry out NAGPRA's provisions.

CONCLUSION

After centuries of discriminatory treatment, the Native American Graves Protection and Repatriation Act finally recognizes that Native American human remains and cultural items are the remnants and products of living people, and that descendants have a cultural and spiritual relationship with the deceased. Human remains and cultural items can no longer be thought of as merely "scientific specimens" or "collectibles."

In interpreting NAGPRA, it is critical to remember that it must be liberally interpreted as remedial legislation to benefit the class for whom it was enacted. This article, hopefully, will aid in the interpretation of NAGPRA in a manner consistent not only with the words of the statute, but also its spirit.

This article was also written to remind people that NAGPRA is a part of a larger historical tragedy: the failure of the United States Government, and other institutions, to understand and respect the spiritual and cultural beliefs and practices of Native people. Governmental policies that threaten Native American religions are not merely historical anachronisms, but continue to have a devastating impact upon contemporary Native Americans. Sites sacred to traditional Indian religious practitioners are currently threatened with destructive development. Centuries-old religious peyote use is threatened by ethnocentric court decisions. Native American prisoners are unable to practice their religions in a manner comparable to the respect accorded Judeo-Christian religious practice. Legislation to address this religious discrimination will be considered by Congress in the near future.

NAGPRA is unique legislation because it is the first time that the Federal Government and non-Indian institutions must consider what is *sacred* from an Indian perspective. Future legislation must be imbued with this same heightened consciousness of the nature of Indian culture and spirituality. The authors hope that the understanding, sensitivity, and moral outrage that gave rise to and is reflected in NAGPRA will likewise result in across-the-board protection and respect for traditional Native American religions—which continued to be under assault in the last decade of the twentieth century.

NOTES

1.   Originally published in the *Arizona State Law Journal*, Volume 24, 1992. Reprinted with permission of the *Arizona State Law Journal*.

2.   Human rights laws that seek to alleviate widespread civil rights violations usually take a long time to implement. For example, the federal civil rights legislation of the 1960s is still being implemented today.

3.   R.F. Martin, Annotation, *Corpse Removal and Reinterment*, 21 A.L.R.2d 472, 475–76 (1950).

4.   See, for example, Stastny v. Tachovsky, 132 N.W.2d 317, 325 (Neb. 1964); Neb. Rev. Stat. § 71-605(5), (6) (1989).

5.   For example, American property-law principles provide that no one may assert a claim to stolen or wrongfully acquired property; nonetheless, it took the Six Nations Confederacy 75 years to negotiate the return of its wampum belts, which are important communally owned patrimony of the Confederacy. *See* Onondaga Nation v. Thatcher, 61 N.Y.S. 1027,1028,1032 (Sup. Ct. Onondaga Co. 1899) (failed judicial attempt to repatriate belts).

6.   Secretary of the Interior, Federal Agencies Task Force, American Indian Religious Freedom Act Report, 77. August 1979.

7.   163 U.S. 537 (1896).

8.   Montoya v. United States, 180 U.S. 261, 265 (1901).

9.   Johnson v. McIntosh, 21 U.S. (8 Wheat.) 543, 569–70 (1823) (the "Marshall trilogy" of cases stripped Indian Nations of their sovereignty and land rights, and converted them into "domestic dependent nations" in a state of "pupilage" to the United States); *see also* Worcester v. Georgia, 21 U.S. (6 Pet.) 515 (1832); Cherokee Nation v. Georgia, 30 U.S. (5 Pet.)

1 (1831). Unlike *Plessy*, which was so devastating to African Americans, these Indian cases have never been overturned by the Supreme Court.

10.   United States *ex rel.* Standing Bear v. Crook, 25 F. Cas. 695 (C.C.D. Neb. 1879) (No. 14, 891).

11.   180 Cal. Rptr. 423 (Ct. App. 1982).

12.   273 N.E. 2d 893 (Ohio Ct. App. 1971).

13.   52 N.E. 126 (Ohio 1898).

14.   Maddox v. State, 121 S.E. 251 (Ga. Ct. App. 1924); Ware v. State. 121 S.E. 251 (Ga. Ct. App. 1924); Ternant v. Boudreau, 6 Rob. 488 (La. 1844); Charrier v. Bell, 496 So. 2d at 607; State v. Doepke, 68 Mo. 208 (1878); Busler v. State, 184 S.W.2d 24 (Tenn. 1944).

15.   Secretary of the Interior, Federal Agencies Task Force, American Indian Religious Freedom Act Report, 64. August 1979.

16.   494 U.S. 872 (1990).

17.   241 U.S. 602 (1916).

18.   370 N.W.2d 737 (S.D. 1985).

19.   United States v. Winans, 198 U.S. 371, 381 (1905).

20.   United States v. Adair, 723 F.2d 1394, 1413 (9th Cir. 1984); *see also* Oregon Wildlife Dept v. Klamath Tribe, 473 U.W. 753, 764–74 (1985); Oliphant v. Suquamish Indian Tribe, 435 U.S. 191, 208 (1978).

21.   S. 2952, 99th Cong., 2d Sess. (1986); S. 187 100th Cong., 1st Sess. (1987).

22.   Senator McCain introduced S. 1021, 101st Cong., 1st Sess. (1989); Senator Inouye introduced S. 1980, 101st Cong., 1st Sess. (1989); Rept. Udall introduced H.R. 1646, 101st Cong., 1st Sess. (1989) & H.R. 5237, 101st Cong., 2d Sess. (1990); and Rep. Bennett introduced H.R. 1381, 101st Cong., 1st Sess. (1989).

23.   135 Cong. Rec. S12397 (daily ed. Oct. 3, 1989).

24.   Senate Report No. 473, 101st Cong., 2d Sess. 1, 3–4 (1990).

25.   136 Cong. Rec. S17174 (daily ed. Oct. 26, 1990) (statement of Sen. Inouye).

26.   Senate Report No. 473, 101st Cong., 2d Sess. 1, 3–4 (1990).

REFERENCES CITED

Bieder, Robert. 1986. *Science Encounters the Indian, 1820-1880: The Early Years of American Eth-nology.* Norman, Oklahoma: University of Oklahoma Press.

——— 1990. "A Brief Historical Survey of the Expropriation of American Indian Remains." On file at the Native American Rights Fund, Boulder, Colorado.

——— 1992. "The collecting of bones for anthropological narratives." *American Indian Culture and Research Journal* 16(2):21–33.

Blair, Bowen . 1979a. "American Indians v. American museums: A matter of religious free-dom." *American Indian Journal of Law* 5(5): 13–21..

——— 1979b. "Indian Rights: Native Americans versus American Museums-a battle for artifacts." *American Indian Law Review* 7:125–154.

Cole, Douglas. 1985. *Captured Heritage: The Scramble for Northwest Coast Artifacts.* Seattle: University of Washington Press.

Davis, Bruce. 1980. "Indian religious artifacts: The curators moral dilemma." *Indian Law Supplement, Ctr. Report 1,* Vol. 2.

Dellios, Hugh. 1991. "Town Fears Burial Mounds May Never Be the Same." *Chicago Tribune,* October 13, p. 1.

Echo-Hawk, Roger C. and Walter R. Echo-Hawk,. 1991. "Repatriation, Reburial and Reli-gious Right." In *Handbook of American Indian Religious Freedom,* edited by C. Vec-sey, pp. 63–80. New York: Crossroad Publishing Company.

Echo-Hawk, Walter R. 1986. "Museums rights vs. Indian rights: Guidelines for assessing competing legal interests in Native cultural resources." *New York University Review of Law and Social Change* 14: 437-453.

Green, Rayna and Nancy Mitchell. 1990. *American Indian Sacred Objects and Skeletal Remains: A Resource Guide.* Washington, D.C.: American Association of Museums.

Harper, Kenn. 1986. *Give Me My Father's Body: The Life of Minik, the New York Eskimo.* Iqalvit, Northwest Territory: Blacklead Books.

Heath, Dwight B. 1986. *Mourt's Relation: A Relation or Journal of the English Plantation Settled at Plymouth in New England [1622].* New York: Corinth.

Horse Capture, George (ed.). 1989. *The Concept of Sacred Materials and Their Place in the World.* Cody, Wyoming: Buffalo Bill Historical Center.

Jackson, Percival E. 1950. *The Law of Cadavers and of Burials and Burial Places.* 2nd ed. New York: Prentice Hall.

Peregoy, Robert. 1992. "The legal basis, legislative history, and implementation of Nebras-ka's landmark reburial legislation." *Arizona State Law Journal* 24(1):329–389.

Price, H. 1991. *Disputing the Dead: U.S. Laws on Aboriginal Remains and Grave Goods.* Colum-bia, Missouri: University of Missouri Press.

Preston, Douglas J. 1989. "Skeletons in our Museums' Closets." *Harper's,* February, p. 68.

Reeves, Bob. 1990. "Pawnee Remains Going 'Home' After Long Wait." *Lincoln Star,* Sep-tember 11, p. 1, 5.

Riding In, James. 1992. "Without ethics and morality: A historical overview of imperial archaeology and American Indians." *Arizona State Law Journal* 24(1):11–34.

Thornton, Russell. 1987. *American Indian Holocaust and Survival.* Norman: University of Oklahoma Press.

Wooley, Wynne. 1990. "Caring for Old Cemetery Has Been a Lifetime Job," *Richmond New Leader,* May 16, p. 1.

Yalung, Catherine and Laurel I. Wala. 1992. "A survey of state repatriation and burial pro-tection statutes." *Arizona State Law Journal* 24(1):419–433.

CURRENT ISSUES AND DIFFERENT PERSPECTIVES

CHAPTER THREE

Ethics and the Past
Reburial and Repatriation in American Archaeology[1]

CHRISTINA E. GARZA AND SHIRLEY POWELL

Reburial and repatriation have been a thorn in the side of archaeology for over 15 years, pitting Native American against archaeologist, and archaeologist against archaeologist. This conflict revolves around one central issue: whether archaeology's claim on human remains and items of cultural patrimony as scientific data outweighs Native American ones based on ancestry and cultural affiliation. This question has been answered, in part, with the passage of NAGPRA; legally, Native American claims to ancestral human remains outweigh those of archaeologists. Yet the passage of NAGPRA has not settled the controversy. Petitions for repatriation of human remains and grave-associated objects are resolved case-by-case, with each case offering opportunities for renewal of the controversy.

How and why did this controversy arise, and what are the implications of reburial and repatriation for the practice of archaeology? We look for our answers in information from a variety of sources: historical, archaeological, and popular. We try to shed some light on how archaeologists view their own practice and on how others (especially Native Americans and the general public) view that same practice. We review archaeological ethics, the context within which archaeologists define their practice, and the history leading up to the reburial and repatriation controversy in the United States. The information presented here paints a fractious picture. Nonetheless, we have observed some positive signs and are confident that the situation is improving. Archaeologists and Indians are reaching compromises, and as a result the discipline will be revitalized by the input of the descendants of some of the people that archaeologists study.

TRADITIONAL ARCHAEOLOGY

Textbooks typically define archaeology as "the study of the human past" (Thomas 1989:649). Archaeologists study the past by making observations on objects (either natural or cultural) found in meaningful contexts (Thomas 1989:7). The kinds of questions asked about the past and the kinds of observations made

on the objects are guided by theory. But regardless of the theory guiding any particular archaeologist's inquiries, it is relatively safe to generalize that archaeologists are interested in the past and try to find out about the past by studying
objects.

One class of objects that archaeologists have collected and investigated in their
study of the past is found in graves—human remains and grave-associated
objects. Archaeologists (and physical anthropologists) contend that these objects
are important to their investigation of the past. The Society for American Archaeology's (SAA) statement on human remains (1987:215) claims:

> Research in archaeology, bioarchaeology, biological anthropology, and medicine
> depends upon responsible scholars having collections of human remains avail-
> able both for replicative research and research that addresses new questions or
> employs new analytical techniques.

The SAA (1987:215) further asserts:

> Whatever their ultimate disposition, all human remains should receive appropri-
> ate scientific study, should be responsibly and carefully conserved, and should be
> accessible only for legitimate scientific or educational purposes.

Archaeologists justify this position by appealing to: (1) the value of scientific
knowledge; (2) the importance of human remains and grave-associated objects
for learning about the past; (3) the relevance of this knowledge to the present; and
(4) the probability that future technological, methodological, and theoretical
advances will produce new ways of looking at the materials (Buikstra 1983:3–4;
Cheek and Keel 1984:198–199). In turn, these justifications support: (1) continued
recovery of human remains and grave-associated objects; (2) study and restudy of
those remains; (3) publication of the results of those studies; and (4) curation of
the objects in perpetuity.

An article in *Science* validates the claim made by archaeologists and physical
anthropologists that it is important to curate objects in perpetuity. In the 1960s a
team led by John Martyn of Bedford College, London, found a fragment of a
hominid skull at Lake Baringo. The site was never dated, and the fragment was
curated in the National Museum of Kenya. Twenty-five years later a team led by
Andrew Hill of Yale University took a new look. They found that the fragment
was actually of the genus *Homo*, and dated to 2.4 m.y.a.—close to half a million
years older than the previous 'earliest *Homo*' find (Gibbons 1992).

The above example, and others, foster archaeologists' attitudes toward archaeological 'data' and their curation. They believe so strongly in the importance of
knowledge and their responsibility to contribute to that knowledge, that to not do
so would be unthinkable and unethical. But these beliefs, however strong, are
culturally embedded and not shared by all. For some, excavation of human
remains, their study, and publication of the results are horrifyingly inappropriate
behaviors. This dissonance in cultural beliefs, coupled with the increasing
involvement of the public (through legislation and regulations) in archaeological
policy, lies at the heart of the reburial and repatriation issues: "Plainly stated, we
are dealing in separate realities" (Hill 1980:24). An examination of archaeological

ethics statements provides a basis for understanding the contexts within which archaeologists believe they operate.

ARCHAEOLOGICAL ETHICS

For whom and in what context do archaeologists practice their archaeology? Founded in 1935, the leading organization of professional archaeologists is the Society for American Archaeology (SAA). The SAA first published by-laws, with guidelines for ethical behavior, in 1948 (Society for American Archaeology, 1948; Davis 1984:14). These guidelines listed inappropriate activities for archaeologists and instituted a penalty for participating in such activities:

> Article I, Section 3: The practice of securing, hoarding, exchanging, buying, or selling of archaeological objects for the sole purpose of individual satisfaction or of personal financial gain is declared contrary to the objects of the Society and, therefore detrimental to the Society.

> Article II, Section 7: The [SAA] Council may drop from the roll of Affiliates and Fellows of the Society anyone who habitually commercializes archaeological objects or sites, or who otherwise has made improper use of his membership, or whose membership is regarded as detrimental to the Society. [Society for American Archaeology, 1948:148]

Later revisions of the SAA by-laws identified "ideals, objects, and accepted standards" for its members (Society for American Archaeology, 1977:308). These are: to promote and to stimulate interest and research in the archaeology of the American continents; to encourage a more rational public appreciation of the aims and limitations of archaeological research; to serve as a bond among those interested in American Archaeology, both professionals and nonprofessionals, and to aid in directing their efforts into more scientific channels; to publish and to encourage the publication of their results; to foster the formation and welfare of local archaeological societies; to advocate and to aid in the conservation of archaeological data; to discourage commercialism in the archaeological field and to work for its elimination [Society for American Archaeology, 1977:308].

In 1961 the SAA published guidelines for ethical behavior focusing on responsibilities to the archaeological record (Champe et al. 1961). These guidelines included grounds for censure or expulsion of violators; however, to date no one has been expelled from the SAA for unethical behavior (Davis 1984:17).

The revised SAA Principles of Archaeological Ethics reiterates the Society's focus on the archaeological record. The first principle pertains to the issue of stewardship:

> The archaeological record, that is, *in situ* archaeological material and sites, archaeological collections, records and reports, is irreplaceable. It is the responsibility of all archaeologists to work for the long-term conservation and protection of the archaeological record by practicing and promoting stewardship of the archaeological record. Stewards are both caretakers of and advocates for the archaeological record (Kintigh 1996:5).

Preserving the *in situ* archaeological record is also addressed in Principle 7, "Records and Preservation," in which the Society "encourage[s] colleagues, students, and others to make responsible use of collections, records, and reports in their research as one means of preserving the *in situ* archaeological record" (Kintigh 1996:17).

In a break with tradition, and in response to the current context of archaeology, the 1996 version of the SAA's ethics do recognize interests other than those of archaeologists. Principle 2 addresses archaeologists' accountability to the public (which pays for most archaeology these days through Federal and State compliance projects), and states that professionals should "make every reasonable effort, in good faith, to consult actively with affected"group(s)" (Kintigh 1996:5). Principle No. 4: Public Education and Outreach explicitly states that "Many publics exist for archaeology including students and teachers; Native Americans and other ethnic, religious, and cultural groups who find in the archaeological record important aspects of their cultural heritage; . . . and the general public" (Kintigh 1996:17; see all Lynott and Wylie 1995a).

However, the SAA's by-laws and guidelines are still primarily focused on the archaeological record and on archaeologists. Indeed, their emphasis is identified in their name; it is a Society *for* American Archaeology (Dincauze 1988:1, emphasis added). Further underscoring the SAA's protective stance on American archaeology is the explicit message that archaeology is a science and that ethical behavior vis-à-vis the archaeological record is based in science. To reiterate, members are encouraged to direct the efforts of professional and nonprofessional archaeologists into "more scientific channels" and to promote a "more rational public appreciation of the aims and limitations of archaeological research" (Society for American Archaeology, 1977:308). Although laudable in and of themselves, such statements have been the basis of charges of scientism that have been leveled against the discipline (e.g., Echo-Hawk and Echo-Hawk 1991; Vizenor 1986).

Other archaeological professional groups generally have either ignored the question of ethical behavior or followed the SAA's lead (Davis 1984:17). "The Society for Historical Archaeology, founded in 1967, makes no mention of unethical behavior and provides no mechanism for chastising its members for wrongdoing" (Davis 1984:17; Society for Historical Archaeology, 1967). The American Society for Conservation Archaeology, founded in 1975, uses virtually the same wording as the SAA's.

In 1976 the Society of Professional Archaeologists (SOPA) broke with tradition, publishing a much expanded and more inclusive Code of Ethics and Standards of Research Performance. SOPA's Code of Ethics directed an archaeologist's ethical responsibilities beyond the archaeological record and colleagues to include the public and employers and clients (SOPA 1981, reprinted in Green 1984:22-27). Furthermore, the ordering of the Code of Ethics gives priority to the public. One of their statements anticipates some of the controversy surrounding reburial and repatriation, by exhorting archaeologists to "[b]e sensitive to, and respect the legitimate concerns of, groups whose culture histories are the subjects of archeological investigations" (SOPA 1981, reprinted in Green 1984:22).

The SOPA guidelines transcend the disciplinary boundaries of previous archaeological ethics statements, and by placing emphasis on the public, echo the concern that anthropological societies place on living peoples (e.g., American Anthropological Association 1976; National Association of Practicing Anthropologists n.d.). The American Anthropological Association (AAA) (1976:1) states:

> In research, anthropologists' paramount responsibility is to those they study. When there is a conflict of interest, these individuals must come first. Anthropologists must do everything in their power to protect the physical, social, and psychological welfare and to honor the dignity and privacy of those studied.

And, the National Association of Practicing Anthropologists (NAPA) affirms that (n.d.:1):

> Our primary responsibility is to respect and consider the welfare and human rights of all categories of people affected by decisions, programs or research in which we take part. . . . It is our ethical responsibility, to the extent feasible, to bring to bear on decision making, our own or that of others, information concerning the actual or potential impacts of such activities on all whom they might affect.

The AAA and NAPA guidelines have their particular emphases on the well-being of living peoples because cultural anthropologists work with living peoples. But, with whom do archaeologists work? To whom are they responsible? Until recently the answer would have been that archaeologists work with deceased populations, and that archaeological research does not impact (or only minimally impacts) living populations. However, reburial and repatriation have challenged these assumptions, and responses are evident in the "First Code of Ethics," recently published by the World Archaeological Congress (WAC) (1991:22–23). The WAC obligates its members to professional activity consistent with the following principles (only some are listed here):

1. To acknowledge the importance of indigenous cultural heritage, including sites, places, objects, artifacts, and human remains, to the survival of indigenous cultures.

2. To acknowledge the importance of protecting indigenous cultural heritage to the well-being of indigenous peoples.

4. To acknowledge that the important relationship between indigenous peoples and their cultural heritage exists irrespective of legal ownership.

5. To acknowledge that the indigenous cultural heritage rightfully belongs to the indigenous descendants of that heritage.

8. To seek, whenever possible, representation of indigenous peoples in agencies funding or authorizing research to be certain their view is considered as critically important in setting research standards, questions, priorities, and goals. [WAC 1991:22]

In the past, archaeological ethics statements have focused on the archaeological record and the profession of archaeology. The Society for Professional Archaeologists, the World Archaeological Congress, and to some extent the Society for American Archaeology, are notable exceptions, emphasizing as well the public, employers, clients, and indigenous populations. Their concern (Society of Professional Archaeologists, 1981, reprinted in Green 1984:22; WAC 1991:22) suggests a sensibility more akin to the ethics statements of anthropological groups like the AAA and NAPA than to other archaeological organizations.

Clearly, over the years the archaeological community's sense of responsibility and awareness of their context has expanded. However, despite this trend, a recurrent theme in recent publications suggests some reaction among professional archaeologists to this broadening. An extreme example, Clement Meighan (1986:7–8), responds strongly to Native American demands for a say about the final disposition of ancestral human remains:

> . . . if I am studying Stonehenge, part of my obligation is to the people who built Stonehenge—they are my informants. Similarly, if I am studying a site in California occupied 5000 years ago, it is the occupants of that site to whom I am obligated to provide a true statement of their life and culture. . . . But if I accept the AAA statement . . . , my paramount responsibility can only be dealt with by a thorough and honest investigation of the archaeological remains.
>
> Avoidance of some or all of the evidence, and failure to communicate all the findings in a free and open way, amounts to destruction of some of the culture history of the people being studied.

Thus, following Meighan's logic, archaeologists (because they think they know the most about their prehistoric informants) are in the position of determining what best contributes to their "physical, social, and psychological welfare" (American Anthropological Association 1976:1). Meighan's conclusion makes archaeologists the final court of appeal regarding the disposition of ancient and/or prehistoric remains, and it limits the context of the practice of archaeology to archaeologists and to the people producing the archaeological record (but *not* their descendants).

Similarly, arguments against reburial that emphasize the importance of the long-term curation of human remains and the potential contributions of restudy with new techniques imply a context for the practice of archaeology (Buikstra 1981, 1983; Turner 1986). Most obviously, access to human remains for study and restudy, and the results of these studies, are important to other archaeologists and physical anthropologists.

Archaeologists and physical anthropologists argue that other constituencies benefit from these analyses as well; however, at least some of these constituencies don't appear to agree. They point out that Native Americans have their own answers to many of the questions that archaeologists and physical anthropologists ask; the fact that the two sets of answers are not the same does not undermine the value of their own answers to Native Americans (e.g., Cecil F. Antone in Quick 1985:103; Weldon Johnson in Quick 1985:41-42). The most extreme critics deny benefits to any groups other than archaeologists; they charge that archaeologists consume the archaeological record for their own ends, converting it into recognition among their peers, jobs, promotions, and raises (e.g., Echo-Hawk and Echo-Hawk 1991:68; Vizenor 1986).

Tim White, author of *Human Osteology*, emphasizes the scientific value of human remains, the importance of long term curation, and the potential contributions of restudy with new techniques (White 1991:422–423). However, on a more balanced note, White (1991:423) also calls for "ongoing dialogue" among "all groups involved in the debate."

Although many archaeologists have broadened their horizons and accept the public in its many guises as part of the context for the practice of archaeology, some do not. And, unfortunately, Native American opposition to archaeology and archaeologists has coalesced around those archaeologists who do not. In narrowing their definition of context, such archaeologists operate as if they believe that their work has no impact on anything or anyone other than archaeological objects and their colleagues. Some critiques of this approach to archaeological practice appear to be reacting to the implicit exclusion from the archaeological decision-making process of all contemporary peoples who are not professional archaeologists. However, as reflected in more recent ethical statements and organizational by-laws, the practice of archaeology occurs in the present and has the potential to impact contemporary people—lineal descendants of the prehistoric peoples under study and others (e.g., Adams 1984; Ferguson 1984; Nichols et al. 1989).

CHANGING ARCHAEOLOGICAL AND PUBLIC OPINION

HISTORICAL BACKGROUND TO THE CONFLICT

To quote historian R. G. Collingwood, the problems we study "ultimately arise out of 'real life' . . . we study history in order to see more clearly into the situation in which we are called upon to act" (quoted in Trigger 1989:13). The development of archaeology and ethnology in the nineteenth century certainly follows that model, and provides a historical context for the present day conflict. By the middle of that century, the majority of America thought Native Americans incapable of becoming civilized, and their "low mental states" forced society as a whole to either actively exterminate them or passively allow them to "pass into extinction . . . to make room for progress" (Gulliford 1996:122). It was believed that the advanced civilizations of Mesoamerica and South America achieved their complexity with the help of outside (that is, European) influence. That influence never reached North America, and it was doubtful that the populations south of the United States were related to those of North America at all (Bieder 1986:123–124; Trigger 1989; Willey and Sabloff 1980).

The Native American's history was, however, part of the history of the whole country. This history was important—the United States needed as long and distinguished a history as Europe to shed its provincial reputation. The Native Americans, and the remnants of older civilizations, provided a historical legitimacy for the country. Therefore, scores of people set out to document the looks and customs of existing tribes, as well as surveying and excavating ancient mounds and ruins (Baigell 1984; Bieder 1986; Gruber 1986; Trigger 1980, 1986,

1989; Willey and Sabloff 1980). One such person was artist George Catlin, a man who could also be considered one of the first ethnographers through his paintings and descriptions of native life. He spent the years 1832–36 traveling among the Plains tribes, documenting every detail with his brush and pen (Baigell 1984; Catlin 1911, 1973). Although he was an early and rare advocate for Native Americans, Catlin was also sure that they had no future:

> . . . the tribes of the red men of North America, as a nation of human beings, are on their wane; that (to use their own very beautiful figure) 'they are fast travel-ling to the shades of their fathers, towards the setting sun'. [Catlin 1973:10]

This surety that Native Americans would disappear in the near future was shared by the American public in general. Native Americans were considered incapable of change. Since they obviously could not adapt to western civilization, they would die out. There was a new order sweeping across the continent, and the Native American was not a part of it (Bieder 1986; Catlin 1911, 1973; Medicine 1972; Trigger 1980, 1986, 1989). American anthropology developed in large part to preserve Native American culture for posterity—not to help them fit into the new society. According to Henry Schoolcraft, that was the primary goal of the field (Trigger 1989:111). Anthropology was also to provide answers as to why Native Americans were racially inferior to other world populations (Bieder 1986; Trigger 1980, 1986, 1989; Willey and Sabloff 1980).

In the search for physical explanations of the inherent inferiority of Native Americans, craniology took an early lead (skull shape and cranial capacity were considered indicative of mental ability [Bieder 1986]). Of course, to investigate any theories skull specimens were needed. Field workers were sent out across the United States to obtain items for study—the Native American was little more than a zoological specimen (Bieder 1980:101; Medicine 1972:23). A government explorer was even quoted as suggesting his expedition "catch" one of the Native Americans along their route and "preserve him in alcohol . . . " (Bieder 1986:101–102). The trade in Native American "specimens" became quite lucrative, and was something of a "cottage industry" on the frontier (Bieder 1986:67). This business continued throughout the nineteenth century, with even respected anthropologists like Franz Boas participating (Bieder 1986).

Ironically, it was during the nineteenth century that archaeologists spent the most time with Native Americans. People like Frank Cushing, Jesse Walter Fewkes, and Ephraim George Squier studied both ethnology and archaeology to reconstruct the prehistory of the United States and the history of Native Americans (Bieder 1986; Trigger 1980, 1986, 1989; Willey and Sabloff 1980). In the early twentieth century, however, archaeologists became much more focused on material culture, and turned their attention away from Native Americans (Trigger 1980, 1986, 1989; Willey and Sabloff 1980). Archaeologists and Native Americans became alienated as the field turned its attention to becoming a science, and this relationship continued even through the processual revolution, when archaeology became anthropology (at least in Binford's [1962] terms). According to Trigger, "archaeologists have turned from using their discipline to rationalize Euro-American prejudices against native people, as they did in the nineteenth century, to simply ignoring native people as an end of study in themselves" (Trigger

1986:206). When archaeology became processual, it became the quest for "explanation[s] in systemic terms for classes of historical events" (Binford 1962:22), and
not the study of human beings.

But Native Americans did not yet quite view archaeology as a lost cause. In
1972, when the political power of Native Americans had just begun to rise and the
backlash against anthropology was very strong, at least one Native American
proposed archaeology be the bridge to anthropological studies that would be relevant to Native Americans:

> The study of archaeology, together with research among the living descendants
> of the Native of the Americas, and an examination of the oral history, is one of the
> most valuable contributions of the scholarly community to an understanding of
> man from his earliest beginnings. In the light of the youthful 'war cry' for rele-
> vant studies, what could be much more relevant than this, if one is looking for
> scholarly excellence, not only excellence in the art of proselytizing (Henry
> 1972:58).

Instead, archaeologists have become victims of their own insensitivity when it
comes to relations with Native Americans (Ortiz 1972:8). Archaeology has a lot to
offer, and Native Americans realize this. Unfortunately, archaeologists have not
realized this, and so conflict has arisen. As Trigger (1989:376-377) says:

> In North America, Australia, and other parts of the world where native peoples
> have been overwhelmed by European settlement, the image of the 'unchanging
> savage' has been demonstrated, with the help of archaeological data, to have been
> a myth that developed as part of the process of European colonization. In this
> context the notion that archaeological data should be used only to formulate and
> test as an end in themselves a potpourri of general theories about human behav-
> ior and cultural change is increasingly being viewed as not only conceptually
> inadequate but also neo-colonialist and insulting to the Third World and to native
> peoples.

These observations suggest that archaeologists and Native Americans perceive
archaeology operating in different arenas. At least some archaeologists operate as
though archaeology exists only for archaeologists, apparently believing that their
activities have no impact on anyone else. Many Native Americans view archaeology in a different context—a context that includes them as well.

REBURIAL AND REPATRIATION WITHIN ARCHAEOLOGY

Most archaeologists would not characterize themselves as racists who exclude
and dehumanize contemporary (and past) Native Americans. But most also view
themselves as operating in a context narrowly constrained by disciplinary boundaries—for the most part archaeology has been by and for archaeologists. However, with federal legislation passed over the last 30 years, these disciplinary boundaries have begun to break down. The vast majority of funding for archaeology
comes from public coffers, and the public (including Native Americans) has
demanded an increasing role in archaeological policy-making. Some of these
demands are based in value systems different from those that guide traditional
archaeology. These demands pit archaeologists against some members of the pub-

lic, and as some archaeologists accept new ways of doing archaeology, they pit archaeologists against other archaeologists.

In a 1971 *American Antiquity* editorial, Charles R. McGimsey, III (1971:1), stated that "Archaeology, like any field of endeavor, cannot and does not exist apart from the world around it. Nonetheless, most of us, much of the time, pretend that it can and does." Subsequent editorials and minutes from the annual meetings reiterated this theme. A few archaeologists were expressing concern in public about archaeologists' relations with Native Americans, and they were predicting the increasing probability of clashes over human remains and grave-associated objects.

Roderick Sprague (1974:1, see also Roderick Sprague in Quick 1985:16) recalled that:

> [a]n attempt was made at the 1968 annual meeting of the Society for American Archaeology to draft and submit a resolution expressing the need for greater respect of American Indian wishes by American archaeologists. This resolution did not make it to the floor.

Elden Johnson (1973:129) questioned whether the SAA's "Four Statements for Archaeology" omitted "a responsibility that we [archaeologists] have not acknowledged"—a responsibility to the "American Indians who are the cultural and biological descendants, particular or general, of the past residents of the sites we excavate." And, in the minutes of the 1974 SAA meeting, "Cynthia Irwin-Williams report[ed] that relationships between native Americans and archaeologists have grown more and more tense over the past few years" (Society for American Archaeology, 1974:668). Such concerns found only occasional published expression in archaeological and anthropological journals over the subsequent years (e.g., Rosen 1980; Trigger 1980).

Despite these early expressions of concern for apparently deteriorating relationships between archaeologists and Native Americans, the SAA endorsed a comparatively unambiguous resolution on human remains in 1984 (Society for American Archaeology, 1984). The SAA resolution is a slightly reworded version of a position unanimously supported in 1982 by the American Association of Physical Anthropologists (White 1991:421):

> THEREFORE BE IT RESOLVED that the Society for American Archaeology deplores the indiscriminant reburial of human skeletal remains except in situations where specific lineal descendants can be traced and it is the explicit wish of these living descendants that remains be reburied rather than being retained for research purposes; and that no remains should be reburied without appropriate study by physical anthropologists with special training in skeletal biology unless lineal descendants explicitly oppose such study (Society for American Archaeology, 1984:216).

The resolution continues by encouraging " . . . close and effective communication with appropriate groups and with individual scholars who study human remains that may have biological or cultural affinity to those groups" (ibid.). Although this resolution passed, and was a majority opinion, there was a voice urging that the SAA not pass any resolution against reburial (see Zimmerman n.d., 1985).

Native American spokespersons reacted strongly and negatively to the SAA's position. The resolution can be (and has been) interpreted as meaning that the research value of human remains is great—so great that to deny archaeologists and physical anthropologists access to them requires an impossibly convincing case. Some argue that demonstrating convincing proof of lineal descent may prove impossible when many Native Americans were forcibly relocated from ancestral homelands to reservations (Echo-Hawk and Echo-Hawk 1991:69). Others dispute the claim that scientific study of their ancestors has benefitted descendant groups in any way (e.g., Mihesuah 1991; Quick 1985:95). And still others argue that the precedence that archaeologists place on their own interpretations of the past devalues Native American accounts as myth or superstition (e.g., Cecil F. Antone in Quick 1985:103; Weldon Johnson in Quick 1985:41–42). Walter Echo-Hawk, a Pawnee and staff attorney with the Native American Rights Fund, views archaeologists' positions on reburial and repatriation as one more example of the long history of Euroamerican racism: "They took everything. . . . Including our dead. *Even* our dead" (Preston 1989:67; see also Hammil and Cruz 1989)

Public Opinion

The media have cast their inquiring eye on reburial and repatriation in articles and newsclips generally sympathetic to the Native American position and critical of archaeology. A 1989 *Newsweek* article headlined "The Plunder of the Past," focused on the ravages of pothunting. However, quoting Native American activist Dennis Banks, the authors suggest that archaeologists are "hardly any better than the graverobbers themselves; only difference is they've got a state permit" (Cowley et al. 1989:60). A *Harper's Magazine* treatment of reburial and repatriation opened with an anecdote about mothballed mummies in the American Museum of Natural History (Preston 1989:66), and continued with the story of six Eskimos who were brought to the American Museum of Natural History in 1986 by Arctic explorer Robert E. Peary. Franz Boas and colleague Ales Hrdlicka went to work measuring and photographing their visitors immediately. The "slight colds" noted upon the Eskimos arrival had turned out to be tuberculosis, and by spring they were dead. Hrdlicka had all four macerated, boiled, and reduced to skeletons that were then added to the museum's collection for scholarly study (Preston 1989:69–70).

The topic of reburial and repatriation has appeared in outlets as different as *Glamour* magazine (a short biography of Suzan Shown Harjo entitled "Honoring Her Ancestors" [Swisher 1990]), a *Saturday Night Live* sketch in which a Native American from Arizona competed on a game show to recover sacred objects and the remains of his great-grandfather, the *National Geographic* coverage of the "crime scene" at Slack Farm in western Kentucky (Arden 1989:378), and the best-selling mystery novel, *Talking God* (Hillerman 1989). Treatment of archaeologists in these pieces has varied from neutral to hostile; however, Native Americans generally are portrayed sympathetically.

In 1989 the SAA opposed federal legislation viewed as favorable to Native Americans (e.g., the Melcher bill, S. 187, approved in committee, but got no further in the 100th Congress). Later, however, the SAA softened its position, and added its support to Morris Udall's Native American Graves Protection and Repatriation Act (NAGPRA, P. L. 101–601), which passed the 101st Congress in November, 1990. Also, Keith Kintigh (former head of the SAA's ad hoc committee on reburial) and Lynne Goldstein (former secretary of the Society) wrote an *American Antiquity* Forum paper in which they conclude that archaeologists must "address our various constituencies, educate all of the publics about the past, and make certain that we don't alienate or disenfranchise past, present, or future generations" (Goldstein and Kintigh 1991:590).

Past generations of Native Americans were alienated, however, and all too often the alienation stemmed from violent and racist behavior on the part of the new Euroamerican society, which was forging its way across North America. Archaeology and anthropology in the United States were born during this period of "manifest destiny," and the influences this had on the two fields are still quite evident. Looking back, it is easy to see the reburial and repatriation conflict as a result of long-held attitudes toward the place of Native Americans in the greater society of the United States.

ARCHAEOLOGY IN THE 21ST CENTURY

THE CONSERVATION ETHIC IN ARCHAEOLOGY

Archaeologists, especially since the early 1970s, have published articles and books expressing their concern with archaeological sites as nonrenewable resources and with the diminishing cultural resource base (e.g., Davis 1972; Lipe 1974, 1977; Schiffer and Gumerman 1977). The resultant conservation model recognizes the invasive and destructive nature of archaeological data collection through excavation, and encourages archaeologists to direct their research efforts to those sites that are threatened by "construction, vandalism, and the looting of antiquities for the market" (Lipe 1977:19). Indeed, SAA's 1996 ethical guidelines place a great emphasis on the stewardship of the archaeological record *in situ* (Kintigh 1996; Lynott and Wylie 1995b). This concern with protecting archaeological remains *in situ* interjects a positive note into this discussion—suggesting a common ground between archaeologists and Native Americans. Native Americans do not want to see sites destroyed any more than do archaeologists.

However 'threatening activities' are poorly defined at present; with some archaeologists including their own activities under that category, while others argue that their excavations protect the archaeological record by distancing it from vandals (in museums or archaeological laboratories). Typically, archaeologists love field work. Some feel ambivalence about the conservation ethic due to their opposing desires to collect new data to answer new questions or look at old ones in new ways (from whatever sites they so choose), and to conserve the resource base.

Unfortunately, for the profession's public image, some Native Americans and others (especially pothunters cited in the public media) have been quick to categorize archaeological excavations as just one more class of destructive activity. A Phoenix newspaper article on the Santa Fe antiquities market charged that "[a]rchaeologists have been just as responsible for destroying sites [as amateurs]" (Hart 1988:AA4).

Despite the ambivalence that archaeologists feel about limiting their own access to sites, and perhaps because of articles like the one quoted above, we note an escalating focus on endangered sites; the conservation ethic is slowly but increasingly becoming a part of archaeological practice. Certainly this trend is encouraged by the fact that the majority of funding for archaeological field work derives from federal legislation intended to protect archaeological resources. We predict that this trend will continue, and that it will lead to collaborative efforts between archaeologists and descendant native populations—thereby lessening the basis for conflict.

NON-INVASIVE ARCHAEOLOGY

Sensitivity to other peoples' world views and the loss of access to human remains do not signal the end of archaeology—scientific or otherwise. Most archaeology does not impact human remains; surface survey is the most notable example, and many excavations do not encounter human remains at all.

Archaeologists can use many techniques to expand their knowledge of the past that do not require the destruction of archaeological remains. Remote sensing, advanced mapping technology, geographic information systems (GIS), and image analysis all offer methods of research that are non-invasive. Remote sensing can easily allow archaeologists to compile a regional perspective including both site and environmental information. It also clearly identifies very large features, provides information on likely areas to look for past human occupation, and allows us to gather information on areas that are very difficult to access or that we do not have the time or personnel to survey (Avery and Berlin 1992; Ebert and Lyons 1983; McAleer 1987; Olsen 1985; Wolkomir 1988). For specific examples of the use of remote sensing techniques in archaeology, see Berlin et al. (1977, 1990), Donoghue and Shennan (1988), Drager and Ireland (1986), Laustrup (1987), McAleer (1988), McKee and Sever (1989), Nichols (1988), Scollar et al. (1990), Sever et al. (1989), Sheets and Sever (1988), and Thompson (1988).

COVENANTAL ARCHAEOLOGY

Archaeology has traditionally been done by and for archaeologists, with their primary justification for their activities being contributions to knowledge. Nonetheless, throughout the history of the discipline, some practitioners have worked *with* indigenous peoples, defining problems and solving them to their mutual benefit, and this trend is becoming stronger.

Archaeologists have worked with Indians on lands claims cases (Anyon and Zunie 1989), revitalization of traditional craft industries (Parezo 1987), and expansion of tribal economic bases (through craft sales [C. Small personal communication 1991; Southwest Arts and Artists Catalogue, 1991] and through tourist development). Additionally, many archaeologists are working with tribal governments to develop their own cultural preservation and archaeological management offices (Adams 1984; Ferguson 1984; Klesert 1992). Some such programs train tribal members as archaeologists and ethnographers—so that they may take over direction and management of their cultural heritages. The Navajo Nation Archaeology Department has entered into such a cooperative arrangement with Northern Arizona University's Anthropology Department to facilitate the formal education of Navajo anthropologists (Klesert 1992).

We feel that such endeavors, while sporadic in the past, are increasing and will become the wave of the future. The new covenantal archaeology will stress cooperation and mutualism at all stages of research, conservation, and preservation. Truly cooperative efforts will be a major step towards reducing conflict and controversy (see Wood and Powell 1993). Cooperation may mean that some topics traditionally investigated by archaeologists may no longer be appropriate subjects of inquiry. However, we feel that new areas of inquiry will open, and that the definition of archaeological 'data' will expand beyond objects to include oral tradition and, for want of a better word, paleoethnography (see Anyon et al. 1996).

Clearly our predictions have a strong postprocessual influence. Postprocessualism does not deny processual interpretations, although this version may deny archaeologists access to some classes of data. It does, however, allow for alternative points of view, and these alternatives to established theoretical orientations open the door for Native American participation. The existence of alternative interpretations does not require that they be uncritically accepted. As Hodder (1991:7) says, postprocessual interpretations still require a "guarded objectivity of the data."

CONCLUSION

Reburial and repatriation have changed and will continue to change how archaeology is done in this country, and both theory and method are affected. Reburial and repatriation have broadened the context within which archaeology is done, increasing the Native voice. Native American involvement in decisions about what constitutes archaeological research introduces a distinctly contextual or postprocessual perspective. The single 'true' interpretation of the processualists will probably never be acceptable to archaeology's new multicultural audience.

Methods, too, will change. Concern with disturbance of human remains and grave-associated objects, coupled with the legally recognized stewardship of the prehistoric peoples' descendants, has already had the effect of redefining 'archaeological data' as the ancestors of living peoples. Surface archaeology, non-invasive techniques, and excavation of only endangered sites will be the rule. Archaeologists will be held to the conservation ethic. This ethic provides the common ground for Indians and archaeologists to work together to protect the heritage of the past.

Within archaeology there must be a shift in attitude concerning accountability before the existing bumps are smoothed out and the potholes filled in. Current ethical guidelines place much more stress on accountability to the profession and the archaeological materials rather than to the public. What is ethically correct treatment of the materials is also judged by the discipline itself, with little or no input from outside sources. An examination of ethics statements shows a deep concern with the improper excavation of materials for the antiquities market and

the ownership of data. On the positive side, there is a growing concern for working with the Native American descendants of prehistoric people, and with Native
American perceptions of the limitations and excesses of archaeology. As one
archaeologist writes:

> I have always explicitly opposed reburial of human remains or of any archaeo-
> logical remains. I still do. However, by accepting Aboriginal ownership and
> control, I accept that a decision to rebury remains, have them studied, dated to
> whatever, is completely in the hands of the relevant community. Clearly, they
> must make these decisions on far more than scientific bases (Pardoe 1991:121,
> N.3).

The first two sentences of this quotation may reflect the majority opinion
today among American archaeologists. However, despite their opposition to
reburial and repatriation, many archaeologists are being confronted with alternative, deeply held beliefs. These diametrically opposed beliefs raise questions
about who has the right to make decisions about archaeological remains. Unfortunately, it looks as if federal courts will be called upon to decide whose concerns
take precedence. The discovery of 9,200 year old human remains on the banks of
the Columbia River near Kennewick, Washington, have spurred the first serious
legal challenge to NAGPRA since its passage nearly ten years ago (Mauro 1997;
Slayman 1997; Watson, this volume). The lawsuit, filed by eight anthropologists,
questions the (lack of) evidence used to determine cultural affiliation with
remains so old. In an interesting twist, the plaintiffs' lawyers seem to be arguing
that their civil rights are being violated—scientists are being denied access to the
remains because "they're not Native Americans" (Slayman 1997:23) The complaint, however, is that "if a pattern of returning [such] remains without study
develops, the loss to science will be incalculable and we will never have the data
required to understand the earliest populations in America" (Douglas W. Owsley
and Richard L. Jantz quoted in Slayman 1997:19).

The bottom line, however, is that archaeologists *have* accepted reburial and are
still able to do archaeology (e.g., Pardoe 1991; Zimmerman 1989). The acceptance
of reburial may mean that traditional archaeology (including invasive research on
human remains) is done with non-indigenous populations or is done with limited samples from Native populations. More likely, a 'new' archaeology will evolve
that studies ancient populations with their descendants' consent and collaboration (e.g., Garza n.d.). "If a cooperative stance is adopted, both Indians and
anthropologists, and as a consequence the general public, will benefit" (Rosita
Worl, quoted in Mauro 1997:22).

Archaeologists are funded primarily from public coffers. Native Americans are
a part of that public, and archaeologists must be responsive to their legitimate
concerns. Many archaeologists individually are doing so. However, with the
exception of SOPA and WAC, archaeological professional organizations do not

recognize this obligation in their ethical statements. A simple revision to archaeological ethical statements that includes accountability to the descendants of peoples studied would remedy this omission.

> [Archaeologists] agree that they have obligations to indigenous peoples and that
> they shall . . . establish equitable partnerships and relationships between [them-
> selves] and indigenous peoples whose cultural heritage is being investigated
> (World Archaeological Congress, 1991:22]

NOTES

1.   Abridged and updated version of Powell et al. (1993). "Ethics and ownership of
the past: The repatriation and reburial controversy," in *Archaeological Method and Theory, Volume 5*, M. Schiffer (ed.), pp. 1–42. University of Arizona Press, Tucson.

REFERENCES CITED

Adams, E. C. 1984. "Archaeology and the Native American: A case at Hopi." In *Ethics in Archaeology*, ed. E. L. Green, pp. 236–242. New York: The Free Press.

American Anthropological Association. 1976. *Professional Ethics: Statements and Procedures of the American Anthropological Association*. Washington, D.C.: American Anthropological Association.

Anyon, R., T. J. Ferguson, L. Jackson, and L. Lane. 1996. "Native American Oral Traditions and Archaeology." *Society for American Archaeology Bulletin* 14(2):14–16.

Anyon, R., and J. Zunie. 1989. "Cooperation at the Pueblo of Zuni: Common ground for archaeological and tribal concerns." *Practicing Anthropology* 11:13–15.

Arden, H. 1989. "Who owns our past?" *National Geographic* 175(3):376–393.

Avery, T.E., and G. L. Berlin. 1992. *Fundamentals of Remote Sensing and Airphoto Interpretation*. 5th ed. New York: MacMillan Publishing.

Baigell, M. 1984. *A Concise History of American Painting and Sculpture*. New York: Harper & Row.

Berlin, G. L., J. R. Ambler, R. H. Hevly and G. G. Schaber. 1977. "Identification of a Sinagua agricultural field by aerial thermography, soil chemistry, pollen/plant analysis, and archaeology." *American Antiquity* 42(4):588–600.

Berlin, G. L., D. E. Salas and P. R. Geib. 1990. "A prehistoric Sinagua agricultural site in the ashfall zone of Sunset Crater, Arizona." *Journal of Field Archaeology* 17:1–15.

Bieder, R. E. 1986. *Science Encounters the Indian, 1820–1880; the Early Years of American Ethnology*. Norman, Oklahoma: University of Oklahoma Press.

Binford, L. R. 1962. "Archaeology as anthropology." *American Antiquity* 28(2):217–225.

Buikstra, J. E. 1981. "A specialist in ancient cemetery studies looks at the reburial issue." *Early Man* 3(3):26–27.

——— 1983. "Reburial: How we all lose." *Society for California Archaeology Newsletter* 17:1.

Catlin, G. 1911. *The Boy's Catlin: My Life Among the Indians*, edited with a biographical sketch by M. G. Humphreys. New York: Charles Scribner's Sons.

——— 1973. *Letters and Notes on the Manners, Customs, and Conditions of the North American Indian; Written During Eight Years' Travel (1832–1839) Amongst the Wildest Tribes of Indians in North America*, Volume I, with an introduction by M. Halpin. New York: Dover Publications, Inc.

Champe, J. L., et al. 1961. "Four statements for archaeology." *American Antiquity* 27:137–138.

Cheek, A. L. and B. C. Keel. 1984. Value conflicts in osteo-archaeology. In *Ethics and Values in Archaeology*, ed. E. L. Green, pp. 194–297. New York: The Free Press.

Cowley, G., A. Murr, N. de la Peña, and V. Quade. 1989. "The plunder of the past." *Newsweek*, June 26, pp. 58–60.

Davis, H. A. 1984. "Approaches to ethical problems by archaeological organizations." In *Ethics and Values in Archaeology*, ed. E. L. Green, pp. 13–21. New York: The Free Press.

Dincauze, D. 1988. "Complementarity between public archaeology and academic archaeology." *Society for American Archaeology Bulletin* 6(4):1–2.

Donoghue, D. and I. Shennan. 1988. "The application of remote sensing to environmental archaeology." *Geoarchaeology: An International Journal* 3(4):275–285.

Drager, D. L. and A. K. Ireland. 1986. "The Seedskadee Project: Remote Sensing in Non-Site Archaeology." Salt Lake City, Utah: Bureau of Reclamation, Upper Colorado Region.

Ebert, J. I. and T. R. Lyons (eds.). 1983. "Archaeology, anthropology, and cultural resources management." In *Manual of Remote Sensing*, 2nd ed., Vol II, edited by J. E. Estes and G. A. Thorley (eds.), pp. 1233–1304. Falls Church, Virginia: American Society of Photogrammetry.

Echo-Hawk, W. R. and R. C. Echo-Hawk. 1991. "Repatriation, reburial, and religious rights." In *Handbook of American Indian Religious Freedom*, ed. C. Vecsey, pp. 63–80. New York: Crossroad Publishing Company.

Ferguson, T. J. 1984. "Archaeological ethics and values in a tribal cultural resource management program at the Pueblo of Zuni." In *Ethics and Values in Archaeology*, ed. E. L. Green, pp. 224–235. New York: The Free Press.

Garza, C. E. n.d. "A history of a reburial policy: Implications for the practice of archaeology." Paper presented at the 56th Annual Meeting of the Society of American Archaeology, New Orleans, 1991.

Gibbons, Ann. 1992. "Human ancestors abound—in museums." *Science* 255:1071.

——— 1991. "Antiquities." *Glamour*, September, p. 247.

Goldstein, L. and K. Kintigh. 1991. "Ethics and the reburial controversy." *American Antiquity* 55:585–591.

Green, E. L. (ed.). 1984. *Ethics and Values in Archaeology*. New York: The Free Press.

Gruber, J. W. 1986. "Archaeology, history, and culture." In *American Archaeology Past and Future: A Celebration of the Society for American Archaeology 1935–1985*, edited by D. J. Meltzer, D. D. Fowler, and J. A. Sabloff, pp. 163–186. Washington, D.C.: Smithsonian Institution Press.

Gulliford, A. 1996. "Bones of contention: The repatriation of Native American human remains." *The Public Historian* 18 (4):119–143.

Hammil, J. and R. Cruz. 1989. "Statements of American Indians against Desecration before the World Archaeological Conference." In *Conflict in the Archaeology of Living Traditions*, ed. R. Layton, pp. 194–200. London: Unwin Hyman.

Hart, W. 1988. "Santa Fe called spot for hot pots: Illegal artifacts allegedly abound." *Arizona Republic*, May 1, AA3–AA4.

——— 1972. *The American Indian Reader: Anthropology*. San Francisco: The Indian Historian Press.

Hill, Richard. 1980. "Indians and museums: A plea for cooperation." *Council for Museum Anthropology Newsletter* 4(2):22–25.

Hillerman, Tony. 1989. *Talking God*. New York: Harper and Row.

Hodder, I. 1991. "Interpretive archaeology and its role." *American Antiquity* 56:7–18.

Holt, H. B. 1990. "Tribal sovereignty over archaeology: A practical and legal fact." In *Preservation on the Reservation: Native Americans, Native American Lands and Archaeology*, edited by Anthony L. Klesert and Alan S. Downer, pp. 9–25. Navajo Nation Papers in Anthropology No. 26. Navajo Nation Archaeology Department and Navajo Nation Historic Preservation Department: Window Rock, Arizona.

Johnson, E. 1973. "Professional responsibilities and the American Indian." *American Antiquity* 38:129–130.

Kintigh, K. W. 1996. "SAA principles of archaeological ethics." *Society for American Archaeology Bulletin* 14(3):5,17.

Klesert, A. L. 1992. "A view from Navajoland on the reconciliation of anthropologists and Native Americans." *Human Organization* 51:17–22.

Laustrup, M. S. 1987. "Potential uses of advanced remote sensing technology in Great Plains archaeology." In *Perspectives on Archaeological Resources Management in the Great Plains*, edited by A. J. Osborn and R. C. Hassler, pp. 179–200. Omaha: I & O Publishing.

Lipe, W. D. 1974. "A conservation model for American archaeology." *The Kiva* 39:214–256.

——— 1977. "A conservation model for American archaeology." In *Conservation Archaeology: A Guide for Cultural Resource Management Studies,* edited by M. B. Schiffer and G. J. Gumerman, pp. 19–42. New York: Academic Press.

Lynott, M. and A. Wylie (eds.). 1995a. *Ethics in American Archaeology: Challenges for the 1990s.* Society for American Archaeology, Special Report. Washington, D.C.

Lynott, M. and A. Wylie. 1995b. "Stewardship: The central principle of archaeological ethics." In *Ethics in American Archaeology: Challenges for the 1990s,* edited by M. Lynott and A. Wylie, pp. 28–32. Society for American Archaeology, Special Report. Washington, D.C.

Mauro, T. 1997. "Bones of contention: Disputing the rights to native human remains." *Preservation* 49(1):21–22.

McAleer, N. 1987. "Archaeology from above." *Space World,* February, 21–25.

McGimsey, C. R., III. 1971. "Archaeology and the law." *American Antiquity* 36:125–126.

McKee, B. R. and T. Sever. 1989. "Remote Sensing in the Arenal Region." Ms. on file, Department of Geography, Northern Arizona University, Flagstaff.

Medicine, B. 1972. "The anthropologist as the Indian's image maker." In *The American Indian Reader: Anthropology,* ed. J. Henry. San Francisco: The Indian Historian Press.

Meighan, C. W. 1986. *Archaeology and Anthropological Ethics.* Calabasas, California: Wormwood Press.

Mihesuah, D. A. 1991. "Despoiling and desecration of Indian property and possessions." *National Forum* 71(2):15–17.

National Association of Practicing Anthropologists. n.d. *National Association of Practicing Anthropologists' Ethical Guidelines for Practitioners.* National Association of Practicing Anthropologists, Washington, D.C.

Nichols, D. L. 1988. "Infrared aerial photography and prehistoric irrigation in Teotihuacán: The Tlajinga canals." *Journal of Field Archaeology* 15:17–27.

Nichols, D. L., R. Anyon, and A. L. Klesert. 1989. "Ancestral sites, shrines, and graves: Native American perspectives on the ethics of collecting cultural properties." In *The Ethics of Collecting Cultural Properties: Whose Culture? Whose Property?,* ed. P. M. Messenger, pp. 27–50. Albuquerque: University of New Mexico Press.

Olsen, J. W. 1985. "Applications of space-borne remote sensing in archaeology." *University of Arizona Remote Sensing Newsletter* 85(1):1–6.

Ortiz, A. 1972. "An Indian anthropologist's perspective on anthropology." In *The American Indian Reader: Anthropology,* ed. J. Henry. San Francisco: The Indian Historian Press.

Pardoe, C. 1991. "Farewell to the Murray Black Australian Aboriginal skeletal collection." *World Archaeological Bulletin* 5(February):121.

Parezo, N. J. 1987. "The formation of ethnographic collections: The Smithsonian Institution in the American Southwest." In *Advances in Archaeological Method and Theory,* vol. 10, ed. M. B. Schiffer, pp. 1–47. New York: Academic Press.

Preston, D. J. 1989. "Skeletons in our museums' closets." *Harper's Magazine* 278(1665):66–76.

Quick, P. McW. 1985. *Proceedings: Conference on Reburial Issues.* Society for American Archaeology and Society for Professional Archaeologists, Washington, D.C.

Schiffer, M. B. and G. J. Gumerman (eds.). 1977. *Conservation Archaeology: A Guide for Cultural Resource Management Studies.* New York: Academic Press.

Scollar, I., A. Tabbagh, A. Hesse, and I. Herzog. 1990. *Image Processing in Archaeology.* Cambridge: Cambridge University Press.

Sever, T., B. McKee, and P. Sheets. 1989. "Prehistoric Footpaths in Costa Rica: Remote Sensing and Field Verification." Ms. on file, Department of Geography, Northern Arizona University, Flagstaff.

Sheets, P. and T. Sever. 1988. "High-tech wizardry." *Archaeology Magazine* 41(6):28–35.

Slayman, A. L. 1997. "A battle over bones." *Archaeology Magazine* 50(1):16–23.

Society for American Archaeology. 1948. "By-Laws of the Society for American Archaeology." *American Antiquity* 14:148.

—— 1974. "Minutes of the annual business meeting." *American Antiquity* 39:668.

—— 1977. "By-Laws of the Society for American Archaeology, as amended." *American Antiquity* 42:308–312.

—— 1984. "Resolution." *American Antiquity* 49:215–216.

—— 1987. "Report of the president." *American Antiquity* 52:214–215.

Society for Historical Archaeology. 1967. "Beginnings." *Historical Archaeology* 1:1–22.

Society of Professional Archaeologists. 1981. "Code of Ethics and Standards of Performance." Directory of Professional Archaeologists, pp. 3–6.

Sprague, R. 1974. "American Indians and American archaeology." *American Antiquity* 39:1–2.

Swisher, K. 1990. "Honoring her ancestors." *Glamour*, April, p. 112.

Thomas, D. H. 1989. *An Introduction to Archaeology.* New York: Academic Press.

Thompson, S. L. 1988. "Discovering Buried Footpaths with Remote Sensing." Ms. on file, Department of Geography, Northern Arizona University, Flagstaff.

Trigger, B. G. 1980. "Archaeology and the image of the American Indian." *American Antiquity* 46:662–676.

—— 1986. "Prehistoric archaeology and American society." In *American Archaeology Past and Future: A Celebration of the Society for American Archaeology 1935–1985,* edited by D. J. Meltzer, D. D. Fowler, and J. A. Sabloff, pp. 187–216. Washington, D.C.: Smithsonian Institution Press.

—— 1989. *A History of Archaeological Thought.* New York: Cambridge University Press.

Turner, C. G. 1986. "What is lost with reburial?" *Quarterly Review of Archaeology* 7(1):1–3.

Vizenor, G. 1986. "Bone courts: The rights and narrative representation of tribal bones." *American Indian Quarterly* 10:319–331.

White, T. D. 1991. *Human Osteology.* San Diego: Academic Press.

Willey, G. R. and J. A. Sabloff. 1980. *A History of American Archaeology.* New York: W. H. Freeman and Company.

Wolkomir, R. 1988. "Looking Down on History." *Air & Space* August/September:62–66.

Wood, John and Shirley Powell. 1993. "An ethos for archaeological practice." *Human Organization* 52(4):405–413.

World Archaeological Congress. 1991. "First Code of Ethics." *World Archaeological Bulletin* 5:22–23.

Zimmerman, L. J. n.d. *Indians, archaeologists and bones: Cooperation and compromise in South Dakota.* Paper presented at the Executive Committee of the Society for American Archaeology, Minneapolis, 1982.

—— 1985. "A perspective on the reburial issue from South Dakota." In *Proceedings: Conference on Reburial Issues,* ed. P. McW. Quick, pp. 1–4. Society for American Archaeology and Society for Professional Archaeologists, Washington, D.C.

—— 1989. "Made radical by my own: An archaeologist learns to accept reburial." In *Conflict in the Archaeology of Living Traditions,* ed. R. Layton, pp. 60–67. London: Unwin Hyman.

CHAPTER FOUR

Yours, Mine, or Ours?
Conflicts between Archaeologists and Ethnic Groups

JOE WATKINS

> Bones represent many things today: political domination, sub-culture identification, cheap thrills in horror movies, and religious iconography. Bones also represent science and history. Past patterns of human social behavior are carved on the skeleton as holes, bony bridges, accessory bones and suture lines, and as shape and size (Pardoe 1994:182).

INTRODUCTION

The 1996 discovery of an ancient skeleton washing out of the banks of the Columbia River in Washington state, and the various public reactions to its discovery, have exposed once again the conflict between archaeologists and Native groups regarding the cultural material of the earliest inhabitants of any recently colonized area. This conflict is nothing new, nor is it limited only to the United States. The struggle of Native groups to obtain, tell or protect their past in the United States (Ferguson 1996; Green 1984; Klesert and Downer 1990; Layton 1989; McGuire 1992; Messenger 1989; Swidler *et al.* 1997; Trigger 1986, 1989) and Australia (Anderson 1985: Archer 1991; Davidson 1991; Mulvaney 1991; Pardoe 1992; Thiele 1991) has frequently been discussed during this past decade. But most of these discussions center around the issues in one particular country or the other. While Hubert (1989:131–166) offers a good overview of repatriation in both the United States and Australia, a comparison of the conflict between archaeologists and Native peoples regarding attitudes toward the disposition of the remains of founder populations (which may be considered ancestral to entire continental populations) suggests that the concerns of Native peoples in these two industrialized countries are quite similar.

THE POLITICS OF REPATRIATION, THE POLITICS OF THE PAST

Bray (1996) is one of the more recent authors to discuss the various political implications of working with another people's past and there have been many other
writings on this subject. Anyone in the field of archaeology anywhere in the
world realizes the extent to which archaeological material and human remains
have been politicized by Native populations, scientists, and elected officials.

Handler (1991:67) divides the various groups competing for ownership of cultural materials into two camps: retentionists and restitutionists. Retentionists
argue that museums have possessory rights over cultural items they have safe-
guarded for years, while restitutionists believe that such things should be
returned to their places of origin. Such places of origin, however, now often have
different boundaries and different occupants than the ones in place at the time the
cultural items were initially removed. How would one define the ancient boundaries of the "Sioux Nation," for instance, when such a "nation" did not exist as a
political unit until the Indian Reorganization Act of 1934?

In *The Plundered Past*, Karl Meyer (1973:203) writes that "the nationalist, the
collector, and the curator . . . each look upon the past as a piece of property.
Another approach is possible—to see our collective cultural remains as a resource
whose title is vested in all humanity." Is there a point in time at which cultural
material may actually cease belonging to any one group or individual and
become the universal property of every one? Warren (1989:22) feels that we
should " . . . rethink the dispute as one of preservation (not, or not simply, as one
of ownership) of the past." In this way, she argues, the importance rests more on
the preservation of an object for the sake of cultural heritage rather than on which
individual or institution retains or regains the physical object in question.

Handler (1991:71) notes that those who wish to retain the cultural property of
others " . . . are quick to condemn the parochial nationalism of their opponents,
but rarely question their own more imperial nationalisms, which they mask in the
name of internationalism." Pardoe (1992:140) suggests that archaeologists have "
. . . legitimized our curiosity by appealing to the noble view of world history, a
democracy of knowledge for all . . . (which) no one person could own . . . "

The situation becomes increasingly volatile when human bones are involved.
As the epigraph to this chapter suggests, bones hold a different meaning for each
group that regards them as important. While archaeologists may be more
amenable to returning human skeletal materials, physical and forensic anthropologists argue that to rebury these remains leads to a significant loss of information on past cultures and civilizations (Landau and Steele 1996; Rose *et al.*
1996). Ubelaker and Grant's (1989) article "Human Skeletal Remains: Preservation or Reburial?" offers a concise overview of the issues from the perspective of
physical anthropology and a rationale for continued study. Providing a list of reasons for the scientific analysis and long-term curation of skeletal remains, a
review of Native American concerns, and a discussion of institutional responses
to the reburial issue, these authors offer a strong argument for the scientific value
of all human remains.

Archaeologists have generally been united in calling for the return of human
remains to ethnic groups who can demonstrate "cultural affiliation" with the

remains (c.f. Dongoske et al. 1997; Ferguson 1996; Leone 1991; McManamon and Nordby 1992; Zimmerman 1989, 1996). There is also some support for the return of remains that may not be demonstrably affiliated with any specific group but which are known to have come from a specific region and may be more generally affiliated with a larger culture group. Repatriation is even taught as a likely outcome in some introductory archaeology text books (Ashmore and Sharer 1996).

However, extremely old skeletal material that is difficult to link with any existing ethnic groups becomes a philosophical sticking point for many archaeologists. In the following discussion I offer three "case studies" regarding the ways that American and Australian archaeologists have reconciled the issue of returning "founder population" material (greater than 7,500 years old) to modern groups who can claim only a generalized descent from those populations.

KENNEWICK MAN

On Sunday, July 28, 1996, Will Thomas and Dave Deacy came upon a human skull eroding out of the banks of the Columbia River near Kennewick, Washington. A brief article in the July 29th edition of the *Tri-City Herald* by John Stang gave little indication of the impact the skull would have on archaeology and physical anthropology in North America. The nearly complete skeleton of the so-called Kennewick Man set into motion a court case that has involved several Native American tribes, individual anthropologists, and the U. S. government in a legal conflict over the control of heritage and human remains.

Shortly after its discovery, the skull was examined by archaeologist James Chatters, acting as agent for the Benton County coroner's office. The physical features of the cranium led Dr. Chatters to conclude that it belonged to a Caucasian male. Two other physical anthropologists, Dr. Catherine J. MacMillan and Grover S. Krantz, also agreed that skeletal characteristics suggested Caucasian origin. The controversy started when a CAT scan ordered by Chatters revealed a projectile point fragment embedded in the hip of the individual. After the projectile point fragment's discovery, the left fifth metacarpal was sent to the University of California at Riverside for radiocarbon testing. The sample returned dates between 9,200 and 9,600 years ago, and Chatters' opinion of "a white guy with a stone point in him" (as quoted in Slayman 1997:16) fell to the wayside. Once the antiquity of the bones was tentatively determined, the Corps took possession of them, citing the Native American Graves Protection and Repatriation Act (P.L.101–601) as authority for its actions.

The Native American Graves Protection and Repatriation Act (NAGPRA), passed in 1990, constitutes human rights legislation. The Act protects Native American burials (Hutt 1992) and requires the repatriation of human remains, burial goods, and cultural patrimony housed in federally-funded museums and institutions to culturally affiliated tribes (Trope and Echo-Hawk 1992, and this volume). As custodian of the property on which the Kennewick remains were found, the Corps was obliged to follow the procedures established under NAGPRA regulations for the inadvertent discovery of human remains (43CFR Part

10.4). Consequently, the Corps halted analysis of the bones and had them transferred to their facility.

As per the clause pertaining to inadvertent discoveries [45CFR Part 10.4(d)(iii)], the Corps was required to notify Native American tribes that were "likely to be culturally affiliated with" the remains, that had "aboriginally occupied the area", or that were "reasonably known to have a cultural relationship to" the human remains. As a result, five tribes, the Umatilla, the Yakama, the Nez Perce, the Colville, and the Wanapum were contacted and subsequently filed a joint claim for the return of the Kennewick remains. The Corps published a "Notice of Intent to Repatriate" in the September 17 and 24, 1996, editions of a local newspaper, the *Tri-City Herald*. But on October 16th, before the mandatory 30-day waiting period after the second publication of the "Notice" expired, eight anthropologists filed suit in District Court to block the repatriation.

The names of the eight anthropologists read like a "Who's Who" of North American archaeology and physical anthropology. They included Robson Bonnichsen, C. Loring Brace, George W. Gill, C. Vance Haynes Jr., Richard Jantz, Douglas Owsley, Dennis Stanford, and D. Gentry Steele. The law suit forced the Corps to halt plans to repatriate the skeletal material until the Court could decide on the merits of the plaintiffs' intervention.

The anthropologists' complaint alleged that the Corps determined the remains were culturally affiliated without sufficient evidence. At issue was the assumption that the skeleton's age automatically meant the individual was Native American. Secondly, since NAGPRA allows the study of remains when the outcome of the study would be "of major benefit to the United States" [45CFR Part 10.10(c)(1)], the anthropologists asserted that the Corps' intent to repatriate would prevent such a study. Thirdly, the scientists asserted that their civil rights were being denied by the Corps' action, claiming that they were being denied the right to study the remains simply because they were not Native American (*Bonnichsen v. United States*, USDC CV No. 96-1481-JE, filed October 16, 1996).

To further complicate matters, a third party entered the fray prior to the expiration of the 30-day notification period. The Asatru Folk Assembly, a pre-Christian, indigenous European religious organization, filed a similar complaint against the Corps alleging they also might be culturally affiliated with Kennewick Man (Horn 1997:511).

On June 27, 1997, United States Magistrate Judge John Jelderks issued a written opinion "to supplement and amplify . . . bench rulings, and to provide additional guidance to the defendants so that this controversy may be resolved in a timely and orderly manner" (Jelderks 1997:3). The opinion provided 17 issues which it felt the Corps should consider, several of which go to the very heart of the NAGPRA legislation (Jelderks 1997:45–51). First and foremost among these was whether the remains in question were actually subject to NAGPRA (Jelderks 1997:45).

Subsequent to the legal proceedings, Congressman Doc Hastings of Washington State, had introduced a bill to amend NAGPRA to allow for scientific access to important, culturally unaffiliated human remains such as in the case of Kennewick Man. The bill, H.R. 2893, was introduced in Congress on November 7,

1997. According to Richard Jantz, one of the plaintiffs in the suit against the U.S. Army Corps, the proposed bill would "make it much easier for [scientists] to gain access to study unaffiliated material, and it would require that [cultural] affiliation be documented to a much greater extent" (as quoted in Lee 1997). The general counsel of the National Congress of American Indians, John Dossett, disagreed with this interpretation. He felt that the proposed amendment would "put scientific study in a place of greater importance than the protection of the graves of Indian ancestors" (quoted in Lee 1997). Though introduced, the amendment never reached the floor of the House for a vote and has since died.

The conflict over Kennewick Man is still far from over. The plaintiffs won the right to have the remains scientifically examined for the purpose of obtaining additional information on cultural affiliation. The analysis is being conducted under tight security at a neutral location. The outcome of this dispute will ultimately have major and far-reaching consequences for the practice of archaeology within the United States.

THE EAST WENATCHEE CLOVIS CACHE

The second case study involves another archaeological site in Washington state where just the possibility of happening upon human remains was enough to create problems between archaeologists and the local Native population. In 1987, an irrigation project in an apple orchard on a terrace above the Columbia River uncovered the a cache of the largest Clovis points ever recorded in North America. Robert Mierendorf, an archaeologist for the National Park Service, and Russell Congdon, a local amateur archaeologist, subsequently performed test excavations at the site that confirmed the existence of *in situ* cultural deposits of Clovis age.

In April of 1988, additional testing was undertaken by professional archaeologists, paleo-Indian specialists, and representatives of the Colville Confederated Tribes. The purpose of this work was to obtain additional data to be used in planning for more extensive excavations in the future. Soil samples from immediately below the artifact level were found to contain an abundance of fine sand and silt-sized Glacier Peak pumice, which dates to about 11,250 B.P. (Mehringer et al. 1984). But excavations were suspended when "apparent bone fragments and associated artifacts—*suggesting* a possible burial—appeared in the floor of one of the excavation units ... " (Mehringer 1989:54, emphasis added). The testing operation was closed after one week; all the units were backfilled and the area protected by covering the surface with over 30 tons of concrete slabs.

In March of 1990, the Buffalo Museum of Science, with Dr. Richard M. Gramly as the Principal Investigator, applied for a permit to conduct archaeological excavations at the East Wenatchee Clovis site. On May 14, 1990, the state issued a permit which allowed for the excavation of 35 square meters to be undertaken between October 15 and December 7, 1990.

Excavations were initiated by Dr. Gramly over the protest of the Colville and Yakama tribes. Because of the political pressure brought to bear by the tribal demonstrations, however, only ten square meters—the units previously opened by Mehringer plus an L-shaped geological trench along the north and east edges of the artifact concentration area—were excavated.

The Colville and the Yakama both claimed cultural ties to the area. Colville Acting Police Chief John Dick was quoted as saying that the excavation of any Clovis remains "would be like somebody trying to dig up the bones of my father" and that " . . . no matter who or where they're at, they're still my people . . . nobody should disturb them" (Wren 1990). The Yakama agreed with the Colville. Yakama Indian Nation Councilman Harry Smiskin said the Yakama feel that " . . . there's a strong probability that Clovis man was ancestral to all local bands" (Wren 1990).

Gramly viewed things differently. He told reporters that he felt the issue was the right to conduct science and that it was pointless to try to connect any modern people, such as the Colville, to remains more than 4,000 years old. "I took that as gospel. Obviously it's not gospel to the Colville" (*Spokane Chronicle*, 1990). His application for the archaeological permit further explicates this view:

> It cannot be assumed, a priori, that human skeletal remains from the East Wenatchee Clovis site, if any are found, are American Indian, however defined. East Asia is home to a variety of genetically-distinct populations. Any or all of these groups could have participated in the peopling of the Americas. Some of these initial immigrants may have left no descendants who survived in the present era (Gramly 1990:9–10).

This topic is open to debate. Meltzer (1989), for instance, writes about the " . . . possibility that the earliest migration was not a single episode, but a multiple series, and that some of those in the multiple series may have failed . . . " (ibid.:482). He also feels that " . . . we lose sight of the fact that Clovis may represents a composite of migratory 'dribbles' . . . " and that " . . . by virtue of the success of the Clovis groups, we miss the possibility that others . . . (pre-Clovis groups) simply disappeared without issue" (ibid.:484). Meltzer does believe, however, that the ancestral Clovis group to which the eastern Washington tribes might belong represent a successful cultural group in the Americas, and that the Colville and Yakama probably represent descendant groups. An alternative interpretation, proposed by Greenberg, Turner and Zegura (1986), suggests that the North American continent was settled by three migrations—the first occurring around 11,000 years B.P., and the other two sometime after 5,000 years B.P. (Greenberg *et al.* 1986:479–480).

Ultimately, an agreement was reached for the purchase of the East Wenatchee Clovis site by the Pacific Northwest Archaeological Society for an amount believed to be around $500,000, with the state of Washington paying $250,000 for the artifacts recovered during excavations (Wheat 1991a). Gramly was pleased at the acquisition, stating that "[w]e were in it for the science; we don't want to keep [the artifacts] permanently in Buffalo and never have" (Wheat 1991a:2).

In conjunction with this purchase, an agreement was drawn up between the Pacific Northwest Archaeological Society and the Colville Confederated Tribes regarding archaeological work undertaken on tribal and aboriginal lands. Upon finalizing this contract, the president of the Society noted that he was "glad to sign what hopefully will become a landmark agreement," and that he felt "it was time to codify a system of ethics for digs" (Wheat 1991b). A complete text of this agreement was published in 1991 in the British journal *Antiquity* (65:917–920). The Colville people also acknowledge that:

> (A)rchaeology on tribal lands can be beneficial both to the public domain and to the tribes insofar as such research may serve to substantiate, or in some cases add new dimensions to, the tribes' oral tradition (Wheat 1991c).

The East Wenatchee Clovis cache is one of the largest, earliest, and best documented in the country. Because no human remains were discovered during excavations, the protests and concerns of local tribes proved to be a moot point. Even so, many of the local archaeologists were quick to side with the tribes against someone they perceived as callous toward Native American concerns.

Kow Swamp

In 1967, Alan Thorne discovered a large number of burials along on the edge of a reservoir named Kow Swamp. These were subsequently excavated between 1968 and 1972. The salvage operation recovered approximately 40 individuals. The burials exhibited a variety of mortuary treatments and contained both artifacts and pigments. According to one of the archaeologists, the remains represented "a crucial statistical assemblage for any investigation of Aboriginal origins" (Mulvaney 1991:14).

While the Commonwealth government of Australia had assumed responsibility for Aboriginal affairs in 1967, administration was generally left to the separate states. The Australian Archaeological and Aboriginal Relics Preservation Act of 1972 (Victoria Act No. 8273/1972, since amended) was the first legislation aimed at protecting the heritage of Aboriginal people in Victoria. A subsequent law, the Aboriginal and Torres Strait Islander Heritage Protection Amendment Act of 1987, later proclaimed that "the Aboriginal people of Victoria are the rightful owners of their heritage and should be given responsibility for its future control and management" (as quoted in Mulvaney 1991:14).

In August 1990, the Museum of Victoria presented the Kow Swamp Collection of human remains and associated grave goods to the Echuca Aboriginal Cooperative on the Murray River in central Victoria, a community that wished to accord those 9,000 to 15,000-year-old human remains a mass reburial. Mulvaney decried the reburial of this collection noting that "the case merits record for its implications for intellectual freedom. . . . It is not simply the Kow Swamp relics which are at stake, but the future of past Aboriginal culture and the freedom of all peoples of any race to study it" (1991:12).

Pardoe (1992) however, feels that scientists have no right to determine the ultimate disposition of human remains. "Some have distinguished between more recent remains, which Aborigines may control, and the older remains, which belong to the world. This denies the concept of full and unfettered Aboriginal ownership of the past" (Pardoe 1992:133).

In *The Australian Journal of Anthropology, Special Issue 2*, entitled "Reconsidering Aboriginality" (1991 2:2), the authors provide a collection of articles reflecting on the status of "Aboriginal Studies" in Australia. Archer (1991:163), for instance, notes that "Aboriginality as a construction for purposes of political action has all the characteristic contradictions of nationalism," while Lewins states that "it is not possible to keep `aboriginality' and politics apart" (1991:177). Thiele (1991:80) argues that `aboriginality' involves "descentism" based solely on the grounds of biological parentage. Another author deconstructs the stereotypical belief that "aboriginal values and practices are somehow more 'ecologically sound' than those of non-Aborigines" (Sackett 1991:235); while still another observes that, in the ever changing relationships between archaeologists and Aborigines, "the motives of Aboriginal and non-Aboriginal peoples have not always been the same" (Davidson 1991:256).

"Aboriginality" in Australia, is thus construed by these scholars as a political, descent-based construction. North American authors involved with Native American issues could easily produce a similar set of papers on the aboriginal peoples of North America. The current state of relations between scholars and indigenous peoples in these two countries is remarkably similar.

CONCLUSIONS

The question has been raised as to whether it is reasonable to assume that a single Native American group or individual, by virtue of their "Indianness" or "Aboriginality", or some genetic relationship, should have rights to control cultural material which may be equally related to an entire population. Should any one of us have the right to determine the fate of the biblical Adam were he to be excavated?

Winter (1980:126) asks whether we should always respond positively to Native Americans, just because they are "Indians." Another anthropologist questions: "who has the right to excavate, or prevent the excavation of, a recent or ancient burial site, and on what authority is that right to be based?" (Rosen 1980:6). While Pardoe (1992:133) notes that "aboriginal demands for ownership and control of their heritage has been consistent for over a decade", he also notes the tension level between archaeologists and Aborigines rises when it is Pleistocene remains (over 10,000 years old) that are slated for reburial.

In the United States, Meighan (1984, 1992) is one of the most outspoken opponents of wholesale repatriation and reburial of human remains that cannot be directly linked with specific modern day groups. He argues that current repatriation agreements "assume all Indian remains of whatever age are the property of contemporary claimants and that it doesn't matter how old things are" (Meighan 1992: 39). Though not alone in his belief that cultural material from extremely old sites is not the property of any particular group of Native Americans, he was, by far, the most vocal in his dissent.

Even the NAGPRA Review Committee, mandated to decide the status of claims by Native American tribes regarding "culturally unidentifiable human remains," is having difficulty establishing a proper process for determining the repatriation of human skeletal material that cannot be assigned to specific cultural groups. Indeed, the Review Committee at its March 1997 meeting proposed a "seminar" to address this topic with hopes that interested parties, including archaeologists, anthropologists and traditional Native peoples, could together devise a workable solution to this dilemma.

Much like Clement Meighan in America, David Mulvaney in Australia feels that, while "archaeologists support the return of remains from recent generations to local communities for reburial, because social and spiritual considerations outweigh other factors," for older remains, "their kin cannot be presumed to have shared the same cultural values or religious concepts of this generation" (1991:16).

As suggested in the title of this paper, there seems to exist a point in time where the relationship to the cultural material from an archaeological site might accurately be described as "ours" (which denotes ownership by the entire world) as opposed to "yours" (which denotes ownership by a specific, bounded cultural group). While the latter portion of this paper contains a plethora of rhetorical questions for which there are no ready answers, archaeology today is immersed in trying to find answers to such questions. As archaeological practitioners like Pardoe, who argues that "a scientific view of the world is not corrupted by advocacy, or by an interest in the wishes of Aboriginal people" (1992:138), and Zimmerman, who openly describes himself as "a radical spokesman for reburial" (1989:66) become more prominent, members of the discipline are as likely to find themselves at odds with one another as with Native people when it comes to Native rights and cultural heritage.

During the conflict over the archaeological excavations at the East Wenatchee Clovis cache, Matthew Dick of the Colville tribe noted that:

> The Colville tribe has said that for many years it has watched the desecration of its grave sites in the name of progress and thirst for knowledge. I still believe there has to be a balance between the thirst for knowledge of our past and the sacredness of our burial grounds (quoted in Wheat 1991d).

Such a balance would ideally be worked out directly by the indigenous populations and the scholarly community. But it appears that it may be up to the courts to decide the fate of human remains in the two former colonial states of America and Australia. The case brought by Bonnichsen *et al.*, ultimately may decide at what point "founder populations" become "aboriginal populations," at least in the United States. It will also help to establish the right of science to pursue answers in opposition to the religious concerns of certain groups. If it must be up to the courts to decide such issues, however, anthropology will come out the loser regardless of the verdict, because it will have demonstrated a failure to understand the cultures about which it endeavors to learn and to prove its worth to the world of which it is a part.

REFERENCES CITED

Anderson, Christopher. 1985. On the notion of aboriginality: A discussion. *Mankind* 15(1):41–43.

Archer, Jeff. 1991. "Ambiguity in political ideology: Aboriginality as nationalism." In *Reconsidering Aboriginality*, Steven Thiele (ed.), pp. 161–170. *The Australian Journal of Anthropology*, Special Issue 2.

Ashmore, Wendy and Robert Sharer. 1996. *Discovering our Past: A Brief Introduction to Archaeology*. Mountain View, California: Mayfield Publishing.

Bonnichsen v. United States. 1996. USDC CV No. 96–1481 JE; filed October 16, 1996.

Bray, Tamara . 1996. "Repatriation, power relations and the politics of the past." *Antiquity* 70(268):440–444.

Davidson, Iain. 1991. "Archaeologists and Aborigines." In *Reconsidering Aboriginality*, S. Thiele (ed.), pp. 247–258. *The Australian Journal of Anthropology*, Special Issue 2.

Ferguson, T.J. 1996. "Native Americans and the Practice of Archaeology." *Annual Review of Anthropology* 25:63–80.

Gramly, R. M. 1990. *Archaeological Excavation Permit Application*. Document on file at the State Historic Preservation Office, Pullman, Washington.

Green, Ernestine L. (ed.) 1984. *Ethics and Values in Archeology*. London: The Free Press.

Greenberg, Joseph, Christy Turner, and Stephen Zegura. 1986. "The settlement of the Americas: A comparison of the linguistic, dental, and genetic evidence." *Current Anthropology* 27(5):477–497.

Handler, Richard. 1991. "Who owns the past? History, cultural property, and the logic of possessive individualism." In *The Politics of Culture*, ed. Brett Williams, pp. 63–74. Washington, D.C.: Smithsonian Institution Press.

Horn, Amanda. 1997. "The Kennewick man loses sleep over NAGPRA: Native Americans and scientists wrestle over cultural remains." Sovereignty Symposium X: Circles of Life, pp. 503–524.

Hubert, Jane. 1989. "A proper place for the dead: A critical review of the "reburial" issue. In *Conflict in the Archaeology of Living Traditions*, ed. R. Layton, pp. 131–166. London: Unwin Hyman.

Hutt, Sherry. 1992. "Illegal trafficking in Native American human remains and cultural items: A new protection tool." *Arizona State Law Journal* 24(1):135–150.

Jelderks, John. 1997. Opinion, Bonnichsen v. United States, USDC CV No. 96-1481-JE. *On-line version available at: http://www.goonline.com/science/kennewic/court/opinion.htm*

Klesert, Anthony L. and Alan S. Downer, (eds.) 1990. *Preservation on the Reservation: Native Americans, Native American Lands and Archeology*. Navajo Nation Papers in Anthropology Number 26. Navajo Nation Archeology Department and the Navajo Nation Historic Preservation Department.

Landau, Patricia and D. Gentry Steele. 1996. "Why anthropologists study human remains." *American Indian Quarterly* 20(2):209–228.

Lee, Mike. 1997. "Doc pushes bill to study old bones." *Tri-City Herald*, November 14.

McGuire, Randall H. 1992. "Archaeology and the First Americans." *American Anthropologist* 94(4):816–836.

McManamon, Francis and Larry Nordby. 1992. "Implementing the Native American Graves Protection and Repatriation Act." *Arizona State Law Journal* 24(1):217–252.

Mehringer, Peter J. 1989. *Age of the Clovis Cache at East Wenatchee, Washington*. Report presented to the Washington State Historic Preservation Office, Pullman, Washington.

Mehringer, Peter J., Jr. and F. F. Foit. 1990. "Volcanic ash dating of the Clovis cache at East Wenatchee, Washington." *National Geographic Research* 6(4):495–503.

Mehringer, Peter J., J. C. Sheppard, and F. F. Foit . 1984. "The age of Glacier Peak tephra in west-central Montana." *Quaternary Research* 21(1):36–41.

Meighan, Clement. 1984. "Archaeology: Science or sacrilege?" In *Ethics and Values in Archaeology.* ed. E. Green, pp. 208–223. London: The Free Press.

——— 1992. "Some scholars' views on reburial." *American Antiquity,* 57(4):704–710.

Meltzer, David J. 1989. "Why don't we know when the first people came to North America?" *American Antiquity* 54(3):471–490.

Messenger, Phyllis Mauch (ed.). 1989. *The Ethics of Collecting Cultural Property: Whose Culture? Whose Property?* Albuquerque: University of New Mexico Press.

Meyer, Karl E. 1973. *The Plundered Past.* New York: Athenium Press.

Mulvaney, D.J. 1991. "Past regained, future lost: The Kow Swamp Pleistocene burials." *Antiquity* 65(246):12–21.

Pardoe, Colin. 1992. "Arches of Radii, corridors of power: Reflections on current archaeological practice." In *Power, Knowledge and Aborigines,* edited by M. Attwood and D. Arnold, pp. 132–141. La Trobe University Press: Melbourne, Australia.

——— 1994. "Bioscapes: The evolutionary landscape of Australia." *Archaeology in Oceania* 29:182–190.

Rose, Jerome, Thomas Green, and Victoria Green. 1996. "NAGPRA is forever: The future of osteology and the repatriation of skeletons." *Annual Review of Anthropology* 25: 81–103.

Rosen, Lawrence. 1980. "The excavation of American Indian burial sites: A problem in law and professional responsibility." *American Anthropologist* 82(1):5–27.

Slayman, Andrew. 1997. "A battle over bones." *Antiquity* 50(1):16–23.

Spokane Chronicle. 1990. History, controversy both buried at Clovis site. December 3.

Swidler, Nina, Kurt Dongoske, Roger Anyon, and Alan Downer. editors, 1997. *Native Americans and Archaeologists: Stepping Stones to Common Ground.* Walnut Creek, California: AltaMira Press.

Thiele, Steven. 1991. "Taking a sociological approach to Europeanness (Whiteness) and Aboriginality (Blackness)." In *Reconsidering Aboriginality,* Steven Thiele ed., pp. 179–201. *The Australian Journal of Anthropology,* Special Issue 2. Vol 2(2).

Trigger, Bruce. 1986. "Prehistoric archaeology and American society: An historical perspective." In *American Archaeology Past and Future,* eds. D. J. Meltzer, D. D. Fowler, and J. A. Sabloff, pp. 187–215. Washington, D.C.: Smithsonian Institution Press.

——— 1989. *A History of Archaeological Thought.* Cambridge: Cambridge University Press.

Trope, Jack and Walter Echo-Hawk. 1992. "The Native Graves Protection and Repatriation Act." *Arizona State Law Journal* 24(1):35–78.

Ubelaker, Douglas H. and Lauryn Guttenplan Grant. 1989. "Human skeletal remains: Preservation or reburial?" *Yearbook of Physical Anthropology* 32:249–287.

Warren, Karen J. 1989. "A philosophical perspective on the ethics and resolution of cultural properties issues." In *The Ethics of Collecting Cultural Property: Whose Culture? Whose Property?,* ed. P. Messenger, pp. 1–25. Albuquerque: University of New Mexico Press.

Wheat, Dan. 1991a. "Gramly applauds Clovis purchase." *Wenatchee World,* August 1.

——— 1991b. "Colvilles to be consulted on digs in future." *Wenatchee World,* May 2.

——— 1991c. "Archaeologists, tribe set forth dig principles." *Wenatchee World,* May 1.

——— 1991d. "Buffalo museum offers $485,000." *Wenatchee World,* April 29.

Winter, Joseph C. 1980. "Indian heritage preservation and archaeologists." *American Antiquity* 45(1):121–131.

Wren, Patricia. 1990. "Tribes want Clovis dig stopped." *Wenatchee World,* July 20.

Zimmerman, Larry. 1989. "Made radical by my own: An archaeologist learns to accept reburial." *Conflict in the Archaeology of Living Traditions.* ed. R. Layton, pp. 60–67, London: Unwin Hyman.

—— 1996. "Epilogue: A new and different archaeology?" *American Indian Quarterly* 20(2):297–307.

CHAPTER FIVE

Repatriation and the Study of Human Remains

BRENDA J. BAKER, TAMARA L. VARNEY, RICHARD G. WILKINSON, LISA M. ANDERSON, MARIA A. LISTON

INTRODUCTION

This chapter is based on a statement originally prepared for presentation at the NAGPRA Review Committee meeting held in November 1994 at the New York State Museum in Albany. As practicing physical anthropologists, we were invited by the National Park Service to share our perspectives on the scientific value of human skeletal remains and discuss how their study contributes to our understanding of the past. Through our experiences at this meeting and in consultations with representatives of different Native American groups, we have found that our views on issues of reburial, repatriation, and the study of human remains have changed.

NAGPRA has forced anthropologists and Native Americans to begin to talk to each other in cases where such dialogue did not previously exist. Through enactment of this legislation, physical anthropologists have been given an impetus to communicate with Native peoples about our interests in their history and their ancestors, to explain why we study human remains, and to share general information. The mandated consultations have also provided the opportunity for us to listen and learn from Native Americans, and our understanding of the issues has grown considerably as a result. We recognize that our approach is only one way of knowing the past and also that it can enrich, and be enriched by, other perspectives.

The purpose of this chapter is to highlight the enormous value that human remains and archaeological materials from all cultures have for understanding our collective past and facing our future. Physical anthropologists specialize in the study of human biology and variation in both present and past peoples. In the United States, physical anthropology had its origin in the perceived need to "scientifically" verify racial differences between groups of people. Means were devised to measure and quantify differences that could then be used as indicators demonstrating the superiority of some groups (e.g., those of European ancestry) over others (e.g., those of Native American or African descent). The benefits of these studies clearly accrued to the dominant culture (see Brace 1982; Gould 1981;

Stanton 1960; Stocking 1968 for cogent discussions of such work). It has taken decades for physical anthropology to shed this racist approach. Physical anthropologists today seek the benefits of studying the remains of past peoples, not just for anthropologists or for Native Americans, but for our society as a whole. As a result, the unique information that we can provide through the study of human remains is increasingly shared with others rather than limited to an academic audience.

Philosophically, anthropologists should embrace repatriation. We have been trained to respect other cultures and beliefs different from our own. On the other hand, most physical anthropologists and archaeologists do not want to lose the physical evidence that constitutes our window on the past. The issue thus centers on the tension between *reburial* (i.e., loss of access) versus *continued access* to the remains for purposes of study. Some Native Americans want both human remains and funerary objects returned to them and some anthropologists want both kinds of remains to paint a larger picture of the past. Some Native Americans ideally want no analysis and immediate reburial, whereas some physical anthropologists ideally want to keep the remains in perpetuity for continuing analysis. These are not mutually exclusive alternatives. A compromise would allow physical anthropologists to study the remains before reburial with agreement on the amount of time for study negotiated between the culturally affiliated Native American groups and the physical anthropologist(s) performing the analysis. In some cases, remains may be repatriated under NAGPRA yet continue to be housed in a museum (e.g., Zuni remains [Anyon n. d.]). In other cases, remains will be repatriated and reburied. In a few cases, cooperative arrangements will be made that provide for reinterment *with* continued access for study (for example, physical anthropologist Phillip Walker has an agreement with the Chumash Indians that allows him access to a repository housing repatriated remains). At the very least, physical anthropologists must acknowledge that we have more to lose than bones—we could lose the bones *and* the benefits of cooperative work with Native Americans. Thus, we must strive to recognize and respect their beliefs even if it means losing the source of our data.

HUMAN SKELETAL REMAINS

Native Americans have been very effective at explaining the spiritual and cultural value of human skeletal remains, and in claiming that physical anthropologists do little of value with the bones. In the following sections, we attempt to explain the scientific and educational values of human remains. Because of the importance that we, as physical anthropologists interested in the past, attach to *all* human remains, we do not distinguish between remains that can be culturally affiliated with a particular group and those that cannot in discussing what can be learned from them.

How can a person's skeleton and the context of a burial tell us about his or her life?

Collections of human remains are the basis for ongoing investigation of the quality of life in the past. What we have to contribute from our studies are accounts of the life of a person or group, based on their skeletons. Physical anthropologists have been accused of looking at a skeleton as just a pile of bones or an interesting laboratory specimen but, to us, no matter how fragmentary, each has a story to tell. Our informants are the people themselves. Each skeleton records the biological "memory" of events that occurred while an individual was alive. It carries a record of the age, sex, health, activity, and death of an individual that gives us a unique perspective on that person's life experiences. Each skeleton becomes a recognizable individual, providing us with information about his or her identity and habits over the course of a lifetime. Through the process of gathering this information some of us feel we begin to know these people on a personal level, and sometimes they affect us deeply.

The following are the stories of two people we have come to know under different circumstances. The burial of the first person was excavated by the New York State Museum in the 1960s. During the course of the museum's inventory work required by NAGPRA, Varney and Baker examined the skeletal remains. These remains will be repatriated. The remains of the second individual described were uncovered during archaeological excavations in the 1950s and subsequently displayed in a privately owned facility. After removal from display in 1993, the remains were studied by Baker and Liston. These remains will be curated in a museum.

The first individual is a Mohawk woman who lived near present-day Albany. She died in her early 30s. Her skeleton indicates her life was not easy. As a child, she experienced nutritional deficiencies that left tiny pits on her skull and grooves on her teeth. Her teeth also show us that her diet consisted largely of starchy corn. Several teeth were lost before she died; others were destroyed by massive cavities. Infection of these teeth left large abscesses in both her jaws and hollowed out the bone of her left cheek. Infection also left its mark on other parts of her skeleton, suggesting she may have suffered from a respiratory disease such as tuberculosis. The bones of her neck still convey her difficulties. One of the vertebral bodies was eaten away and the two bones below it did not separate as they developed, limiting her mobility. Despite these limitations, she was a robust, active woman throughout her life, as we see from the size of her upper arms and their muscle attachments. Without reading the record preserved in her skeleton, we would not know of these challenges or, as importantly, that she survived them.

The second individual is a young man who died at Fort William Henry, far from his home and family. He may have been one of our ancestors. Historical accounts tell us only that he was a British or provincial soldier in the 1750s. His skeleton tells us more. Though he was only in his twenties, the wear and tear on his bones reveal that he led an arduous existence. His skeleton also shows us that he endured tuberculosis for many years, but the disease was not what killed him. Death came in battle, with a shot from a musket and a blow to his head.

We also know from our studies of past groups that many enjoyed long, healthy lives. Despite the common misconception of mainstream society, some people lived to a ripe old age. Without their remains, these personal narratives could not be told. Their stories enrich our appreciation of the past and benefit us all. We come to know these people well through our work, and our respect for them has increased with what we have learned about them.

Our description of a person is not complete without knowing the context of how they were buried. A full understanding of a person who lived in the past comes not just from the individual's skeletal remains but also from the manner of burial and any items accompanying him or her. We can learn even more about a person from evidence of other burials and activities nearby. Cumulatively, individuals from one burial place, or from several places throughout a region, can reveal information about the group to which they belonged. Areas rich in oral traditions or written records can aid in deciphering some of the meaning behind the burial ritual, from objects placed with the deceased to choice of burial location. We derive the most meaning from remains when we have knowledge of their associated context.

In many cultures, burial practices serve as a rite of passage in the transition from life into death, and as a way of maintaining continuity with the living. Objects buried with the deceased can reflect the identity and role of the individual in life, and ways in which a person's death is viewed by the society. Objects placed with the body may have many different meanings. Objects may be necessary for use by the deceased or the soul on the journey to an afterworld or in an afterlife. An object could also serve to protect the living from a restless spirit. Items placed with a body may, thus, have functional or symbolic significance. On another level, objects placed with the deceased may be personal possessions or gifts from family and friends. These objects might signify the person's socioeconomic status, age and gender, or the relationship the individual had with other members of the society.

For example, the woman described previously was buried in a grave with two other individuals—an infant and a child ten to twelve years old. The three individuals were probably members of the same extended family or had close clan affiliation. By the woman's head was a ceramic vessel with four effigy figures on the collar. The pot may have contained perishables needed to sustain the deceased or the spirit. The decoration on the pot may symbolize clan affiliation. The infant was buried between the woman and the older child, who was placed in the grave wearing a necklace of glass trade beads and a beaded bracelet. The child was also wearing a garment that appeared to have beads and a brass bell sewn on it. By the child's left arm were a pewter spoon, an iron awl, and two ceramic vessels. These offerings indicate that the children were recognized as valued members of the society. Perhaps the greater number of objects buried with the children signifies their greater vulnerability. The physical qualities of the objects that were placed with the children may also have been culturally significant. Among the Iroquois, for example, metal and glass are bright and reflective and act as material metaphors for cultural well-being (George Hamell, personal communication 1995).

As a highly symbolic act wholly integrated with religion and ideology, mortuary behavior may be one of the few links to worldview in the deep past. While some may argue that it is not appropriate or even possible to understand past meaning, it has become a topic with great potential for reevaluating our interpretations of prehistory. An ancient burial site in central New York state, for example, was defined some fifty years ago as typifying an enigmatic mortuary complex believed to date from 2,000 to 3,000 years ago (Ritchie and Dragoo 1960; Ritchie 1965). A recent reassessment of material and skeletal remains from the site suggests that it may have been used well beyond the period originally defined (Anderson 1996). The earliest funerary events at the site may have marked it as a focal point for repeated ritual activity by later, possibly unrelated groups. Associations between this site and death persist to this day in Iroquois oral tradition. A revised interpretation of the site's history would reflect the participation of numerous groups and present a more complex picture of past activity and cultural affiliation.

We can also learn about changes that occur through time by examining groups of burials from different locations and different time periods. For example, information from seventeenth-century Native American cemeteries in New England reveals much about change and persistence in relation to contact with another culture. Examination of the human remains indicates considerable change in health status and the age and sex distribution of the population. Despite these changes, burial traditions that existed before European contact persisted throughout the seventeenth century (Baker 1994).

Unfortunately, not even all anthropologists have recognized what can be gained from contextualizing each burial. It is disturbing to us that some of our colleagues divorce the human remains from the funerary objects buried with them in their studies and in discussions of repatriation and reburial. They deem it important to return the human remains, while overlooking the fact that the associated cultural remains are also a part of who that person was. Some of this internal dissension in the discipline stems from the fact that archaeologists want to protect their access to cultural remains, while physical anthropologists want to protect access to human remains. To understand the meaning of the associated artifacts, however, they must be interpreted in the context of the entire burial.

WHAT IS THE VALUE OF PAST HEALTH AND ACTIVITY INFORMATION FOR MODERN MEDICAL RESEARCH AND TREATMENT?

In a broader context, studying human remains can tell us not only about the past, but about present human conditions. Such study has contributed to several developments in modern medical treatment. The study of environmental and infectious diseases in prehistoric Native American populations and other groups has shown some patterns that are instructive for modern peoples (Hill and Baker 1989). For example, back problems stemming from upright posture have plagued human populations for millennia. Many daily activities place excessive stress and strain on the spinal column, and back pain is one of the most frequently cited reasons for missing work (Clark 1985). Orthopedic surgeons have used the work of anthropologist T. Dale Stewart as a standard reference in their identification and treatment of a spinal disease known as spondylolysis, which causes severe back problems. Stewart (1935, 1956), an M.D. and renowned physical anthropologist, examined this pathology in skeletons from several sites in Alaska and correlated it with daily subsistence activities. This research and its conclusions have assisted physicians in prescribing treatment and therapy for patients today.

Certain diseases resulting from daily activity and diet, such as arthritis, osteoporosis, and nutritional anemia, were common in many prehistoric groups. With increased longevity and an aging population in industrialized countries, degenerative diseases that affect the skeleton have become serious problems in modern populations. Many modern biomedical conditions are very difficult to study in living individuals because the skeleton is obscured by soft tissue and cannot be examined directly. Researchers must rely on x-rays, CT scans, or MRI images of the bone. As a result, medical research on skeletal conditions tends to focus on clusters of individual case studies. In contrast, investigations of ancient remains provide direct examination of the bone as well as larger samples and cross-sections of populations. In this context, health information from past groups provides a broader perspective on the relationship between certain activity patterns and health problems. Conclusions derived from these studies advocate diet and lifestyle adjustments for people at early ages that assist in curtailing health problems fostered by specific living patterns. Bioanthropological research on human remains supports the provision of better social services and health practices in contemporary societies. The examples given here are just a few of many that demonstrate how research on past populations is of value for improved health in modern societies.

Archaeologists and physical anthropologists study many types of past events and the cultural contexts in which they occurred (Hill and Baker 1989:2). *All* groups are of interest in such studies. In North America, extensive research has been carried out on the remains of all populations, including those of European, African, and Asian ancestry (Owsley 1990). Studies of military personnel are numerous. Standard osteological methods of estimating age and stature were developed from examination of skeletons of U.S. Army soldiers killed during World War II and the Korean War (McKern and Stewart 1957; Trotter and Gleser 1952, 1958). The remains of soldiers from the Civil War and later frontier battles have also been studied (Scott et al. 1989; Sledzik and Moore-Jansen 1991). Many such skeletal remains are stored and displayed at the Armed Forces Institute of Pathology/National Museum of Health and Medicine. The skeletons of British and provincial soldiers from the French and Indian War (Baker and Liston 1995a, 1995b; Liston and Baker 1994, 1995, 1996; Steegman 1986) and American soldiers from the Revolutionary War (Sciulli and Gramly 1989) and the War of 1812 (Pfeiffer and Williamson 1991) have provided windows into conditions during particular periods in American history. Investigations of the skeletons of poorhouse and almshouse residents (Elia and Wesolowski 1991; Grauer and McNamara 1995; Higgins and Sirianni 1995; Lanphear 1988, 1990; Steegman 1991; Sutter 1995) have revealed much about the living conditions and medical care at these facilities that would otherwise be unknown. Burials of Euro-American colonists, plantation owners, and pioneers, as well as European explorers, have also been examined (Aufderheide et al. 1985; Beattie and Geiger 1987; Finnegan 1976; Gill et al. 1984; Larsen et al. 1995; Little et al. 1992; Murray and Perzigian 1995; Pfeiffer et al. 1989; Rathbun and Scurry 1991; Saunders et al. 1995; Saunders and Lazenby 1991; Shapiro 1930; Thomas et al. 1977; Winchell et al. 1995). Studies of the remains of enslaved and free African Americans enable us to learn about a segment of American society that was largely denied a voice in historical writings and records (Angel et al. 1987; Aufderheide et al. 1985; Blakey et al. 1994; Crist 1995; Finnegan 1976; Hill et al. 1995; Hutchinson 1987; Kelley and Angel 1987; Mack et al. 1995; Martin et al. 1987; Owsley et al. 1987; Parrington and Roberts 1990; Parrington and Wideman 1986; Rankin-Hill 1990; Rathbun 1987; Roberts and McCarthy 1995; Rose 1985; Rose and Hartnady 1991; Thomas et al. 1977). Finally, forensic and autopsied remains of all North American groups have been significant in the identification of individual remains and in the investigation of disease processes (El-Najjar 1981; İşcan et al. 1984; Krogman and İşcan 1986; Rathbun and Buikstra 1984; Roberts et al. 1994; Stewart 1970; Todd 1920).

WHAT IS THE VALUE OF HUMAN REMAINS FOR FUTURE RESEARCH AND TRAINING?

In addition to the value of human remains for exploring our past, another reason for continued access to skeletal remains is to train future students in the area of human osteology. From crania, physical anthropologists can determine with a fairly high degree of probability whether remains are those of Native Americans; this identification will not be possible without Native American remains to serve as models for instructing graduate students in this type of identification. There is a world of difference between plastic replicas of bone and real bone. Any artificial model fails to provide the range of variation in all aspects of observation that real bone can provide. We would not trust a surgeon trained exclusively through computer-generated anatomy programs, and we should not trust a skeletal biologist whose training was similarly artificial. To fully understand human skeletal biology requires Native American remains, as well as remains of all other peoples of the world.

Curated skeletal remains can be restudied as new questions arise. Extensive museum collections that have been amassed over the last century or more have been examined repeatedly as new theoretical and methodological approaches have developed (Buikstra and Gordon 1981). When we realize that radiocarbon dating is only fifty years old, or that techniques to aid in reconstructing diet are only 20 years old, the value of curated collections is especially clear. We can now extract DNA from archaeological bone. Although this technique is in its infancy, it will help establish modern Native American affinities in relationship to known periods in the past. Reburial of human remains without first obtaining samples will preclude any chance of tracing genetic relationships between present and past populations.

Not only do new methods help us gain a more complete picture of past lifeways, but the study of a single skeleton by several investigators is essential. No single analytical procedure, or set of procedures, can reveal all the information contained in human remains. No one analyst can know all of the possibilities or have the expertise to explore *all* the features of a skeleton. Methods continue to improve and change, questions and problems expand, and the ability to restudy populations means that new information can be cumulative and complementary. Older collections of human remains are often used in the development of new analytical techniques and in population comparisons with more recently collected remains (Buikstra and Gordon 1981). As an example, no reliable technique for determining the sex of sub-adult skeletal remains has been established. However, recent research (Hall 1995) may help bridge this gap in our expertise.

In sum, the curated remains of *all* peoples are important for training future investigators to unlock the biological memories preserved in skeletons. Human remains will be inadvertently uncovered in the future and we must continue to train students to document these remains accurately and thoroughly. The reburial of all or most Native American remains will make it difficult to teach students in this area, and will shift the focus of future study in skeletal biology to other geographic areas and peoples. While Native Americans may applaud such a shift, it will eventually result in a gap in anthropological knowledge of the world's people.

WHAT IS THE VALUE OF "CULTURALLY UNIDENTIFIABLE" HUMAN REMAINS?

The issue of repatriation becomes increasingly complicated where cultural identifications with modern groups are not possible for anthropologists to trace. For remains that are unprovenienced or more than a few hundred years old (that is, before about A.D. 1300), direct cultural affiliation between past and present populations is not always discernible through the archaeological record. Because humans have migrated through time, it is possible that the descendants of one group live in an area occupied by a different group in the past. Some groups may have joined together in past centuries, whereas others may have moved apart. The question thus becomes with which, if any, of these groups were these remains affiliated. The question is further complicated by fundamental differences in the ways that anthropologists and Native Americans trace ancestry.

It is often *assumed* that remains should be returned to the Native group currently residing in the area where the remains were found, whether or not this group occupied the area in the past. This assumption can lead to situations in which an intent to repatriate unidentifiable human remains to a specific group may violate the interests of others who may be descendants. An example of such a situation arose in the town of Waterford, in upstate New York, in May 1995.
The remains of three individuals were encountered during a town sewer construction project (Conlon 1995a, 1995b, 1995c, 1995d). These remains did not fall under the provisions of NAGPRA.

The upper Hudson Valley area, where these burials were found, was the aboriginal homeland of the Mohicans, an Algonkian group whose descendants are now known as the Stockbridge Munsee Band of Mohican Indians. After A.D. 1600, the Mohicans were forced out of the Hudson Valley by the Mohawks. Today, the Stockbridge Munsee reservation is located in Wisconsin. Upon discovery of the burials during the construction in Waterford, officials notified an Iroquois chief from Onondaga, in central New York. Negotiations were initiated with him for reburial of the remains. The Stockbridge Munsee were not notified directly, but eventually learned of the discovery and took immediate action. The ensuing dispute concerning the remains also involved the Governor's office and other state officials. The Onondaga wished to rebury the remains in a nearby State Park, whereas the Stockbridge Munsee (Mohican) wanted to rebury the remains in their established tribal burial site (Conlon 1995d). Because the remains are thought to be about 1000 years old, it might be argued that they are culturally unidentifiable.

The remains were reburied at the State Park in July 1996 in a ceremony conducted by the Onondaga chief (Gardinier 1996). About 50 Stockbridge Munsee made the trip from Wisconsin to attend the reburial. Many state officials and area anthropologists (including Baker) observed the ceremony. The Onondaga were given primacy in this reburial, while the Stockbridge Munsee, who claim the area as their homeland, were denied any significant role in decisions regarding the treatment and disposition of these remains. This is but one example from New York in which the return of culturally unidentifiable remains to a specific group infringed upon the wishes of other Native Americans with equal or greater claim as descendants.

There is no consensus on these issues among anthropologists or Native Americans (see Ubelaker and Grant 1989). Some groups, like the Zuni, do not want human remains returned to them because of their religious beliefs about the dead. Others, like the Chumash, have made arrangements for reburial that allow for continued access by physical anthropologists (Phillip Walker, personal communication 1994). Some groups want remains reinterred without study by physical anthropologists, while others are interested in osteological analysis and how it may benefit them (the Hopi [Ferguson et al. 1995:11], Pima and Maricopa [Ravesloot 1995]). From the standpoint of physical anthropology, it is not appropriate to rebury culturally unidentifiable remains because much can be learned about the lives of these people from their skeletons. As new methods of study are developed, group membership may eventually be deciphered, allowing the remains in question to be returned to the appropriate group and treated according to that group's wishes. The difficulties inherent in these issues require dialogue between anthropologists and Native Americans for resolution. Anthropologists and Native Americans need to work together to resolve conflicts; insisting upon self-righteousness produces no solutions. This is not idealistic rhetoric on our part, but a practical perspective that stems from our own developing relationships with certain groups of Native Americans in the U.S. (see below).

Another issue concerns the humanistic, scientific, and educational value of poorly provenienced or fragmentary remains. It is widely assumed that there is little to learn from such remains; however, small fragments of a skeleton can reveal clues about a person's identity to those willing to search for them. Even cremated remains, though broken and burned, shed light on an individual and his or her culture (Barbian 1994; Barbian and Magennis 1994; Liston 1993; Magennis 1986). Each and every skeleton is important in providing a view of the past.

Some regions, like the Northeast, were occupied in antiquity by small groups who are often underrepresented in the archaeological record. Even isolated burials, fragmentary skeletons, and those that are unprovenienced can provide information on a region and for time periods about which we know very little

(Schindler et al. 1981; Shaw 1988). It is only through careful attention to each and every individual that we can build a more complete picture of the past.

SHARED RESPONSIBILITY

It has been our responsibility as anthropologists and museum personnel to care for collections in order to preserve them, to learn from them about our plurality of pasts, and to provide the public with access to this information. Francis McManamon (1994:2), Departmental Consulting Archeologist for the National Park Service, states that archaeological "collections are an irreplaceable part of our national heritage, which is why laws were passed to collect and protect them for present and future generations." Perhaps future generations will be interested in learning about their past through studying the cultural material and skeletal remains of their ancestors. The type of information to which we assign value changes through time and varies from culture to culture. It is our professional obligation to preserve as much information as possible for future generations.

At the NAGPRA Review Committee meeting at the New York State Museum in November 1994, Sebastian "Bronco" LeBeau (Cheyenne River Sioux Tribe) stated that "we are all related—*all* of us are part of the family of humanity." The study of all cultures in both the past and present, together with shared concerns about our survival in the future, promotes understanding and acceptance of cultural diversity. Studying and restudying the physical remains and material evidence of our pasts has helped to promote this understanding. Our histories are as diverse as the peoples who participated in them, and it is of benefit to all people to preserve as much of the past as possible for future generations. As anthropologists, we feel we have a unique and valuable perspective to contribute to recording these histories that should not be lost.

While we acknowledge that museum collections were often excavated without consideration of the descendants, the current generation of professional anthropologists was not responsible for these excavations. We are, however, responsible for these collections, no matter how they were obtained. As such, we should try to help rectify past problems resulting from the manner in which some collections were made. Future students should be trained to be aware of others' needs and others' voices, and strive to work cooperatively with Native peoples in a way that is productive and satisfactory to all. Cooperation provides the opportunity to exchange information. In these exchanges, traditional and scientific ways of learning about the past complement each other (see, for example, Ferguson et al. 1995; Ravesloot 1995). The understanding we gain from cooperative efforts fosters mutual respect. Some museums have already opened their collections to Native American groups for purification or blessing ceremonies. Such access should be maintained and expanded for materials that may not be repatriated very soon or are not even subject to NAGPRA. This access promotes increased interaction between Native Americans and anthropologists.

Improving relationships with Native Americans is clearly in the best interests of physical anthropologists and we hope that the Native communities would see the benefits as well. Our personal experiences may serve to illustrate the positive outcome of such interactions. Over the past several years, one of us (Wilkinson) has had extended interactions with members of Native American communities in the process of analyzing and reburying skeletal remains. More recently, others of us (Anderson, Baker, and Varney) have interacted with Native Americans in the process of complying with NAGPRA.

Wilkinson's analysis of skeletal material from sites affiliated with the Pequot and the Oneida Nation serve as examples of cooperation. In the first instance, Charlene Prince, a member of the Mashantucket Pequot tribe was present throughout the process of removing remains from the historic Pequot site of Long Pond and assisted with the subsequent analysis. In the second case, a small collection of remains was found eroding out of a riverbank north of Syracuse, in an area occupied in historic times by the Oneida Nation. In this instance, Wilkinson was joined by Brian Patterson, a member of the Oneida Men's Council, and they had an opportunity to spend the day talking about the skeletal analysis and Mr. Patterson's feelings about the bones and their destiny. Wilkinson recounts these experiences as follows:

> In both of these instances, I was struck by the intensity of interest shown by my Native American associates in what we could say about the lives of the people represented by the skeletal remains. These people were genuinely excited about the information provided, and the process of interpretation leading to the information. As a professor, it was the equivalent of having the smallest possible class with the most highly motivated students, and it was a joy leading the "students" through the analysis. No small part of my delight at the reaction of Ms. Prince and Mr. Patterson to my work was based on my prejudicial expectations that they would be hesitant at best, most likely obstructionist, and possibly even hostile enough to prevent the analysis. The very positive interactions afforded me the opportunity to evaluate my prejudices, and come to a much better understanding of at least some Native American people's desire to know the past.

> The reburial ceremony on the Mashantucket Pequot reservation was held on a cold spring morning. In addition to members of the tribe and visiting Indians, the archaeologists who excavated the site were also invited. Circular pits were dug, duplicating the original burial pits in number, and approximating them in size. Woven mats were placed in the bottom of the pits, and the mats were covered with blankets, as was the original practice. The skeletal material was arranged in the same position as found, and the funerary objects were placed in their original positions with the remains. Sweet grass was burned, the drum was sounded and words were said; circling the graves, we each added a handful of earth to them. The Pequot appeared deeply moved by the reburial ceremony. I found myself entering the process as an anthropologist, with an academic interest in the proceedings. I emerged from the ceremony with much less objectivity, and a deeper understanding of the significance of the event to the people.

> The reburial ceremony was followed immediately with a ceremony to dedicate the new children's center on the reservation, and the relationship between the two life-defining events was made explicit in speeches and conversations. At lunch, more speeches were made and plaques were presented to the anthropologists, making it clear that we were considered integral parts of this important Pequot event. Something was lost during this lengthy process. Anthropologists lost information about these particular Pequots who died 300 years ago, and it is

irretrievable. Something was also gained. Anthropologists gained a measure of respect for the Pequot community and from the community as well.

Anderson and Baker experienced similar feelings at a reburial ceremony to which they were invited by the Stockbridge Munsee tribe in July 1994. Prior to the reburial, they were asked by the tribe's NAGPRA representative to examine human remains that were being returned to them by the son of the man who had collected them over sixty years ago (Baker 1996).

> Initially, we were very pleased that we would be allowed to observe the ceremony, although we were somewhat apprehensive regarding our role. As the anthropologists delivering the remains to be reinterred, we were unsure how we would be received by people to whom our profession represented sacrilege for disturbing their ancestors. It soon became evident that everyone present, whether Native American or not, would be participants rather than observers. People from all walks of life attended the ceremony, including the Stockbridge Munsee, Native Americans from other groups, Buddhist monastics, Catholic nuns, several archaeologists, the son of the man who collected the remains, and other interested people. Because of this inclusiveness, the ceremony took on added meaning. Despite feeling torn that we were reburying remains we would like to have learned even more about, we were part of something that felt right because the ceremony brought together a diverse group of people and evoked a sense of closure and new beginnings at the same time.

In retrospect, it is apparent that we, as physical anthropologists, benefitted from this reburial in several ways. Because of the interest expressed by the Stockbridge Munsee in their past, we were consulted prior to the reburial regarding information we could provide to them about the individual. As a result, we established a cooperative working relationship, and we acquired information that was not previously recorded. We also gained an understanding of the importance of these remains to the descendant community. The Stockbridge Munsee also benefitted from the reburial by learning about one of their ancestors and by returning him to the ground to complete his journey. Perhaps we all made a journey that day along the way to understanding.

This cooperative relationship has been solidified over the past three years. Stephen Comer, the NAGPRA representative of the Stockbridge Munsee, volunteers at the New York State Museum to aid with inventories for sites in the Hudson Valley, his traditional homeland. A ceremony was also performed by his group for the human remains from the Hudson Valley region that are held in the collections of the New York State Museum. As at the reburial ceremony, all who attended were allowed to participate. As participants, Anderson, Baker, and Varney came to a better understanding of, and appreciation for, the feelings of our Native American colleagues. The ceremony helped us begin to bridge a gap between anthropologists and Native Americans, and between science and tradition.

In addition, Anderson, Baker, and Varney have conducted NAGPRA consultations at the New York State Museum with representatives of several Iroquois nations. Again, we entered these consultations with some apprehension based on our expectation that our work would be perceived negatively. Instead, the consultations proved to be very positive experiences. From the great number of questions about our inventory process, the museum's collections, and especially the human remains, it was obvious that the Iroquois representatives had a great interest in what we do and why we do it. Many showed a considerable understanding of the task with which we are faced and expressed their appreciation for our efforts to put individual people back together (storage practices sometimes resulted in the dispersal or commingling of several individuals' remains) and to reassociate them with the objects buried with them. Many found it difficult to understand why we feel compelled to dig people up and put them on museum shelves. We thus had the opportunity to explain on a one-to-one basis our fascination with the people of the past. We are extremely interested in who these people were, and what their lives and cultures were like, whether they were Native Americans, Europeans, or ancient Egyptians. Interestingly, one of the representatives found herself agreeing that ancient Egypt is fascinating, thereby forming a link that helps foster mutual understanding. Rather than being a negative experience, these consultations have had the very positive result of generating further discussion and the sharing of information.

As physical anthropologists, we would like to think that Native Americans are interested in the work we do, because we sincerely believe we are unlocking a past whose record is unwritten. From these limited experiences, we can say that there are, indeed, Native Americans who appreciate what we can tell them, and the skills we bring to the task. This appreciation, however, does not preclude an even deeper respect for the significance of their spiritual beliefs, an area that has been avoided or denied by the majority of physical anthropologists. The Native Americans with whom we have worked have been fascinated by the skeletal analyses, and fully appreciative of the information to be gained from the bones, but they are also extremely happy that the remains were or will be reburied.

This kind of productive exchange can go far toward healing the wounds of the past, and the impetus for change has to come from the anthropologists. In the cases described here, the benefits far outweigh the costs. In other cases, like that of the Kennewick, Washington, remains that are over 8,000 years old (Chatters 1997), the loss of information that would result from reburial may be the greater cost. It is important to establish a dialogue about costs and benefits with Native Americans, and not simply assert that "our" losses as scientists always outweigh theirs (see also Ubelaker and Grant 1989:280–282).

CONCLUSION

There is much value in learning about the past. The experience that physical anthropologists are gaining in working with Native Americans is essential to explaining what we know, how we know it, and what we have yet to learn. People can benefit from learning about past health and disease, demographics, migration, group relationships, kinship, and subsistence, to name but a few areas, and many are interested in how we recover this information from the human skeleton. In summary, human remains are important for reconstructing history, understanding human health and adaptations through time, valuing diversity and educating future generations.

In our view, it would be inappropriate to rebury the people who have resided in museum collections for decades without first learning their stories. They have not been neglected for lack of interest in who they were, but because there are very few of us to undertake such investigations. There are presently only about 250 human osteologists in the United States and Canada, many of whom are graduate students (American Association of Physical Anthropologists, 1992). Many of our number teach full-time in colleges across the country and have little time to pursue other work. In addition, our analytical techniques, including photographs, x-rays, CAT scans, radiocarbon dating, stable isotope analysis, DNA extraction, and others are extraordinarily costly. Funding for documentation of human remains is limited, though after the passage of NAGPRA it increased slightly. We are also faced with too little time to really learn about the lives of these people. Thorough documentation requires us to record enormous quantities of information. The *Standards for Data Collection from Human Skeletal Remains* (Buikstra and Ubelaker 1994), developed from a seminar organized by Jonathan Haas (a member of the NAGPRA Review Committee), describes minimal standards for documenting information that should be obtained from human skeletal remains. It contains over 200 pages. The difficulty of trying to meet these standards in the time allowed is tremendous.

A critical part of the value of human remains is in the unique potential they have for providing an understanding of a people's past that is not based on misconceptions and which may otherwise be unknown or unknowable. We take the recent motto of the Society for American Archaeology to be essential: "Save the past for the future." One thing we have learned through studying the history of various groups is that culture changes, as do religious beliefs and spirituality. Ironically, it is the work of anthropologists that aids the repatriation process by using culture histories and archaeological interpretations to determine cultural affiliation. Like most disciplines, however, archaeology is built upon the continual testing and re-testing of ideas as new approaches and data are available. Unlike Native histories, the way we interpret the past is an ever-changing process. We propose repatriation with continued access as a possible solution for reducing the tensions between the scientific and spiritual values of human remains. We approach this problem as physical anthropologists, yet we are beginning to understand other values of human remains beyond the scientific and educational value we place upon them. We cannot predict what our grandchildren and their children will want, or need, to know but we have a professional obligation to preserve at least part of their past for their future.

By offering our expertise as physical anthropologists to Native American communities who wish to learn about their ancestors through our studies of skeletal remains, new relationships can be forged. In this manner, physical anthropology can benefit through the addition of further information, Native Americans can benefit from what we can tell them through our analysis prior to reburial and by caring for the spiritual well-being of their ancestors. As anthropologists, we need to do more to recognize and respect the voices of the people who are emotionally and spiritually affected by our work. We urge our colleagues to take the first step toward reconciliation. Invite Native Americans to work with you, and encourage them to learn about your work. We have found many Native American people to be sincerely interested in their past and in our contributions toward understanding it. Substantial mutual benefits can be derived from such close interaction. Perhaps, as was suggested by more than one person during our NAGPRA consultations, the ancestors are in collections for a reason—to bring us together.

ACKNOWLEDGMENTS

We would like to thank Carol Raemsch (Hartgen and Associates) and Lorraine Saunders (SUNY-Brockport and Rochester Museum and Science Center) for their contributions to the original statement prepared for the NAGPRA Review Committee meeting in November 1994. George Hamell of the New York State Museum has also provided us with insight into symbolism of mortuary behavior. We also thank the NAGPRA representatives and other individuals from the Native American groups with whom we have had the opportunity to work. Although not all of these individuals would agree with many of our statements, we have benefitted from our discussions with them.

REFERENCES CITED

American Association of Physical Anthropologists. 1992. "Proceedings of the Sixty-First Meeting of the American Association of Physical Anthropologists." *American Journal of Physical Anthropology* 89:505–515.

Anderson, Lisa M. 1996. "Vine Valley Revisited." In *A Golden Chronograph: Papers in Honor of Robert E. Funk,* edited by Christopher Lindner and Edward V. Curtin, pp. 155–161. Occasional Papers in Northeastern Anthropology, No. 15. Archaeological Services, Bethlehem, Connecticut.

Angel, J. Lawrence, Jennifer O. Kelley, Michael Parrington, and Stephanie Pinter. 1987. "Life Stresses of the Free Black Community as Represented by the First African Baptist Church, Philadelphia, 1823–1841." *American Journal of Physical Anthropology* 74(2):213–229.

Anyon, Roger. n. d. Letter to New York State Museum, October 9, 1995, from Director of Zuni Heritage and Historic Preservation Office.

Aufderheide, Arthur C., J. Lawrence Angel, Jennifer O. Kelley, Alain C. Outlaw, Merry A. Outlaw, George Rapp, Jr., and Lorentz E. Wittmers, Jr. 1985. "Lead in Bone III. Prediction of Social Correlates from Skeletal Lead Content in Four Colonial American Populations (Catoctin Furnace, College Landing, Governor's Land, and Irene Mound)." *American Journal of Physical Anthropology* 66:353–361.

Baker, Brenda J. 1994. "Pilgrim's Progress and Praying Indians: The Biocultural Consequences of Contact in Southern New England." In *In the Wake of Contact: Biological Responses to Conquest,* edited by Clark Spencer Larsen and George R. Milner, pp. 35–45. New York: Wiley-Liss.

Baker, Brenda J., and Maria A. Liston. 1995a. "Infection in Eighteenth-Century Military Remains at Fort William Henry." Poster presented at the 64th Annual Meeting of the American Association of Physical Anthropologists, Oakland. Abstract in *American Journal of Physical Anthropology Suppl.* 20:61.

——— 1995b. "War is Hell: Eighteenth-Century Military Remains at Fort William Henry." Poster presented at 60th Annual Meeting of the Society for American Archaeology, Minneapolis.

Barbian, Lenore T. 1994. *A Case Study of Northeastern Late Archaic Mortuary Behavior: Turner Farm, Maine.* Ph.D. dissertation, Department of Anthropology, University of Massachusetts, Amherst. University Microfilms, Ann Arbor.

Barbian, Lenore T., and Ann L. Magennis. 1994. "Variability in Late Archaic Human Burials at Turner Farm, Maine." *Northeast Anthropology* 47:1–19.

Beattie, Owen B., and John Geiger. 1987. *Frozen in Time: Unlocking the Secrets of the Franklin Expedition.* Saskatoon, Saskatchewan: Western Producer Prairie Books.

Blakey, Michael L., Teresa E. Leslie, and Joseph P. Reidy. 1994. "Frequency and Chronological Distribution of Dental Enamel Hypoplasia in Enslaved African Americans: A Test of the Weaning Hypothesis." *American Journal of Physical Anthropology* 95(4):371–383.

Brace, C. Loring. 1982. "The Roots of the Race Concept in American Physical Anthropology." In *A History of American Physical Anthropology, 1930–1980,* edited by Frank Spencer, pp. 11–29. New York: Academic Press.

Buikstra, Jane E., and Claire C. Gordon. 1981. "The Study and Restudy of Human Skeletal Series: The Importance of Long-term Curation." *Annals of the New York Academy of Sciences* 376:449–466.

Buikstra, Jane E., and Douglas H. Ubelaker. 1994. *Standards for Data Collection from Human Skeletal Remains.* Arkansas Archeological Survey Research Series No. 44, Fayetteville.

Chatters, James C. 1997. "Encounter with an Ancestor. " *Anthropology Newsletter* 38(1):9–10.

Clark, George A. 1985. *Heterochrony, Allometry, and Canalization in the Human Vertebral Column: Examples from Prehistoric Amerindian Populations.* Ph.D. dissertation, Department of Anthropology, University of Massachusetts-Amherst. University Microfilms, Ann Arbor.

Conlon, Kevin. 1995a. Another Indian Skeleton Found. *The Daily Gazette*, May 16, p. B5.

——— 1995b. "Finding Artifacts Creates Delicate Balance for Municipalities." *The Sunday Gazette*, June 4, p. B6.

——— 1995c. "Sacred Site: Two Indian Skeletons Found in Waterford." *The Daily Gazette*, May 4, p. A1.

——— 1995d. "Skeletons' Nationality in Dispute." *The Daily Gazette*, May 5, pp. A1, A5.

Crist, Thomas A. J. 1995. Bone Chemistry Analysis and Documentary Archaeology: Dietary Patterns of Enslaved African Americans in the South Carolina Low Country. In *Bodies of Evidence: Reconstructing History through Skeletal Analysis,* edited by Anne L. Grauer, pp.197–219. New York: Wiley-Liss.

Elia, Ricardo J. and Al B. Wesolowski (editors). 1991. *Archaeological Excavations at the Uxbridge Almshouse Burial Ground in Uxbridge, Massachusetts.* BAR International Series 564. British Archaeological Reports, Oxford.

El-Najjar, Mahmoud Y. 1981. "Skeletal Changes in Tuberculosis: The Hamann-Todd Collection." In *Prehistoric Tuberculosis in the Americas,* edited by Jane E. Buikstra, pp. 85–97. Northwestern University Archeological Program, Scientific Papers No. 5. Evanston, Illinois.

Ferguson, T. J., Kurt Dongoske, Mike Yeatts, and Leigh Jenkins. 1995. "Hopi Oral History and Archaeology. Part II: Implementation." *Society for American Archaeology Bulletin* 13(3):10–13.

Finnegan, Michael. 1976. "Walnut Creek massacre: Identification and analysis." *American Journal of Physical Anthropology* 45:737–742.

Gardinier, Bob. 1996. "Quiet ceremony of reburial: Native Americans laid to rest in Waterford Park." *Times Union*, July 21, pp. D-1, D-5.

Gill, George W., John W. Fisher, Jr., and George M. Zeimens. 1984. "A pioneer burial near the historic Bordeaux trading post." *Plains Anthropologist* 29:229–238.

Gould, Stephen Jay. 1981. *The Mismeasure of Man.* New York: W. W. Norton.

Grauer, Anne L., and Elizabeth M. McNamara. 1995. "A piece of Chicago's past: Exploring childhood mortality in the Dunning Poorhouse cemetery." In *Bodies of Evidence: Reconstructing History Through Skeletal Analysis,* edited by Anne L. Grauer, pp. 91–103. New York: Wiley-Liss.

Hall, L. J. 1995. "Sexual dimorphism in the deciduous dentition and dental arch of modern Native American Indians." Poster presented at the 64th Annual Meeting of the American Association of Physical Anthropologists, Oakland. Abstract in *American Journal of Physical Anthropology Suppl.* 20:104.

Higgins, Roseanne L. and Joyce E. Sirianni. 1995. "An assessment of health and mortality of nineteenth-century Rochester, New York, using historic records and the Highland Park skeletal collection." In *Bodies of Evidence: Reconstructing History Through Skeletal Analysis,* edited by Anne L. Grauer, pp. 121–136. New York: Wiley-Liss.

Hill, M. Cassandra and Brenda J. Baker. 1989. "Human skeletal populations: Bones of contention in biomedical and biocultural research." In *Archaeological Ethics and the Treatment of the Dead.* Unpublished papers from the First Inter-Congress of the World Archaeological Congress, University of South Dakota, Vermillion, South Dakota.

Hill, M. Cassandra, Michael L. Blakey, and Mark E. Mack. 1995. "Women, endurance, and enslavement: Exceeding the physiological limits." Abstract in *American Journal of Physical Anthropology Suppl.* 20: 110–111.

Hutchinson, Janis 1987. "The age-sex structure of the slave population in Harris County, Texas, 1850 and 1860." *American Journal of Physical Anthropology* 74:231–238.

İşcan, M. Yaşar, Susan R. Loth, and Ronald K. Wright. 1984. "Metamorphosis at the sternal rib end: A new method to estimate age at death in white males." *American Journal of Physical Anthropology* 65:147–156.

Kelley, Jennifer O. and J. Lawrence Angel. 1987. "Life stresses of slavery." *American Journal of Physical Anthropology* 74:199–211.

Krogman, Wilton M. and M. Yaşar İşcan. 1986. *The Human Skeleton in Forensic Medicine*. 2nd ed. Springfield, Illinois: Charles C. Thomas.

Lanphear, Kim M. 1988. *Health and Mortality in a Nineteenth Century Poorhouse Skeletal Sample*. Ph.D. dissertation, Department of Anthropology, University at Albany, SUNY. University Microfilms, Ann Arbor, Michigan.

────── 1990. "Frequency and distribution of enamel hypoplasias in a historic skeletal sample." *American Journal of Physical Anthropology* 81:35–43.

Larsen, Clark S., Joseph Craig, Leslie E. Sering, Margaret J. Schoeninger, Katherine F. Russell, Dale L. Hutchinson, and Matthew A. Williamson. 1995. "Cross homestead: Life and death on the midwestern frontier." In *Bodies of Evidence: Reconstructing History Through Skeletal Analysis*, edited by Anne L. Grauer, pp. 139–159. New York: Wiley-Liss.

Liston, Maria A. 1993. *The Human Skeletal Remains from Kavousi, Crete: A Bioarchaeological Analysis*. Ph.D. dissertation, Department of Anthropology, University of Tennessee. University Microfilms, Ann Arbor, Michigan.

Liston, Maria A., and Brenda J. Baker 1994. "Military burials at Fort William Henry." In *Archaeology of the French & Indian War: Military Sites of the Hudson River, Lake George, and Lake Champlain Corridor*, edited by David R. Starbuck, pp. 11–16. Queensbury, New York: Adirondack Community College.

────── 1995. "Trauma in eighteenth-century military remains at Fort William Henry." Poster presented at the 64th Annual Meeting of the American Association of Physical Anthropologists, Oakland. Abstract in *American Journal of Physical Anthropology Suppl.* 20:135–136.

────── 1996. "Reconstructing the massacre at Fort William Henry, New York." *International Journal of Osteoarchaeology* 6(1):28–41.

Little, Barbara J., Kim M. Lanphear, and Douglas W. Owsley. 1992. "Mortuary display and status in a nineteenth-century Anglo-American cemetery in Manassas, Virginia." *American Antiquity* 57:397–418.

Mack, Mark E., Michael L. Blakey, and M. Cassandra Hill 1995. "Preliminary observations of the dental pathologies of the African burial ground skeletal population." Abstract in *American Journal of Physical Anthropology Suppl.* 20:138.

Magennis, Ann L. 1986. "The physical anthropology of the Indian Neck ossuary." In *The Indian Neck Ossuary: Chapters in the Archeology of Cape Cod, V*, by Francis P. McManamon, James W. Bradley, and Ann L. Magennis, pp. 49–183. Cultural Resources Management Study No. 17, Division of Cultural Resources, North Atlantic Regional Office. Boston: National Park Service.

Martin, Debra L., Ann L. Magennis, and Jerome C. Rose. 1987. "Cortical bone maintenance in an historic Afro-American cemetery sample from Cedar Grove, Arkansas." *American Journal of Physical Anthropology* 74(2):255–264.

McKern, T. W., and T. D. Stewart 1957. *Skeletal Age Changes in Young American Males*. Technical Report EP-45. Headquarters Quartermaster Research and Development Command, Natick, Massachusetts.

McManamon, Francis P. 1994. "A time for seamless cooperation." *Federal Archeology* 6 (Summer):2.

Murray, Elizabeth A., and Anthony J. Perzigian. 1995. "A glimpse of early nineteenth-century Cincinnati as viewed from Potter's Field: An exercise in problem solving." In

Bodies of Evidence: Reconstructing History Through Skeletal Analysis, edited by Anne L. Grauer, pp. 173–184. New York: Wiley-Liss.

Owsley, Douglas W. 1990. "The skeletal biology of North American historical populations." In *A Life in Science: Papers in Honor of J. Lawrence Angel*, edited by Jane E. Buikstra, pp. 171–190. Center for American Archeology, Scientific Papers no. 6, Kampsville, Illinois.

Owsley, Douglas W., Charles E. Orser, Jr., Robert W. Mann, Peer H. Moore-Jansen, and Robert L. Montgomery. 1987. "Demography and pathology of an urban slave population from New Orleans." *American Journal of Physical Anthropology* 74:185–197.

Parrington, Michael and Daniel G. Roberts. 1990. "Demographic, cultural, and bioanthropological aspects of a nineteenth-century free black population in Philadelphia, Pennsylvania." In *A Life in Science: Papers in Honor of J. Lawrence Angel*, edited by Jane E. Buikstra, pp. 138–170. Center for American Archeology, Scientific Papers 6, Kampsville, Illinois.

Parrington, Michael and Janet Wideman. 1986. "Acculturation in an urban setting: The Archaeology of a black Philadelphia cemetery." *Expedition* 28(1):55–62.

Pfeiffer, Susan, J. Christopher Dudar, and Shawn Austin. 1989. "Prospect Hill: Skeletal remains from a 19th-Century Methodist cemetery, Newmarket, Ontario." *Northeast Historical Archaeology* 18:29–48.

Pfeiffer, Susan and Ronald F. Williamson (editors). 1991. *Snake Hill: An Investigation of a Military Cemetery from the War of 1812*. Toronto: Dundurn Press.

Rankin-Hill, Leslie M. 1990. *Afro-American Biohistory: Theoretical and Methodological Considerations*. Ph.D. dissertation, Department of Anthropology, University of Massachusetts, Amherst. University Microfilms, Ann Arbor, Michigan.

Rathbun, Ted A. 1987. "Health and disease at a South Carolina plantation, 1840–1870." *American Journal of Physical Anthropology* 74:239–253.

Rathbun, Ted A. and Jane E. Buikstra (editors). 1984. *Human Identification: Case Studies in Forensic Anthropology*. Springfield, Illinois: Charles C. Thomas.

Rathbun, Ted A. and James D. Scurry. 1991. "Status and health in colonial South Carolina: Belleview Plantation, 1738–1756." In *What Mean These Bones? Studies in Southeastern Bioarchaeology*, edited by Mary Lucas Powell, Patricia S. Bridges, and Ann Marie Wagner Mires, pp. 148–164. Tuscaloosa: University of Alabama Press.

Ravesloot, John C. 1995. "The road to common ground." *Federal Archeology* 7(3):36–40.

Ritchie, William A., and Don W. Dragoo. 1960. *The Eastern Dispersal of Adena*. New York State Museum and Science Service Bulletin 379. The University of the State of New York, The State Education Department, Albany, New York.

Ritchie, William A. 1965. *The Archaeology of New York State*. Garden City, New York: Natural History Press.

Roberts, Charlotte, David Lucy, and Keith Manchester. 1994. "Inflammatory lesions of ribs: An analysis of the Terry Collection." *American Journal of Physical Anthropology* 95(2):169–182.

Roberts, Daniel G. and John P. McCarthy. 1995. "Descendant community partnering in the archaeological and bioanthropological investigation of African-American skeletal population: Two interrelated case studies from Philadelphia." In *Bodies of Evidence: Reconstructing History Through Skeletal Analysis*, edited by Anne L. Grauer, pp. 19–36. New York: Wiley-Liss.

Rose, Jerome C. (editor). 1985. *Gone to a Better Land: A Biohistory of a Rural Black Cemetery in the Post-Reconstruction South*. Research Series No. 25. Fayetteville: Arkansas Archaeological Survey.

Rose, Jerome C. and Philip Hartnady. 1991. "Interpretation of infectious skeletal lesions from a historic Afro-American cemetery." In *Human Paleopathology: Current Syn-*

theses and Future Options, edited by Donald J. Ortner and Arthur C. Aufderheide, pp. 119–127. Washington, D.C.: Smithsonian Institution Press.

Saunders, Shelley R., Ann Herring, Lawrence A. Sawchuck, and Gerry Boyce. 1995. "The nineteenth-century cemetery at St. Thomas' Anglican Church, Belleville: Skeletal remains, parish records, and censuses." In *Grave Reflections: Portraying the Past through Cemetery Studies,* edited by Shelley R. Saunders and Ann Herring, pp. 93–117. Toronto: Canadian Scholars' Press.

Saunders, Shelley R. and Richard Lazenby. 1991. "The links that bind: The Harvie family nineteenth-century burying ground." *Occasional Papers in Northeastern Archaeology,* No. 5. Dundas, Ontario: Copetown Press.

Schindler, Debra L., George J. Armelagos, and M. Pamela Bumsted. 1981. "Biocultural adaptation: New directions in northeastern anthropology." In *Foundations of Northeast Archaeology,* edited by Dean R. Snow, pp. 229–259. New York: Academic Press.

Sciulli, Paul W. and Richard M. Gramly. 1989. "Analysis of the Ft. Laurens, Ohio, skeletal sample." *American Journal of Physical Anthropology* 80:11–24.

Scott, Douglas D., Richard A. Fox, Jr., Melissa A. Connor, and Dick Harmon. 1989. *Archaeological Perspectives on the Battle of the Little Bighorn.* Norman: University of Oklahoma Press.

Shapiro, H. L. 1930. "Old New Yorkers: A series of crania from the Nagel burying ground, New York City." *American Journal of Physical Anthropology* 14(3):379–404.

Shaw, Leslie C. 1988. "A biocultural evaluation of the skeletal population from the Nevin site, Blue Hill, Maine." *Archaeology of Eastern North America* 16:55–77.

Sledzik, Paul S., and Peer H. Moore-Jansen. 1991. "Dental disease in nineteenth-century military skeletal samples." In *Advances in Dental Anthropology,* edited by Marc A. Kelley and Clark S. Larsen, pp. 215–224. New York: Alan R. Liss.

Stanton, William. 1960. *The Leopard's Spots: Scientific Attitudes Toward Race in America 1815–59.* Chicago: The University of Chicago Press.

Steegman, A. Theodore, Jr. 1986. "Skeletal stature compared to archival stature in mid-eighteenth century America: Ft. William Henry." *American Journal of Physical Anthropology* 71:431–435.

——— 1991. "Stature in an early mid-19th century poorhouse population: Highland Park, Rochester, New York." *American Journal of Physical Anthropology* 85:261–268.

Stewart, T. Dale. 1935. "Spondylolisthesis without separate neural arch (Pseudo-spondylolisthesis of Junghanns)." *Journal of Bone and Joint Surgery* 17(3):640–648.

——— 1956. "Examination of the possibility that certain skeletal characters predispose to defects in the lumbar neural arches." *Clinical Orthopaedics* 8:44–59.

Stewart, T. Dale (editor). 1970. *Personal Identification in Mass Disasters.* Washington, D.C.: National Museum of Natural History.

Stocking, George W. 1968. *Race, Culture, and Evolution: Essays in the History of Anthropology.* New York: The Free Press.

Sutter, Richard C. 1995. "Dental pathologies among inmates of the Monroe County poorhouse." In *Bodies of Evidence: Reconstructing History Through Skeletal Analysis,* edited by Anne L. Grauer, pp. 185–196. New York: Wiley-Liss.

Thomas, David H., Stanley South, and Clark S. Larsen. 1977. Rich man, poor man: Observations on three antebellum burials from the Georgia coast. *Anthropological Papers of the American Museum of Natural History* 54(3):393–420.

Todd, T. Wingate. 1920. "Age changes in the pubic bone." *American Journal of Physical Anthropology* 3:285–334.

Trotter, Mildred and Goldine C. Gleser. 1952. "Estimation of stature from long bones of American whites and negroes." *American Journal of Physical Anthropology* 10:463–514.

———— 1958. "A re-evaluation of estimation of stature based on measurements of stature taken during life and of long bones after death." *American Journal of Physical Anthropology* 16:79–123.

Ubelaker, Douglas H. and Lauryn Guttenplan Grant. 1989. "Human skeletal remains: Preservation or reburial?" *Yearbook of Physical Anthropology* 32:249–287.

Winchell, Frank, Jerome C. Rose, and Randall W. Moir. 1995. "Health and hard times: A case study from the middle to late nineteenth century in eastern Texas." In *Bodies of Evidence: Reconstructing History Through Skeletal Analysis,* edited by Anne L. Grauer, pp. 197–219. New York: Wiley-Liss.

CHAPTER SIX

Desecration
An Interreligious Controversy[1]

RONALD L. GRIMES

Are we then to give up their sacred graves to be plowed for corn? Dakotas, I am for war!

—Red Cloud, 1866 (in McLuhan 1971:94)

They stumble all night over the bones of the dead
And feel they know not what but care
And wish to lead others when they should be led.

—William Blake, 1794, *Songs of Experience*, plate 54

The subject matter of religious studies is the sacred, and sacrality is often close-ly associated with power. In religious studies it is widely assumed that differences between religions are fundamentally rooted in divergent ways of nam-ing and conceptualizing power, for example, *mana, taboo, anima, tapas, rta*, or *tao*.[2] One scholarly strategy has been to appropriate and generalize these terms for theoretical use. Another has been to employ the rhetoric of power itself. Gerardus van der Leeuw in *Religion in Essence and Manifestation* (1963) made the notion of power central to his understanding of religion, thus implicitly challenging the separation of religion from magic and calling attention to religion's interest in the capacity to effect, cause, and originate events. Mircea Eliade (1957) coined the term "kratophany" to refer to any appearance of the sacred characterized by power, especially when such power is generated by a ritualistic or mythic return to origins. Rites are often a nexus connecting religious cosmologies and political ideologies, hence their embeddedness in power struggles. Power, like space, is never neutral, never abstract, except in inadequate philosophical conceptions of it. Conceptualizations of power are secondary to specific embodiments and enact-ments of it. Power is always "power to" and "power of." We desire and judge power on the basis of its intentions and origins.

Neither van der Leeuw nor Eliade had much to say about the relation of sacred power to social or political power. This link was made explicitly by Max Weber who, in *The Sociology of Religion* (1922), developed the notion of charisma, which denoted the convergence of personal and/or spiritual power with social-political power. One of the main preoccupations of recent scholarship in religious studies has been to maintain a conceptual connection between sacred and social power without reducing either to the other.

This connection is nowhere more evident than in the current struggle of Native American people to control the display of indigenous burial remains and sacred artifacts. Because of charges by, and pleas from, Native people, it is essential that European Americans, that is "White" people, reflect critically on the ethical and religious implications of their own actions in supplying, maintaining, and visiting public sites such as museums where sacred artifacts and mortuary remains are displayed.

Controversy over the disposition of Native burial remains has been in the public eye since at least 1971. Two examples illustrate the issue as it has appeared on both sides of the U. S.–Canadian border. In 1971 members of AIM (American Indian Movement) disrupted a dig outside Minneapolis-Saint Paul. Even though there were no burials at the site, the symbolism of the confrontation was important to AIM members who felt the excavation was proceeding without consideration of Native values and beliefs. According to the Arlie House Report (McGimsey and Davis 1977:90) the public was largely sympathetic with Native people while archaeologists were not.

In 1977, after a controversy over a burial site at Grimsby, Ontario, and a sit-in by First Nations peoples at the Royal Ontario Museum, a meeting was convened among representatives of Native and archaeological groups in order to begin the formulation of ethical guidelines to ensure "proper dignity and reverence for the remains" (Douglas Tushingham, cited in Savage 1977:35). In this case a number of archaeologists, including the president of the Ontario Archaeological Society, were sympathetic, and insisted that the permission of the nearest Native band should be obtained before any excavation begins. Despite the passage in 1978 of the American Indian Religious Freedom Act, desecration of burial sites and unceremonious methods of handling excavated remains continued until the 1990s and remains a problem, though of smaller proportion, today.

At a brief forum held in Denver in 1984 at the American Anthropological Association's (AAA) annual meeting, Native representatives asked scholars to formulate professional guidelines against excavation of Native burial remains. Repeatedly, they insisted that the issue is a religious one, but the responses they received, even the most sympathetic ones, were of the political-legal variety.

With Jan Hammil, head of AIAD[3] (American Indians against Desecration), present at the AAA meetings in 1985, another forum was held, this one larger and more formal. There were actually two forums held on the issue, one conducted largely by scholars; the other conducted largely by Native Americans. Many physical anthropologists and archaeologists stayed away from both forums, though a few attended, along with a number of cultural anthropologists. As might be expected, one of the meetings was cool and low key, while the other was laden with emotion.

Three main questions were at issue: Should researchers excavate burial sites at all? If so, how should they be treated and the remains handled? Who has, or should have, the power to make decisions on these questions? As the epigraph by Red Cloud illustrates, the roots of the conflict are old and deep.

The most militant statement on the Native side was issued by the American Indians against Desecration in 1984. They insisted that no further digging be done in Native cemeteries, that accidental disinterments (for example, by bulldozing for subdivisions and roads) lead to immediate reburial, and that all remains in museums and laboratories be returned for ritual reburial. More moderate positions called for full consultation with nearby Native groups and for reburial once archaeological analysis was complete. Some government bodies (the state of Iowa, for example) as well as various professional associations (for instance, the American Association of Museums) had already formulated guidelines.[4]

The problem as articulated by scholars appeared complex. A common position among anthropologists was that the desire for repatriation of burial remains was merely a political ploy to gain national attention, that it had little or nothing to do with the maintenance of religious or ethnic integrity.

In the scholarly view the issues were thorny and seldom solved by being reduced to the question: Should non-Natives be allowed to excavate Native cemeteries in the name of science? A list of some of the recurring questions raised at the AAA meeting and elsewhere illustrates this complexity:

1. Are the remains historical or prehistoric? Are they identifiable as relatives of existing Native groups? If so, which one(s)? How related, genealogically and ritually, are the living to the disinterred dead?

2. What is it that is sacred, and thus subject to desecration? All land in general? A specific site? Human remains? The location and position of the remains? Burial goods? Who owns the land on which the remains were found? Who owned or used it at the time of burial?

3. How were the remains initially interred, if at all? Ritually? By slaughter? Abandonment? What is the history of the care of the site? How should this history influence present practices?[5] What if the contentious grave sites were unmarked, neglected, or the result of mere disposal rather than ritual burial? Should they not fall in the public domain?

4. Was the exhumation deliberate or accidental? If deliberate, for what purpose (for example, secondary burial, research, looting)? What consultations were held and permissions obtained? What if sites are accidentally disinterred by developers? Isn't it better that archaeologists rather than construction crews or vandals excavate the remains?

5. How will the remains be treated? How long will they be kept? How and by whom will they be reburied, if at all? If by AIAD or some other intertribal group, where should they be buried? By what authority does such a group act? What will be the disposition of sacred mortuary artifacts? Will they be used in museum displays? What Native attitudes and practices does such handling contravene? What if there are no direct, living descendants of the deceased? Does a Native group, especially one that was historically at war with the exhumed, have any more right to claim the remains than a non-Native group?

6. Whom does the research on human remains and sacred sites benefit? How much does it benefit them? What about the rights of North Americans to know their past? Would not repatriation and reburial violate these rights? Don't Native Americans benefit from archaeologists' reconstruction of the prehistoric, indigenous past? Aren't rights notoriously culture-bound? Why should Whites accept the Native view of the dead rather than their own? Isn't this really a legal, rather than an ethical or religious, issue?

7. Do the dead have rights? How do the various groups of the living define the transitions from person to corpse to skeleton to remains to earth?

8. What are the religio-ethical values and practices of the researchers, and how significantly do these figure in deciding whether and how to dig or retain possession of remains? How long is it justifiable to store remains in anticipation of new research techniques? To what extent is the issue the sacrality of sites and remains, and to what extent is it the power to decide what happens to them?

Many of the questions are themselves ethno- or religio-centric.[6] In addition, any one of them could tie those who debate them in such intellectual and emotional knots that they might be tempted to avoid the hard decisions at hand. It is unlikely that one can untangle all of them before being called upon to make further decisions about policy and action.

At the AAA meeting there were conflicting definitions of the situation. Native people defined the issue as essentially religious, not just political or scientific; they spoke of burial sites and remains as sacred and the act of excavating and doing research on human remains as desecration. Many felt that the issue was simpler than social scientists made it out to be. The resort to complexity was viewed by some Native Americans as a political tactic typical of academics. AIAD insisted that it the issue was a religious, ethical, and legal one. AIAD convened conferences, made appeals, initiated legal proceedings, and provoked confrontations on the issue of the disposition of Native mortuary remains.

RELIGION, RITUAL, AND REBURIAL

What has religious studies generally and ritual studies specifically to say about this issue?[7] There seem to be three related tasks: (1) from the point of view of the history of religions to discuss conflicting mortuary attitudes of scholars and Natives and to account for the "neutral" attitude of the former; (2) from the point of view of comparative religion to define desecration and show how it is a function of this neutrality; and (3) from the point of view of ritual studies and ethics to offer some brief reflections on the notion of ritual responsibility.

As it has appeared in anthropology, the controversy over the treatment of Native American burial sites and human skeletal remains has seemed to be either a legal question, a matter of professional ethics, or a science versus religion debate. However, from the point of view of religious studies, it appears differently in three respects: (1) Native American intertribalism and scholarly humanism are seen as conflicting religious ideologies; (2) desecration is understood to be the result of a historical process and defined independently of the intentions of those accused of committing it; and (3) the act of exhumation and the procedures for doing mortuary research are considered tacitly ritualized processes for which scholars must assume responsibility.[8]

Matthew King, a spiritual leader and a chief of the Lakota nation, when asked to comment on the excavation of human skeletal remains, said:

> This is nothing new. After the immigrants came into our country, they started digging for graves, I don't know why. They have no respect. They show their ignorance. They don't know God. Religion is praying with all the heart, mind, body, and soul, nothing else. You could know a lot of things, but if you change your whole life, that's religion. Let the people sleep in peace. It [the land] is a burial ground and also a church, for our Indian people (Hammil and Zimmerman 1983:3-4).

To illustrate the communication problem that arises when Native Americans and scholars discuss burials, consider the following passage. Notice the rhetorical parallels and divergences between King's plea and the summary statement, made by three respected archaeologists on the archaeology of death:

> The archaeology of death is not a new subject. An interest in the mortuary practices of past human cultures has been evident throughout the development of archaeology to its present disciplinary status. Indeed there is little to match the discovery of an impressive new grave assemblage in generating both professional and public enthusiasm and demonstrating "the universal impact of death." Among the shortcomings of social analyses published in the last decade we have discussed the insufficiently explicit attention given to the formation and transformation of the archaeological record, the inadequate treatment of symbolism, the relative neglect of spatial patterning in the location of disposal areas and the absence of a regional perspective in the analysis of mortuary practices (Chapman et al. 1981:1, 23).

King says digging up other people's graves is not new. Chapman Kinnes, and Randsborg say the archaeology of death is not new. King complains that he does not know why non-Natives are digging up Native bones. Chapman *et al.* note that mortuary data are central to the archaeological enterprise. King bemoans the lack of respect. Chapman, Kinnes, and Randsborg put "the universal impact of death" in quotation marks and note the enthusiasm that greets an impressive mortuary find. King accuses excavators of not knowing God and implies that knowing lots of data is of less worth than religious knowledge. Chapman *et al.* are silent on the matter of their religiosity. King regards the earth not only as a burial ground but as a "church," that is, a sacred space. For Chapman, Kinnes, and Randsborg the earth is a "disposal area" in which graves display "spatial patterning."

These two passages have little in common except the topic of burial, and it seems that comparing them is as futile and misguided as comparing snails and doorknobs. King is speaking religious language, while Chapman *et al.* are speaking scientific language. So one might argue that communication would be better served if King would speak scientifically or Chapman, Kinnes, and Randsborg, religiously, about human burials. But what would have to happen for this to occur? What sort of magic or confrontation could bring about a situation in which physical anthropologists and Native people could stop talking past one another? One possibility would be for one party to speak the language of the other. But King already speaks English, the language of the dominating culture. Have scholars any right to expect him also to speak scientific language? Would that really change the outcome of the debate or just extend it? What if one required Chapman, or any physical anthropologist for that matter, to respond religiously? What sort of face, credibility, and reputation would archaeologists lose if they responded religiously to what Native people insist are religious issues?

The worst possible situation is one in which the debate gets reduced to the polarity, science versus religion, especially if this sort of terminology is thought to imply non-Native science versus Native religion. The situation seems to require interlocutors, Native archaeologists and anthropologists, for example. But there are very few of these.[9]

A religion scholar must consider not only the so-called world religions or major denominations but also examine the interplay and conflict between several sources of mortuary attitudes that are likely to lie behind local controversies: i. e., Jewish, Catholic, Protestant, scholarly-humanistic, civic-professional (for instance, funeral-directing ethics), tribal, and inter-tribal. Some of these overlap. For instance, some Natives are Catholics and some civic practices have become standard in distinctly religious institutions.

The disagreement between Native Americans, on the one hand, and archaeologists and physical anthropologists, on the other, is not a science versus religion controversy but a clash between conflicting religions. No doubt, there will be immediate and vigorous resistance to this claim: Which religions? Is AIAD a religion? As an intertribal group, whom does it represent? Is it an example of Lakota religion? Also of Pueblo and Ojibwa religions? After all, aren't there important tribal and individual differences that ought not be glossed over by an intertribal plea?

As a result of recent North American religious history, a religiologist would consider it as proper to speak of an intertribal religion of indigenous people as it is to conceptualize either civil religion or ecumenical Christianity, provided one does not claim too much for the term. On certain issues—and desecration of the dead seems to be one of them—the consensus among tribes and factions, along with the moral weight of the appeal, outweighs the differences. Just as one can be, say, a Presbyterian and at the same time an ecumenical Christian, so one can be a Pima and an intertribally religious person. AIAD may not speak for every Native person or equally well for every tribe, but neither does the World Council of Churches or the pope speak for every Christian. Modern intertribal religiosity has the same religious (or quasi-religious, if you prefer) authority (and problems) as modern ecumenicity does. Denominationalism and tribalism are social realities no scholar or religious person ought to ignore, but so are intertribalism and ecumenism. It is a political tactic, not a matter of scientific principle, when scholars focus on tribal differences as an excuse for ignoring an intertribal appeal.

So much for the kind of religiosity that motivates those who plead for reburial. What about the religiosity of archaeologists and anthropologists? There are those who espouse humanistic codes of professional ethics, thereby rejecting explicit religiosity, and they, no doubt, would prefer to speak of conflicting "ethics" or "value systems" rather than "religions." My argument is that the term religion is appropriate, because it includes not only values and ethics but myths, symbols, and rituals as well. But let us not quibble about terms. It is enough if one can arrive at the point of admitting the clash is between competing value systems rather than religion and science (two different kinds of systems). If we speak of the "religion" of social scientists, we can, for the sake of the discussion, put the term in quotation marks.

Let us assume that, despite the reputed agnosticism of social scientists, some are Catholics, Jews, Protestants, and other. How has this religiosity anything to do with their scholarship, since, as a matter of principle, they intend to bracket it out of their research—at least insofar as it is written and published in scholarly books and journals? We would be claiming too much if we were to imply that archaeologists, as archaeologists, when they are excavating burial mounds, are doing so as Southern Baptists, as Reformed Jews, or as Zen Buddhists. Everything hinges on the mysterious "as," a grammatical cue indicating that one is distinguishing roles. Role differentiation is a cardinal tenet in the tacit religiosity of many scholars, including archaeologists. It facilitates a compartmentalization, a division of life into sectors, that is tenaciously defended as a sacred proposition. This religion[10] one might call "scientistic" humanism. If archaeologists are Hindus or Christian Scientists or atheists, they are also likely to be humanists.[11] So, to be precise, the conflict as focused in the last quarter of the twentieth century is between two religions, Western humanism and Native American intertribalism, both of which have distinct histories with relatively recent origins.[12]

Humanism usually assumes, and occasionally argues, that its practices are universal and therefore neutral. But research is not value-free. It may be true (though I doubt it) that the rules of scientific procedure are value-free, but the motives, side-effects, and consequences of research are not. Consequently, scientists, especially social scientists, formulate codes of professional behavior, for example, the American Anthropological Association's "Statements on Ethics and Professional Responsibility." To the religiologist such statements should not be understood apart from their historical derivation from identifiable religious traditions (notably, Judaism and Christianity) and longstanding cosmologies and epistemologies (especially classical Greek ones). Although not reducible to these traditions, the ethics of scholarly humanism are secularized derivations from them.

If one does a textual analysis of general statements on professional responsibility or specific ones on reburial, they are recognizable as documents of a specific culture, era, and ethos. One needs only to count the number of times words like "sensitivity" and "communication" occur in the Arlie House Report (McGimsey and Davis 1977) and its appended code of ethics "as promulgated by the Society of Professional Archaeologists" to notice how culture-bound they are. Along with terms such as "reasonable," "dignity," and "preservation," there are the old humanist stand-bys "universal" and "human." These virtues are treated as if they were the moral equivalent of travelers checks. Even though some have the illusion that they can be cashed anywhere in the world market, they are (to pursue the analogy a bit further) drawn on a national currency. American Express is still very American. As values, they have their limits, because the definition of humanness is precisely what is at issue. In the eyes of Native Americans it is inhuman to disinter skeletal remains, while in the eyes of archaeologists and physical anthropologists, it is human to want to expand the horizons of scientific understanding.

Scholars who would never assume the universality of their research conclusions have sometimes assumed the universality of their codes of ethics. But claims to universal ethics have the same status as denominational claims to universality. When Christian evangelism, Jungian archetypalism, or Bahai inclusivism claims universal validity, this claim usually means that some local, regional, or historical symbols are being *imposed* on others or, euphemistically, imagined to encompass all others. The tacit religiosity of scholarly humanism is no different in this respect. Its universalistic aspirations easily become universalistic pretensions or platitudes. To a religiologist vagaries like "dignity" and "respect" are meaningless until we see the shape of the practices they engender. Many scientists do not consider it undignified to put skeletal remains in bags, because they have been trained to believe that they serve humanity by doing sound research. But this belief is being flatly contradicted by those Native Americans who insist that exhumation does not serve them.

Alongside the claim that research has universal value is the assumption that it is neutral. In comparative religion a neutral attitude toward the dead is anomalous, a rarity in the 70,000 or more years people have been burying their dead. Neutrality, not veneration, needs explanation or, if not explanation, then historical context to be comprehensible. We ought not busy ourselves with doing further studies of Native spirituality to account for "their" attitudes if, in fact, "ours" are the peculiar ones. Our skeletons, not theirs, need to come out of the closet. How have we arrived at the attitude that scientific exhumation of other people's burials is not desecration or, if it is, that it is worth it?

Philip Aries's (1981) history of Western attitudes toward death is probably the best single treatment, but it does not directly address the topic of attitudes toward *other people's* dead nor toward the land that contains them. So the best one can do for the moment is to list some possibilities, which, by the way, are not *causes*; they may simply be *expressions* of this so-called neutral attitude:

- Early Christian eschatological indifference ("Let the dead bury the dead") and subsequent beliefs in the immortality of the soul may have led to indifference toward the fate of human remains.

- Various dualisms (body/soul, mind/body, body/spirit) that directly encourage indifference toward the body may have precipitated the objectification of the body that became obvious by the eighteenth century.

- The nineteenth-century removal of the dead from churchyards and the centers of town to "gardens" on the edge of towns, along with zoning laws that disallowed funeral homes in residential areas, may have contributed to the modern alienation from death and the dead.

- Symbolization of the earth as an object or machine may have fostered a sense of disconnectedness between the human body and the earth.

- Ideas of private and public property, that is, belief that land must be either owned by individuals or else equally open to all, may have encouraged a feeling that the prehistoric dead are public property.

- The privatization of death and the professionalization of funeral directing may have desensitized us to communal bonds with the dead.

- The parochialization and folklorization[13] of death in anthropology itself may have contributed to social scientists' indifference.

Aries (1981) has chronicled the process by which Euroamerican culture repressed the reality of death. People alienated from their own deaths are likely to vacillate between objectification of, and fascination with, the dead.[14] Much more historical research would have to be done to demonstrate this claim or to prove that any of the factors isolated has, in fact, led to the "neutral" attitudes of scholars toward sacred burial sites. Such neutrality is probably compounded of objectification and fascination, two attitudes that exercise considerable torque on one another.[15]

An important question is that of the Lakota elder who asked, "What good will it do anybody?" (Hammil and Zimmerman 1983:3). What do the bones, mortuary goods, and grave sites tell us? Scholars say the archaeology of death can provide information about the age, sex, social position, stress level, fertility, marital status, profession, religion, health, and diet of the deceased. Current American archaeology, if one may take Chapman *et al.'s* (1981:8) summary as accurate, also relates the disposal of the dead to the reconstruction of social organization.

Suppose that it *might* do Matthew King some good to know more about the social organization of his prehistoric ancestors. We must say "suppose," because he clearly says such information will do him and his people no good. Even if it did, he would probably still object that data gained in an unholy manner cannot lead to understanding. He might also respond ironically, as one Native spokesman did in one South Dakota discussion (Hammil and Zimmerman 1983:20-21), that authentic understanding of bones best comes from ritual divination of them, or, as other spokespersons have claimed without irony, from oral traditions about burial. In short, however useful the information is to humanistic scholars, its traditional, non-consultative mode of acquisition is an affront to Native religious values. There is no denying that archaeologically gained information about mortuary practices is useful. The question is: Useful to whom? And the answer to that question in most cases is clear, although some Native Americans, for example Zunis, have instituted projects that indicate that archaeology of some kinds is in fact useful to them.

DESECRATION AND RITUAL RESPONSIBILITY

The charge leveled at scientists is that exhumation and subsequent analysis and handling of human remains constitute desecration, that an attitude of neutrality is, in fact, an ethic spawning practices that amount to covert or unwitting sacrilege. To assess such an accusation, we would need to know whether accused persons (1) maintain on principle that desecration is impossible, (2) claim that in such-and-such a case they did not desecrate, or (3) believe that scientific discoveries are worth the cost of admitted desecration.

But this kind of information is just the beginning. The seriousness of the charge demands that attention be paid to the definition of desecration. Doing so is essential for legal as well as scholarly purposes. Since the literature on the concept is almost nonexistent, our discussion will of necessity constitute a proposal rather than a consensus. Much more energy has been spent in describing the sacred and modes of sacralization than in understanding profanation, desecration, and other forms of ritual negation.

To begin the work of understanding the ritual dimensions of scholarly excavation, we need some basic concepts. Several terms require distinguishing: profanation, desecration, desanctification, and to a lesser extent, secularization and taboo. *Taboo* refers to an intrareligious avoidance. As I propose to use the term here, one must be an insider to violate or observe a taboo. When some act, place, object, or person is taboo, it is too power-laden to approach directly.

Deconsecration applies to an intrareligious act. For example, a priest may deconsecrate an altar when the destruction of a church building is necessary. When something becomes *secularized*, it is part of a historical process whereby a religion becomes differentiated, leaving it in either a compartmentalized or a covert relation to other cultural domains. Whereas the tabooed is so positively charged that it exerts a negative effect, the secularized appears to be simply neutral. Archaeological excavation in cemeteries is the outcome of a long process of secularization, which functions as a powerful invisible religion (Luckmann 1967). When a researcher is capable of suspending fear, reverence, and awe in order to treat human remains as data, a remarkable transformation has occurred. Secularization as such is not desecration, though it may lay the groundwork for it.

The two most important terms for the present discussion are *profanation* and *desecration*. "Profanation" implies a charged relation to the sacred. When people profane, they take the sacred seriously but invert or violate it. For example, in the case of profane language one draws upon the sanctity of religious or sexual imagery for the sake of the power that this sanctity provides. The one who profanes is not necessarily an insider or a believer, but by definition the profaner is not indifferent to the power implicit in the violated object. When someone chisels out the name of the deceased from an Egyptian tomb, this is an act of profanation.

Desecration, I suggest, is an interreligious violation in which one discounts or ignores the sacredness of what is violated. It is, one might say, a ritual blunder even though perpetrators may deny that they intended to violate or to engage in a ritual act. Desecration is not counter-ritual, as is the case in profanation; nor is it a neutralization of ritual, as in instances of deconsecration. Rather, it seems to arise in two sorts of circumstances: when one is ignorant of ritual consecration or when one refuses to admit the sacred as a relevant category. Desecration is a possible ritual consequence of the historical process of secularization. There may be varying degrees of desecration ranging from the ignorant to the willful, but, just as ignorance of the law is no excuse, choosing to overlook sacred zones and remains is not either. The cultural milieu in which desecration is likely to occur is one in which a highly secularized society (in which religion is compartmentalized and/or covert) and a more traditional one (in which religion more thoroughly permeates other cultural domains) impinge upon one another.

Little has been said about the purely ethical dimensions of this conflict, namely, that those who have power also have responsibilities to allow the living to bury their dead without fear. Since few would disagree, at least in principle, with this view, we need to look at the ritual dimensions that parallel the ethical ones that bear on direct dealings with the long-buried dead. Desecration is a form of tacit ritualization. Whatever scientists' *intentions* may be, the *actions and consequences* of exhumation include ritual ones: they are stylized enactments of culturally sacralized gestures.[16]

The ethical and ritual traditions of most White North American scholars predispose us to desecration, which may occur *despite* (perhaps even *because of*) our noblest intentions. There is no point in claiming that all exhumation constitutes desecration. Nevertheless, our religious heritages make the likelihood of it high. Because of this predilection, we are obliged to assume a higher degree of ritual responsibility. We ought to assume an ethic of respect that bears directly upon habitual practices and bodily comportment in sacred places and in the presence of sacred objects and skeletal remains.

It is a mistake in discussions of mortuary behavior to make too absolute a distinction between tacit ritualization, codes of professional responsibility, and scientific procedures. We scholars must assume explicit responsibility for the implicitly ritualistic dimensions of our research. Our professional and scientific conduct at burial sites is itself a form of mortuary behavior. Whatever its practical consequences, it has inescapable symbolic and quasi-ritualistic dimensions.

As a bare minimum, full consultation and proper permission should be obtained from Native descendants or spiritual kin, and, if denied, no excavation whatever should occur. However, we should go further. If permission is granted, or when no such descendants are found, leaving archaeologists free to dig, fieldworkers have an obligation to develop minimal practices that are in keeping with the most reverent we know—whether or not we are believers in any orthodox sense. In addition to our ethical responsibilities to obtain permission, we have ritual ones that bear on bodily comportment. And we are ill-prepared for the latter because humanism has been so notoriously oblivious to the ritual implications of its ethics.

Certainly, in any field study of the rites of another culture we would typically show our respect for indigenous sacredness by walking softly, as it were, and other means of handling with care. In short, we should behave with ritual decorum—either by drawing on our own gestural canons of sanctity or by imitating those of others on whose sacred precincts we tread. We should allow ourselves to be tutored; we should suspend or modify our usual manners out of respect for our hosts. The same decorum is appropriate when visiting a society of the dead as it is when visiting a society of the living. If we neither have conventions of our own nor are sure what were the practices of the prehistoric people we may have unearthed, then we may have to invent ways of embodying our ritual responsibilities.

I emphasize the idea of ritual, rather than merely ethical, responsibility in order to remind us that in situations of cultural conflict the importance of symbolic gestures escalates, because we can no longer assume a shared moral consensus. It would be a mistake to assume that exhumation of Native burials is analogous to autopsies or anatomical research on donated cadavers. In the latter instances the dead have shared the value systems of the living; they are bound by a common legal, ethical, and ceremonial code. But in cases characterized by intercultural conflict, recourse to ritual is sometimes a necessary prelude or accompaniment to moral negotiation. If we show no respect (a ritual quality), how can we expect to be taken seriously (a moral necessity)?

Probably these suggestions, if taken seriously, will at first result in awkwardness. Archaeological digs are not noted for their air of sanctity but, rather, for their sweat, bawdy humor, and iconoclasm.[17] We have little other than our aesthetic sense of appreciation and some vague sense of respect to draw upon. We approach grave sites in a state of ritual ignorance; we may not even know how to display respect. Most of us have never known how to walk in a sacred manner, so we can expect considerable self-consciousness until we relearn what we may never have known, namely, how to let those whose bones we transmute by a strange alchemy into data rest in peace.

NOTES

1.   Updated and edited from a version that first appeared in *American Indian Quarterly*, Volume 10, No.4, 1986. © University of Nebraska Press. Reprinted with permission of the *American Indian Quarterly*.

2.   For a concise summary, see Alan L. Miller's article "Power" (1987).

3.   Originally known as AID.

4.   As far as I know there are no statements regarding the ethics of research on dead subjects that parallel those on living subjects (for instance, by the Social Sciences and Humanities Research Council of Canada), and there should be.

5.   Unfortunately, using answers to these questions to make decisions about whether or not to excavate is almost impossible, since excavation is usually required to answer them.

6.   This term means "being so centered in one's own religious tradition as to be unable to understand that of another." Thus it parallels "ethnocentrism."

7.   In a video by Philip L. Walker called "Science or Sacrilege" (reviewed by Merbs 1985), a religiologist was asked to respond to the issue. Another religiologist, Robert Michaelsen (1980:109), in his analysis of the American Indian Religious Freedom Act, urged colleagues in religious studies to become actively involved in cross-cultural and comparative studies of "the phenomenology of sacralization, desacralization, and resacralization of land forms and particular sites."

8.   Excavation, cataloging, and analysis of human remains are not just "procedures," they are "practices," the acting out of sacredly held and defended cultural values. As practices they are power-laden, and the rhetorical ploy of claiming neutrality is a power play despite claims that this was not the intention of White scientists.

9.   Since I am neither an archaeologist nor a Native American, I have little to lose in this debate, which means my opinion is either valuable because it is comparatively non-partisan or useless because it costs me nothing—neither my research nor my ancestors.

10.   Anthropologists' codes of ethics and behavior in the field qualify as religious according to numerous definitions. Among them are these: "A religion is a system of symbols which acts to establish powerful, pervasive, and long-lasting moods and motivations in men by formulating conceptions of a general order of existence and clothing these conceptions with such an aura of factuality that the moods and motivations seem uniquely realistic" (Geertz 1973:90). "Religion is a synthesis of thought, emotion and behavior expressing man's attitude towards his environment and towards his existence within it" (Gaster 1951:374).

11.   Note that I do not use this term to mean teachers in humanities divisions of universities but subscribers to humanistic codes of ethics.

12.   Whether or not one agrees that professional codes are quasi-religious documents should not deter scholars from recognizing that many codes governing research on humans require that, if there is any conflict between the aims of research and the welfare of the people being studied, the latter, not the former, should take precedence.

13.   See Fabian (1973) for a discussion of the folklorization of death.

14.   See Grolnick and Lengyel (1978) on burial symbols as "transitional objects."

15.   In discussions about excavation and reburial one finds several types of attitudes toward the dead: (1) remains-as-data, the object constituted by scientism. As Gerald Schaus (Wilfrid Laurier University 1988: 11) put it, "Dead is dead. . . . When living beings die their bodies are inanimate objects; " (2) remains-as-dead-person, that is, one with human rights that exceed the imperatives of research; (3) remains-as-sacred-memory, the conventional religious view; (4) remains-as-sacred-ancestor, a Native view: remains are more-than-person, they constitute the seat or home of spirit.

16.   Laird Christie (Wilfrid Laurier University, 1988:15) suggested that scholars, by "exploitatively commodifying and purveying for our own interests those cultural patterns we study," engage in morally questionable behavior. Of this I have no doubt, but our recognition of the widespread ambiguities of scholarly research does not obviate our responsibility for dealing with the specific issue at hand.

17.   Lawrence Toombs, an archaeologist colleague, suggests that such humor and iconoclasm may be our culture's nervous way of recognizing the presence of the sacred.

REFERENCES CITED

American Indians against Desecration [AIAD]. 1984. "A Resolution on the Protection, Avoidance, and Treatment of Ancestral Remains and Sacred Objects." Vermillion, South Dakota.

Aries, Philip. 1981. *The Hour of Our Death*. Translated by Helen Weaver. New York: Knopf.

Chapman, Robert, Ian Kinnes, and Klaus Randsberg (eds.). 1981. *The Archaeology of Death*. Cambridge: Cambridge University Press.

Eliade, Mircea. 1957. *The Sacred and the Profane*. New York: Harper & Row.

Fabian, Johannes. 1973. "How others die: Reflections on the anthropology of death." In *Death in American Experience*, ed. A. Mack, pp. 177–201. New York: Schocken.

Gaster, Theodor. 1951. "Errors of method in the study of religion." In *Freedom and Reason: Studies in Philosophy and Jewish Culture*, ed. Salon Baron et al., pp. 29–53. New York: Conference on Jewish Relations.

Geertz, Clifford. 1973. *The Interpretation of Cultures*. New York: Basic Books.

Grolnick, Simon A. and Alfonz Lengyel. 1978. "Etruscan Burial Symbols and the Transitional Process." In *Between Reality and Fantasy: Transitional Objects and Phenomena*. New York: Jason Aronson.

Hammil, Jan and Larry J. Zimmerman. 1983. "Reburial of Human Skeletal Remains: Perspectives from Lakota Spiritual Men and Elders." ms. on file with the American Indians Against Desecration and the University of South Dakota Archaeology Laboratory, Rapid City, South Dakota.

Luckmann, Thomas. 1967. *The Invisible Religion: The Transformation of Symbols in Industrial Society*. New York: Macmillan.

McGimsey, Charles R., III and Hester A. Davis. 1977. "Archeology and Native Americans." In *The Management of Archeological Resources: The Arlie House Report*, pp. 90–97. Washington, D.C.: Society for American Archeology.

McLuhan, T. C. 1971. *Touch the Earth: A Self-Portrait of Indian Existence*. New York: Outerbirdge & Dienstfrey.

Merbs, Charles F. 1985. Review of *Science or Sacrilege* by Philip L. Walker. *American Anthropologist* 87:490–491.

Michaelsen, Robert S. 1980. "The significance of the American Indian Religious Freedom Act of 1978." *Journal of the American Academy of Religion* 52:93–115.

Miller, Alan L. 1987. "Power." In *The Encyclopedia of Religion*, vol. 11, edited by Mircea Eliade. New York: Macmillan.

Savage, Howard G. 1977. "Meeting of Representatives of Indian Groups and Archaeologists of Ontario." *Arch Notes* (October–November): 34–36.

van der Leeuw, Gerardus. 1963. *Religion in Essence and Manifestation*, 2 vols. Translated by J. E. Turner. New York: Harper & Row.

Weber, Max. 1922. *The Sociology of Religion*. Translated by Ephraim Fischoff. Boston: Beacon Press.

Wilfrid Laurier University. 1988. *The Point: Newsletter of the Wilfrid Laurier University Archaeological Society* 4: 3–20.

CHAPTER SEVEN

A Zuni Perspective on Repatriation

EDMUND J. LADD

L ong before it was vogue or fashionable, when the Native American Graves Protection and Repatriation Act (NAGPRA) was still a dream, Zuni religious elders made a link between the removal of sacred objects and the current state of the world. Searching their collective memories and relying on their wisdom of Zuni belief systems, they came to the conclusion that the present state of world unrest, manifest in catastrophic earthquakes, volcanoes, fires, floods, hurricanes, typhoons, and wars, might be due to the loss of control over certain powerful and mischievous spirit beings. In council, the leaders of the Deer and Bear clans agreed that it could be because the *Ahayu:ta*, or Twin Gods, had been removed from their shrine homes and were being held captive in different museums around the world where they were exhibited as "objects of art."

THE AHAYU:TA

In Zuni culture, the Twin Gods are the patrons of sports. They were created by Sunfather at the beginning of time. Images of the Twin Gods are recreated annually by the Deer and Bear clans. These representations are placed at various shrines around Zuni land for the protection of the Zuni people and the world at large. The bow priests (also sometimes called war priests) are entrusted with the responsibility of placing these images in their shrines. This is why the *Ahayu:ta* are sometimes referred to as the "War Gods." Beyond the fact that they are attended by the bow priests, they have nothing to do with war. Rather they are considered the protectors of the Zuni people and the world in general, guarding against both human-produced and natural disasters.

When a new image of the *Ahayu:ta* is installed in a shrine, the 'old' one is removed to `the pile,' which is where all the previous gods have been lain (fig. 7-1). This act of removal specifically does NOT have the same connotations as `throwing away' or `discarding.' The image of the god that has been replaced must remain at the site to which it was removed and be allowed to disintegrate there. Like a chain, each god that is replaced adds to the continuum that

Fig. 7–1. Shrine on Twin Mountains with newly installed Ahayu:ta in foreground. The images that have been replaced are piled to the rear where they will continue to disintegrate. *From the National Anthropological Archives, Smithsonian Institution/2332-B.*

augments and reinforces the protective powers of the *Ahayu:ta*. It is through the process of disintegration that these gods realize their protective powers. It is therefore imperative that they not be removed, collected, or preserved; such acts are both dangerous and insensitive. They are dangerous because these gods are mischievous and can play havoc with nature if removed from their shrines. It is insensitive because the Zuni did not produce the images of these gods to be preserved or displayed but rather to be destroyed by nature. They are not art objects but "Spirit Beings" that have the power to either benefit or harm society if improperly removed from their shrines and the oversight of appropriate religious people. According to Zuni belief, the mishandling of these images can result in serious harm.

THE LOSS OF ZUNI SACRED OBJECTS

For many years students, collectors, art dealers, anthropologists and tourists have bought, traded, and in some cases, illegally removed, objects of sacred, religious, and ceremonial value from Zuni lands. Many of these objects have found their way into museums both in the United States and abroad where they are treated as art or objects of curiosity. Such treatment shows no regard for their true significance and value in Zuni culture. This insensitive treatment has long been a concern of Zuni religious and tribal elders. On May 30, 1978, in consultation with the tribal elders and the governor, Tribal Resolution No. M70–78–991, was signed into effect, officially sanctioning the position of the elders in condemning the misappropriation and mistreatment of Zuni sacred objects and initiating a formal procedure to rectify this very serious situation. Tribal Resolution No. M70–78–991 reads, in part, as follows:

> Whereas, the Zuni Tribal Council has for several years been aware of the increasing problems posed for the Zuni people by loss, theft or unauthorized removal from Zuni lands of items of sacred religious significance to the Zuni people; and,

> Whereas, on May 30, 1978, the Tribal Council initiated a formal process by which this problem and related problems of securing proper care for and/or return of such items as may be now in possession of museums or other third parties might be addressed and resolved; and,

> Whereas, it was recognized and stated by the Tribal Council in its May 30th memorandum that "because this effort ultimately involves protection and return of objects which are intimately bound up with the traditional religious practices and doctrines of the Zuni tribe, the appropriate tribal religious leaders should have final control over the process of policy making and decisions making in this matter."

ZUNI APPROACH TO RECOVERY OF SACRED OBJECTS

Zuni religious leaders and official tribal policy advocates a three-pronged approach to rectify the mistreatment of expropriated Zuni sacred properties. Of first concern is to request the return of all *Ahayu:ta* illegally removed from their shrines. As no one has the right to alienate these objects, all *Ahayu:ta* found outside of Zuni land are, by definition, stolen property. Secondly, for the protection and proper care of Zuni objects of religious significance housed in museums, appropriate curatorial treatment must be instituted. Finally, the third aspect of Zuni policy calls for sensitive treatment in the display and exhibition of all Zuni materials. The tribal council and elders are available to consult with museums on curatorial and exhibition issues upon request.

The Zuni have established a clear and successful strategy for the proper treatment, protection, and return of certain of our sacred materials. Over the past two decades, Zuni religious elders and the Tribal Council have successfully handled the problems of repatriating religious and sacred objects by negotiating each return on a case by case basis. This strategy has been employed with national and state institutions as well as private collectors and art galleries. The official tribal position, which is to recover objects of sacred religious significance to the Zuni, is not presented as a demand to museums. Rather, contact is initiated in the form of a request to enter into negotiations with the holders of sacred objects. It is not the intention of the Zuni tribe to raid museum collections. The major focus to date has been the recovery of the Twin Gods, the *Ahayu:ta*, and their associated gaming objects. In only one case thus far has it been necessary to resort to legal means to recover an *Ahayu:ta* that was being offered for sale at auction (General Federal Criminal Protection Law, 18 U.S.C. Section 1163). In all the other cases, negotiations have resulted in the voluntary return of these objects to the Zuni homeland.

I must be clear that all religious objects, no matter how small or insignificant they may seem to others, hold great spiritual value for our culture. Among the Zuni, items created for religious, ceremonial, and ritual purposes are not meant to be preserved. Their power is realized through the process of disintegration. These objects constitute religious offerings to the spirit world. They are spiritually received into the after-world as they are transformed into earth and air through decomposition.

The rationale for the recovery of *Ahayu:ta* from museums and private collections has been fairly straightforward given that these items had to have been illegally taken from the Zuni people. Guidelines for reclaiming other religious objects are not as clear cut, though the elders have provided some basic recommendations and directives. Almost all objects created for religious purposes have great significance and spiritual power. They embody the spiritual essence of Zuni life and culture. Many religious objects are owned by and in the care of individuals but they are still used in collective ritual activities for the good of the tribe. All religious objects are treated in very specific ways in Zuni culture.

To facilitate discussions and negotiations with holding institutions, the religious elders have developed a five part classification scheme for sacred objects (Table 1). This system is only valid for ethnographic objects and is presented only as a point of departure for further discussion.

REPATRIATION AT THE MUSEUM OF NEW MEXICO

Museums around the country have devised different approaches for dealing with the repatriation mandate. The Museum of New Mexico in Santa Fe offers one example of a particularly successful repatriation program. In what follows, I outline the collaborative approach that was developed between the Laboratory of

Anthropology, a unit of the Museum of New Mexico, and the Pueblos of Zuni and Nambe for purposes of inventorying and assessing the approximately 20,000 Zuni items in the Museum for possible repatriation.

Table 1. Zuni System for Classification of Ethnographic Material.

CLASS	TYPE OF ITEMS	RECOMMENDED ACTION
I	Unique objects; communally-owned items; objects of cultural patrimony (i.e., Twin Gods)	Repatriation; ownership non-negotiable
II	Items removed from Zuni lands without consent; communally-owned items	Repatriation requested, but negotiable
III	Items of special concern legally sold by individuals; include replicas of ceremonial masks	Special curatorial treatment
IV	Other less highly sensitive items sold by individuals or removed from local shrines, i.e. prayer plumbs	Special curatorial treatment
V	Items of daily use such as pottery, tools, dance paraphernalia and other household artifacts	No special restrictions apply; exhibition consultation recommended

The first step in the process was to create an inventory of all Zuni and Nambe ethnographic objects in the museum's collection. The item by item inventory was made from museum records, catalogue cards, accession records, purchase documents, and any other relevant sources. Each item was checked against the catalogue cards to make sure all objects listed were still in the possession of the museum. Catalogue cards were also cross referenced with objects to verify object name, storage location and tribal affiliation. Human remains were treated separately.

Following the verification process, the next step was to evaluate and sort the objects by levels of sensitivity. This was the most important stage of the repatriation process. The evaluation of cultural and religious sensitivity was based on card catalogue information, general observation, and available literature, and was conducted by knowledgeable curatorial staff. The classification scheme used in this process recognizes five levels of sensitivity and was based on the one outlined by the religious elders given above. As a preliminary evaluation, it was understood that the sensitivity levels assigned to objects by the curatorial staff were not necessarily the final word on any particular item's significance. It was simply a means of reducing the scope of objects that would need to be discussed immediately with the tribe. It should be noted that from the Zuni perspective, all cultural materials are considered sensitive to some degree and appropriate tribal members should be consulted prior to undertaking curatorial action on any of them.

Based on the initial curatorial evaluation of the Zuni ethnographic collection in the Museum of New Mexico, a total of 123 items were identified as `very sensitive.' The four Twin Gods previously in the possession of the Museum, which would have been the only items classified as `highly sensitive,' had already been repatriated to the tribe in 1980. Following the inventory, a letter was sent to the Zuni Tribal Council informing them of the general contents of the Zuni collections and listing the items identified as very sensitive, suggesting that these would be the most likely candidates for repatriation discussions.

Two Zuni councilmen and four religious elders reviewed the inventory and then visited the collections. The tribal representatives down-graded the status of nearly three-quarters of the items listed as `very sensitive' to lower levels of sensitivity. They suggested that the remaining 32 objects originally identified as `very sensitive,' be repatriated to the Zuni, if appropriate religious elders concurred. Shortly thereafter, a delegation of nine religious elders came to the Museum of New Mexico to review the collection. They agreed that these items were very sensitive and should be repatriated to the tribe. With respect to the other 91 items originally classified by the curatorial staff as very sensitive, they indicated that the Zuni would be happy to receive them if offered for repatriation by the museum and that they would be welcomed home. In the meantime, however, they recommended that these items be accorded special curatorial treatment.

The "sensitivity scale" described above was also applied to the Zuni collections at the National Museum of the American Indian (NMAI). After the computer inventories and collections were examined, a preliminary assessment of the collections was made by the tribal representatives. Of the 1,429 Zuni ethnographic objects in the NMAI collection, 132 items were classified as being either highly sensitive or very sensitive. These items will be the focus of upcoming discussions on repatriation with the NMAI.

REPLICA ITEMS

Among the objects identified for repatriation by the elders at the Museum of New Mexico were several replicas of Zuni religious paraphernalia constructed of colored paper and feathers. These items were produced by non-Zuni individuals in the 1930s during the Works Progress Administration (WPA) era. The Museum asked the Zunis to explain why they were requesting the repatriation of these poorly made replicas. In a letter to the Museum Director written on behalf of the religious elders and council in November 1990, Zuni Governor Robert E. Lewis offered the following explanation:

1. Information is power; the replicas embody powerful information that belongs to the Zuni people that should not be revealed to uninitiated people;

2. The "replica" artifacts are sensitive objects intended only for use of the Zuni people;

3. The display of these artifacts in your museum would be disruptive to our traditional methods of teaching our young people about the Zuni religion;

4. As replicas, the artifacts have very little artistic value from the Zuni perspective and are highly offensive to Zuni cultural values;

5. There is no valid educational purpose in your retaining the artifacts. Any display or exhibit of the replicas would likely mislead the public because they would be presented outside of their proper context; similarly, museum storage is also an improper context for these items.

REPATRIATION OF HUMAN REMAINS

While the Zuni have focused most of their repatriation efforts on the recovery of the Twin Gods and other religious, ceremonial, and ritual objects, another category of materials has also been under scrutiny. This is the highly volatile and extremely sensitive category of human remains and funerary offerings. In 1987, the Laboratory of Anthropology at the Museum of New Mexico established an ad hoc committee to handle matters relating to sensitive cultural materials, with it first priority being human remains and grave goods. Two years later, the ad hoc committee became a permanent standing committee within the Museum.

In September 1989, the Director of the Museum of New Mexico informed the Zuni Tribal Council that there were human remains and grave goods in the museum's collections from Zuni lands. The museum needed to know how the Zuni wished to proceed with respect to these remains. The Governor of Zuni responded that according to the Zuni belief system, when a person dies, the spirit leaves the body after four days and never returns to the skeletal remains. Death is a clan and family matter and a very sad event. To remind one of death in the family and return bones desecrated by exhumation would be extremely insensitive from the cultural perspective of the Zuni. Questions would arise as to which clan would accept the remains, feed them, wash them, ready them for reburial, plant prayer plumbs, and conduct the fast. In closing, the Governor noted that although human remains were not sacred to Zuni, they should nonetheless be treated with respect.

For the above reasons, and after consultation with appropriate tribal members, the Zunis decided that the human remains and grave goods now in the museum's collections should remain in the custody of the museum.

The decision about the Zuni ancestral remains was formalized in a Letter of Agreement and a Tribal Resolution authorized by the Zuni elders. The November 1989 letter from Zuni Governor Robert E. Lewis to the Museum Director, reads, in part, as follows:

> ... After careful deliberations, the Zuni Pueblo has determined that the Museum of New Mexico should continue to be custodians of these human remains.

Human remains and their associated grave goods that have been removed from Pueblo lands have been desecrated through removal from our lands. The Pueblo has decided that bringing these remains and their associated grave goods back to our land for reburial would serve no useful purpose. We respectfully request that the Museum of New Mexico, as custodians of culturally sensitive materials such as human remains, refrain from displaying these remains.

We wish to make it clear that this policy applies to human remains and their associated grave goods already removed from our lands. Any burials that are now excavated on Zuni lands must be re-buried with their associated grave goods, after in-field analysis, as close as possible to their original resting place and out of harm's way. This policy of re-burial has been applied to all burials excavated in recent past and will continue to be the policy of the Zuni Pueblo.

The Pueblo of Zuni has made its decision and policy regarding human remains after careful deliberations among appropriate members of our tribe. The decision and policy are only those of the Pueblo of the Zuni and may not be the same as those adopted by other tribes for their ancestral remains.

It was also stipulated that the Museum consult with tribal leaders prior to introducing studies on the extant collection of Zuni ancestral remains now in the Museum collections. The intent of this provision was not to require that the Museum request permission but rather that it inform the tribe of any such undertaking. A condition of this pact is that the results of all such studies be made available to the tribal council, the Zuni school system, and the reservation libraries.

COLLABORATION BETWEEN TRIBES AND MUSEUMS

The Museum of New Mexico's success in working with Zuni and other tribal governments is based in large part on the open and collaborative approach employed. Each tribe has its own unique religious and government institutions that must be treated with honesty and respect. While initial contacts are made through the tribal governing body, typically the tribal council, it is only the religious elders who have the final authority to determine what is sacred. The Governor and tribal council function only as the conduit for relaying information and knowledge from the elders and completing the paper work involved in this very complex process. These tribal bodies are not vested with the authority to make religious decisions for the tribe.

The key to a smooth collaborative relations during the repatriation process is honesty and frequent personal contacts. Museums should not write to tribes saying "if we don't hear from you in three weeks, we will assume you agree". It should be kept in mind that every tribe has received notices from hundreds of museums, each of which may require a response. Every tribe is also beset by all of the ills that plague any government organization, i.e., its members are underpaid, overworked, and sometimes unmotivated.

The *A:shiwi*, or Zuni people, have withstood the impacts of cruelty, greed, and insensitivity for over five hundred years. Although much scarred and bruised, they still prevail as a culture with their own unique language, their own lands, however much diminished, and, most importantly, their own sacred ways. Zuni tribal religion has endured, in spite of intense pressure from both the west (Spanish) and the east (United States) to eradicate it. Some of the ceremonies have become extinct over the years and there has been much change, but the religion is just as viable as it was two thousand years ago.

The National Graves Protection and Repatriation Act (NAGPRA) is seen as a very important law for the Zunis that will allow them to gain control of their cultural heritage and determine what material elements of that heritage have been stored in museums for the past two hundred years. Zunis are also aware of the expenses associated with curation and are happy, in many instances, to let museums continue to provide this service. They recognize the mutual benefit, for instance, when the newly established *A:shiwi awan (Zuni) Museum and Heritage Center* is able to request loans of particular objects with ease. The Zuni also recognize that this law puts museums on notice: you will inventory your collections, you will notify tribes of your holdings, you will consult with tribes, and you will repatriate culturally and religiously sensitive material. All that remains for the Zunis (and other tribes) to do is review two million sheets of computer print-out from two thousand museums and make their claim!

The Zuni approach to repatriation is based on the collaborative model discussed above. The motivation of the Zunis to reclaim objects of sacred religious significance goes back over twenty years when the clan leaders requested the tribal council's assistance in the recovery of their sacred Twin Gods. Over the years, they have searched various museums and they now know what objects will be requested for repatriation. With the exception of the Twin Gods, whose return to their Zuni homeland is a matter of some urgency, there is no rush. The Zuni will use the law to recover what belongs to them.

CHAPTER EIGHT

Sacred Under the Law

Repatriation and Religion Under the Native American Graves Protection and Repatriation Act (NAGPRA)

JONATHAN HAAS

The Native American Graves Protection and Repatriation Act (NAGPRA) was passed by the U.S. Congress and signed into law by President George Bush in November 1990. On various occasions I have heard this Act compared to a hot dog, that is to say, "you do not want to know what went into it." But in trying to understand how the law functions on a practical basis, it is important to know how the specific language and definitions in the Act were formulated as this wording has implications for the implementation of the Act.

In the Fall of 1990, as it became apparent to the interested parties that Congress would pass some form of repatriation legislation before the end of the session, fairly intense negotiations were underway behind the scenes over the precise language to be included in the proposed Act. Largely mediated by the American Association of Museums, these discussions aimed at balancing the concerns of museums, universities, and various Native American constituencies. From the museum's perspective, it was imperative that the language in the law make clear that not *all* collections were susceptible to repatriation and that it afford some protection with respect to the property rights of the institutions. Native Americans, in turn, wanted language that would enable them to effectively seek the return of certain kinds of objects that were considered to be of great spiritual and cultural importance. The resulting wording in many sections of the final legislation enacted represented a compromise between the various interested parties. In many cases these compromises were not wholly satisfying to either side. In most areas the results were considered "workable."

To provide a better understanding of the kinds of concerns raised by different parties to this discussion and the practical implications of the compromises reached, this paper will focus on the category of objects designated as "sacred" under NAGPRA. As Curator of North American Archaeology at the Field Museum of Natural History, I was involved in the behind the scenes dialogue regarding how "sacred objects" would ultimately be defined in the Act. Later, as a member of the NAGPRA Review Committee from 1992–1996, I played a role in explicating the term "sacred object" for the Federal Regulations developed by the

Department of the Interior, the agency charged with overseeing implementation of the Act. Since the passage of NAGPRA, I have also worked directly with several tribes to accomplish the repatriation of sacred objects.

Under Section 2(2)(C) of NAGPRA, "sacred objects" are defined as "specific ceremonial objects which are needed by traditional Native American religious leaders for the practice of traditional Native American religions by their present day adherents." In the NAGPRA Regulations, published December 4, 1995, there is a limited effort to clarify this definition:

> While many items, from ancient pottery sherds to arrowheads, might be imbued with sacredness in the eyes of an individual, these regulations are specifically limited to objects that were devoted to a traditional Native American religious ceremony or ritual and which have religious significance or function in the continued observance or renewal of such ceremony. The term traditional religious leader means a person who is recognized by members of an Indian tribe or Native Hawaiian organization as:
>
> > *(i)* Being responsible for performing cultural duties relating to the ceremonial or religious traditions of that Indian tribe or Native Hawaiian organization, or
> > *(ii)* Exercising a leadership role in an Indian tribe or Native Hawaiian organization based on the tribe or organization's cultural, ceremonial, or religious practices (CFR, 12 December 1995, p. 62160).

Both the definition provided in the Act and the expansion of this in the Regulations illustrate the fact that the notion of "sacred" used in this law does not correspond to the more common, everyday uses of the term. Webster's Collegiate Dictionary, for example, defines sacred as something 1) "dedicated or set apart for the service or worship of a deity;" or 2) "worthy of religious veneration"; or 3) "of or relating to religion: not secular or profane." The definition of sacred under the NAGPRA is distinct from such everyday definitions in a number of ways.

ON THE NOTION OF "NEEDED" IN
DEFINING THE SACRED

First, the inclusion of the notion that sacred objects are those "needed" by traditional religious leaders in the definition was a deliberate effort to reduce the number of objects potentially affected by the law to a comparatively small subset of the full range of religious and ceremonial material held by museums. The term "needed" in this context is inherently ambiguous and is not further clarified in either the law or the Federal Regulations. If a tribe has been actively practicing their traditional religion without an object that has been lying in a museum for 100 years, how can that object be "needed" for the practice of that religion? If such a concept of "needed" was applied to other, non-Native religions, there would be little indeed that would fall within the parameters of "sacred." For instance, if this definition was applied to Catholicism, a crucifix would not be considered "sacred" because no specific crucifix is "needed" for the practice of any particular Catholic ritual. Most religious paraphernalia for Christian religions is readily available on the commercial market and no specific piece can be held up as uniquely necessary for the practice of any particular ritual. Similarly, in most Native American cultures, new ceremonial objects are made as they are needed.

What continues to be needed in a ceremonial sense has been worked out on a case by case basis by tribes working with museums around the country. One of the strongest and most effective arguments made by tribes for needing specific objects for religious practices is to explain that certain kinds of objects are spiritually alive and individually powerful. Such living objects are a continuing source of spiritual health and/or danger for the tribe regardless of how long they have been held in museums. Furthermore, tribes have made the argument that there is a clear "need" to have these objects repatriated so the living spirits can be appropriately venerated in the proper religious context. The *katsina* masks of Southwestern Pueblo groups are a good example of this type of "needed" sacred object. The Pueblo *katsinas* are living spirit messengers to the gods and they carry the prayers of the people.

Another avenue open to tribes for establishing artifacts as sacred under NAGPRA is to demonstrate that they are needed to renew ceremonies that have been not been practiced in recent years. The historical record of virtually every American Indian tribe contains instances of rituals that were eradicated for economic, social, or political reasons. In such cases, contemporary religious leaders of a tribe may demonstrate an overt *need* for specific objects to aid their efforts to revive particular ceremonies and rituals that have not been practiced for a generation or more. Sometimes the removal of the object itself was the reason the ceremony was stopped. In other cases, objects may have been lost because tribes were unable to carry on specific religious traditions due to specific historical or cultural circumstances.

TRADITIONAL RELIGIOUS LEADERS

The Act and the Federal Regulations essentially mandate that all tribes have a religious hierarchy with recognized and designated religious leaders. This particular component of the NAGPRA definition of "sacred" effectively reduced the number of individuals who would have standing to assert the sacredness of any given object for a tribe. Although the language of the Act is relatively open as to who may claim to be a religious leader, it is made clear elsewhere (e.g., Sec. 7 (a)) that only the tribe has standing to request the repatriation of sacred objects. Therefore, the federally recognized tribal government is placed as a structural intermediary between the religious leaders of the tribe and the museums and federal agencies from whom the objects would be requested. Given that the secular government of many tribes is often quite separate and distinct from tribal religious organization, the language of NAGPRA imposes a cumbersome, Western pattern on the great diversity of social, political, and ceremonial relationships found in Native American communities.

THE NOTION OF "TRADITIONAL"

In defining sacred objects as only those needed for the practice of "traditional Native American religions," the language of the Act again reduces the scope of affected objects, limiting them to items clearly devoted to religious activities. Such wording was also intended to forestall any efforts to "invent" new ceremonies that might incorporate or venerate any conceivable object from the past. Whether or not such concerns were well-founded, the emphasis on "traditional" in NAG-PRA tends to deny or ignore the inherent dynamics of Native religions. Most of the sacred objects held by museums today were acquired in the period from about 1880 to 1920 and were intimately related to religious practices at that time. Accordingly, "traditional" has a tendency to be interpreted as "the way things were" in the late-nineteenth and early-twentieth centuries. This is certainly the case with Native American art, where "traditional" styles and designs of pottery making or beading, for example, are taken to be those of some romantic, idealized past that is usually traceable to the nineteenth-century.

Such a concept of "traditional," with its focus on the past, fails to recognize that just as cultures grow, develop and change over time, so, too, do traditions. Religious beliefs and practices of the late twentieth century are rarely the same as they were 100 years ago. Just as the traditions of the Catholic Church, for example, have changed over the past century, so have the traditions of most Native American tribes. At the same time, religious items that had a specific role in the ceremonial life of a tribe in the nineteenth-century may come to have a different but nevertheless important role in the ceremonial life of the twentieth (or twenty first) century.

While the language of NAGPRA may be murky, patronizing, clumsy and unrealistic, the law in many ways is working. All parties concerned with collections and repatriation, e.g. curators, lawyers, tribal officials, traditional leaders and many others, are finding ways to deal with both the letter and the spirit of the law. With a decade of experience since the passage of the Act, it appears that many of the dire predictions of vast collections flowing out of museums have simply not come to pass. Increasingly, we see that the idea of repatriation in most museums, with certain notable exceptions, is viewed less and less as a threat and more commonly embraced as an opportunity to build new kinds of relationships with the Native communities whose objects are represented in their collections and exhibit halls. Museums have also sought to play an active role in helping define basic principles of repatriation to address the concerns of Native Americans while simultaneously maintaining consistency with respect to the intellectual, educational, and fiduciary responsibilities of the institution.

ARAPAHO SUN DANCE WHEEL

An example drawn from the experiences of the Field Museum may help illustrate the intricacies of steering through the language of NAGPRA and trying to grapple substantively with the illusive notion of "sacred objects." The details provided below are a matter of public record and I am not revealing any information given to me in trust or confidence. Confidential information would add another layer of complexity to the story, though its very confidentiality is itself a part of the story. In dealing with sacred issues, at least some tribes have found it advantageous to reveal certain kinds of information to individuals in museums with the (often implicit) understanding that such information is not for public dissemination. The sharing of this kind of information is a manifestation of new kinds of personalized relationships of trust developing between individuals in museums and Native groups.

In January of 1993, the Field Museum received a request signed by the Chairman of the Northern Arapaho Business Council and the Secretary of the Ceremonial Elders for the repatriation of an Arapaho Sundance Wheel. The Museum's records indicated that this piece had been collected from the Wind River Reservation of the Northern Arapaho by George Dorsey, a Museum curator, in 1900. Dorsey reportedly paid 25 cents for the Wheel. Even for the time, this was a very small amount to pay for an important piece and it raises unanswered questions about how Dorsey acquired the object.

In April of 1993, an invited delegation from the Northern Arapaho Tribe visited the Field Museum at the institution's expense. The group included the Chairman of the Business Council, a second Council member, two of the four recognized Ceremonial Elders of the Sun Dance, and one member of the Cheyenne and Arapaho Tribe Business Council, representing the Southern Arapaho of Oklahoma. As such, the group contained both federally-recognized tribal representatives and "traditional religious leaders" as identified under NAGPRA. While at the Museum the group had the opportunity to view the entire Arapaho collection and spent a considerable amount of time with the specific Sun Dance Wheel in question.

During the visit, there ensued a respectful if sometimes heated discussion about the possibility of expediting the repatriation of the Wheel. This brought the spiritual and ceremonial concerns of the Tribe face-to-face with the legal and policy concerns of the Museum. Tribal representatives wanted the Wheel back as soon as possible so it could be properly cared for and hopefully readied for the annual Sundance held in July. The Museum representatives articulated the institutional obligations to follow both the mandates of NAGPRA, as well as state laws and internal policies. The group left with a promise that the repatriation request would be reviewed as quickly as possible.

In accordance with the Museum's internal repatriation policy (adopted by the Board of Trustees), the Arapaho request was first reviewed within the Anthropology Department. As part of this review, a determination had to be made about whether the Wheel fit the definition of "sacred object" according to the NAGPRA legislation. Fortunately, in this case, Dorsey himself had written extensively about the Arapaho Sundance and explicitly about the Wheel. Dorsey concluded: "This object [the Sundance Wheel] next to the great tribal medicine, the flat pipe, in the keeping of the Northern Arapaho, is the most sacred possession in the tribe."

The substance of the review along with a recommendation of the Curator to repatriate the Wheel was forwarded to the Museum administration and ultimately to the Board. The curator's recommendation was formally reviewed following Museum policy (see Boyd and Haas 1992) by the Department Registrar, the Department Chair, the Museum's internal legal counsel, the Museum President, a subcommittee of the Board of Trustees (responsible for overseeing the academic programs), and finally by the full Board of Trustees.

The eventual decision to repatriate the Wheel was then sent to the office of the Illinois Attorney General for informational purposes only. The Illinois Attorney General has a mandated oversight role to insure the fiduciary responsibilities of nonprofit institutions in the State of Illinois. This admittedly long list of concerned parties illustrates the bureaucratic tangle involved in deaccessioning an object held in good faith by the Museum for almost a century.

Once the Board had approved the recommendation to repatriation the Wheel, a notice of intent to repatriate was sent on August 3, 1993, to the U.S. Department of Interior for publication in the Federal Register. Clearly the deadline had passed for returning the Wheel in time for the annual Sundance. Actually, the Arapaho traditional people had indicated that the Wheel would had to have been returned well before July to be ritually prepared. The notice of intent to repatriate the Wheel was published in the Federal Register on August 24, 1993, and read as follows:

> Notice is hereby given under the Native American Graves Protection and Repatriation Act of 1990 of the intent to repatriate a cultural item in the possession of the Field Museum of Natural History, Chicago, that meets the definitions of "sacred objects" and "object of cultural patrimony" under section 2 of the Act.
>
> The carved wheel with beads and eagle feathers, approximately 21 inches in diameter with an overall length of 30 inches, was collected in May 1900 at the Wind River Reservation, Wyoming, by George A. Dorsey, Chief Curator of Anthropology for the Field Museum. The original museum catalogue records describe the object as "catalogue number 61397; accession number 694; field number 548; Wheel (hoti)–from Sun dance pavilion—cottonwood; Arapahoe".
>
> The form of the object, its source and documentation lead the museum to believe that it is a Sun Dance Wheel. Copies of the museum records and photographs of the object have been provided to the Northern Arapaho Business Council and members of the appropriate Sun Dance religious body. Authorized representatives of the Arapaho tribe have viewed the object in person and concur with this identification of the object as a Sun Dance Wheel. The Northern Arapaho Business Council has requested repatriation of the object from the Field Museum of Natural History in a letter dated January 19, 1993. The Field Museum of Natural History has no objections.
>
> Authorities of the United States Fish and Wildlife Service have been contacted regarding applicability of Federal endangered species statutes to this transfer and have concurred in the conclusion that the object is not covered due to its age. (Federal Register, August 24, 1993).

This public notice again brings into focus the somewhat incongruous juxtaposition of Native American religion with the formal language and requirements of federal law. At the same time, it illustrates that a public notice of intent to repatriate a sacred object need not reveal any sensitive or confidential information about the object or the context within which it is used by the group. Why the object is considered sacred by the Arapaho and fits the NAGPRA definition of "sacred" is not addressed in the public notice.

Following a 30-day waiting period after publication of the notice in the Federal Register, a letter was sent to the Chairman of the Northern Arapaho Business Council and the Secretary of the Ceremonial Elders on September 30, 1993, informing them that it was possible for the Tribe to take possession of the Wheel. On October 24, two Arapaho traditional people, including the senior member of the Ceremonial Elders, came to the Museum, picked up the Wheel and signed a formal transfer of title of the Wheel from the Museum to the Tribe. The entire process, from beginning to end, thus took approximately nine months.

The eventual return of the Wheel and the administrative and legal details preceding the return are only one part of the whole story of the repatriation of the Sun Dance Wheel to the Northern Arapaho Tribe. There was also a parallel story unfolding in the Arapaho communities of Wyoming and Oklahoma. This parallel story starts shortly after the visit to Chicago by the Northern Arapaho delegation in April 1993. Later that same month, the designated Arapaho NAGPRA representative of the Cheyenne and Arapaho Tribe of Oklahoma wrote to the Museum to express concerns about the return of the Wheel. The gist of these concerns was that the Arapaho people already had a Sun Dance Wheel that was danced every year and had been appropriately initiated in proper ceremonies. The recommendation was that the Wheel should not be repatriated but kept by the Museum. Additional communications were received from traditional people in Wyoming, all of whom had responsibilities for the annual Sundance and for keeping the current Sun Dance Wheel. Specific concerns were raised about the authenticity of the Wheel as well as general spiritual concerns about whether the Wheel should be returned.

Additional communications continued during the months leading up to the actual repatriation in October of 1993. Much of the conversation took place over the telephone and there was an effort on the part of all the Arapaho individuals to help the Museum representatives understand some of the ceremonial and political complexities surrounding the Wheel, the two different Arapaho communities (in Oklahoma and Wyoming), and the Sundance in general. The tenor of these communications, though at times highly emotional, was always respectful. It is perhaps best reflected in a statement made in a letter dated September 9, 1993, from Virgil Franklin, Sr., a member of the Cheyenne and Arapaho Tribe of Oklahoma to Timothy McKeown in the NAGPRA office of the National Park Service: "Believe me that there is no animosity involved but only an interest in protecting the sacred objects that we respect and in resolving ... our present concerns."

These discussions largely ignored the niceties of NAGPRA. The concern was not about federal definitions of "sacred objects" or "traditional religious leaders" but rather about the social and spiritual well-being of the Arapaho people and whether it was a good idea to try to reintegrate this object back into the ceremonial life of the community. Clearly there was not agreement within the two tribes. The tribes themselves were not in opposition to one another as there were individuals from both groups taking differing positions. There was an effort to get the Museum to understand their cultural concerns and to make its decisions based on that understanding.

Realistically, in the end, although the discussions were useful in airing differences they had little impact on the decisions and actions of the Museum. The Museum was obliged by federal law to consider the repatriation request only according to the criteria given in NAGPRA and with respect to its own repatriation policy. Those who raised concerns about the repatriation did not raise a formal objection nor make a competing claim for the Wheel. They raised deeply felt human concerns for which there is no corresponding mechanism in the formal language of the law. For their own, culturally-defined reasons, none of the individuals concerned about the repatriation chose to engage the formal, and very public, dispute resolution process built into NAGPRA (by appeal to the Review Committee). No one wanted to discuss these matters in an open confrontational forum. They wanted people to listen and understand that this was an Arapaho issue that should be resolved by the Arapaho people—not by federal law or anthropologists and administrators in a distant museum. The Museum, in turn, was placed in the uncomfortable, if not simple, position of having to give precedence to the voices and formal requests of only those individuals who had been given explicit authority by the secular tribal councils. Ultimately, federal law prevailed. The repatriated Sun Dance Wheel is today being kept by one of the Ceremonial Elders of the Northern Arapaho Tribe. As of the summer of 1997 it had not been danced in a Sundance ceremony.

In 1995, the Field Museum received a NAGPRA grant from the National Park Service for purposes of consultation with the Northern and Southern Arapaho tribes. As part of this grant, Arapaho interns came to the Field Museum to fully inventory the Arapaho collection. There were also visiting delegations of traditional people from both tribes who came to familiarize themselves with the collection and provide counsel on appropriate treatment and care for specific kinds of objects. The collection was fully photographed and copies of the photo albums were given to representatives of both tribes.

Bob Spoonhunter, the intern from the Northern Arapaho Tribe and one of the active initiators of the joint project, supervised special photography of a sample of artistically outstanding artifacts. He then mounted an exhibit of these objects together with historic photographs of tribal members back on the Wind River Reservation in Wyoming. He also used his research on the collection to reintroduce historical quillwork techniques to the Arapaho artists on the reservation. Tragically, Mr. Spoonhunter died before he could complete arrangements to travel the photography exhibit to the Southern Arapaho community in Oklahoma. Active discussion with members of both tribes continues to the present and the relationship between the Museum and the Arapaho communities is very positive.

The relationship between museums and Native Americans is one that has been characterized as "bittersweet." Museums must shoulder the positive and negative responsibilities of collecting a broad range of objects that can be variously referred to as "ritual," "ceremonial," "sacred," or "religious." On the plus side, many of these objects are in existence today only because they have been cared for in the vaults of museums. On the negative side, many of these objects never should have been taken from Native American communities in the first place. NAGPRA represents a good-faith effort on the part of the federal government to mandate a process for the possible repatriation of certain kinds of sacred objects that should not have been removed from tribes. There are also a growing number of successful repatriations which demonstrate that the law is having positive effects in many situations. At the same time, it should not be a big surprise that an effort to legislate a concept such as "sacred" has inevitable problems when applied to the huge diversity of cultures found amongst the Native American tribes of North America.

REFERENCES CITED

Boyd, Thomas and Jonathan Haas. 1992. "The Native American Graves Protection and Repatriation Act: Prospects for new partnerships between museums and Native American groups." *Arizona State Law Journal* 24(1):253–282.

CHAPTER NINE

Regenerating Identity
Repatriation and the Indian Frame of Mind

RICHARD W. HILL, SR.

About forty generations ago, the Iroquois of upstate New York received a message of peace, power and unity that formed the basis of what is called The Great Law of Peace. This Great Law served as the founding constitution for the Six Nations Iroquois confederacy. The oral tradition surrounding the formation of this confederacy and its procedural requirements were encoded in a series of sacred belts and strings of tubular shell wampum beads assembled about 1,000 years ago. Messages, beliefs, and hopes were spoken into these belts as a way to preserve their power for future generations. Through this wampum, the Iroquois were connected to previous generations and acted as a cultural bridge to future ones.

Unfortunately, this continuity was ruptured through the coercive sale, theft, and removal of many of these belts during the nineteenth century. The wampum documents have since become the center of strained relations between the 45,000-strong Iroquois nation and several major museums that hold these sacred items. In this paper, I focus on the struggle of the Iroquois to recover these wampum belts as a way of illustrating the cultural issues behind the politics of repatriation.

It has been 25 years since I first heard of the sacred wampum. Even growing up as an Iroquois though, I never saw any of these pieces in our communities. Most of the known wampum belts were locked away in museums. As a young man, I learned of their fate and was part of a movement to recover the wampums. It seemed to many Native people that the glorious beauty of the past, as well as the spiritual legacy of the future, was imprisoned in museums. I felt strongly that if we were to survive as a people, we needed to hear the messages from the past and be empowered to carry this knowledge forward.

Culture is, indeed, more than objects, but for many Native American nations, there are certain objects that are essential to manifesting that culture. Most Native American children were growing up without ever having seen the treasures of their cultural heritage. To me and many Native Americans of my generation, it seemed that the sanctioned institutions of culture in our society were actually contributing to our cultural decline, and this became intolerable.

THE CHANGING POLITICAL LANDSCAPE

It is important to remember that the Native American Graves Protection and Repatriation Act (NAGPRA) was preceded by decades of confrontations between museums and Native Americans over the issues of cultural patrimony, representation, religious rights, and human rights. During the 1960s, a period of intense political unrest, the federal government had begun to redefine its relationship to Native Americans. An era of forced relocation and assimilation was coming to an end and a new age of self-determination loomed on the horizon. Native Americans were growing stronger in their own sense of identity, and consequently became more vocal and aggressive in addressing social inequities. Museums were just one sector of American society to come under scrutiny as part of the associated spiritual revitalization movements, and repatriation needs to be understood as one component of these larger social reforms.

It is difficult to explain how deeply these movements affected Native Americans. Generations of poverty, oppression and self-doubt had to be overcome. Leaders came to see the restoration of traditional cultural values as one of the most important avenues for enabling change. A stronger cultural base, it was thought, would provide Native people with a stronger sense of self, a stronger sense of place, and a stronger sense of destiny. But as more college-aged Native Americans began to seek out their spiritual heritage in order to reconnect with traditional values, they found many of the paths blocked because the objects needed to perform necessary ceremonies and rites were in the possession of museums. When those same Indian students began to visit these institutions, they found the material component of their cultural heritage behind glass and strangely silent, the objects of non-Native's gawking stares. Freeing the objects from their ethnological fate came to be equated with the struggle for the liberation of the Native American mind and spirit.

Around this same time, museums and the field of anthropology were undergoing their own kind of reformation. Various policies, programs and practices were being questioned with regard to standards of fairness and equity. African Americans, Asian Americans, Hispanic Americans, women, and the alternative arts were all demanding more attention from museums. Museum trustees were just beginning to address inconsistencies in standards of conduct on issues of accessioning and deaccessioning. The mishandling and outright illegal activities of some museums caused administrators to take a hard look at their practices and critically examine whether they were in fact upholding the public trust with which they were charged.

With demands for the reburial of human remains, the removal of sacred objects from public display and the repatriation of cultural patrimony, Native Americans forced standard museum policies and practices onto the public stage. I cannot say which museum was the first to return human remains or which was the first to formally recognize the rights of Native Americans to their own cultural patrimony. Some museums, mainly smaller ones, responded immediately to the claims of Native peoples without requiring the force of law to compel them. But the Native American Graves Protection and Repatriation Act came about because many of the major museums would not address our concerns. While NAGPRA was the final resort for Native Americans at the time, we now see it as a new beginning.

THE IROQUOIS WAMPUM CASE

In 1970, the New York State Assembly Subcommittee on Indian Affairs recommended that the century-old Wampum Law be amended to allow the return of five wampum belts to the Onondaga Nation. The amendment was proposed in recognition of the Onondaga's traditional role as the wampum keepers of the Iroquois Confederacy, an alliance which also includes the Seneca, Cayuga, Oneida, Mohawk, and Tuscarora Nations. When we learned of the proposed amendment, it came as surprise to many of us that the Wampum Law even existed. How had New York State become the wampum keeper for the Iroquois? How had wampum, one of the Iroquois' most sacred objects of cultural patrimony, ever left our possession?

In many ways, the Iroquois experience is similar to that of other Native nations. Many Native Americans of my generation were born into communities rent asunder by the divergent beliefs of their own members. Differing views of religion, governance, education, economy, and culture tore at the very fabric of our common identities. We had become confused about who we were, what we were supposed to do, and how well our traditional culture served our needs in Cold War America.

Visits to museums exacerbated this cultural disorientation. Museums were painful because Native bones, as well as objects we believed to be sources of power for our communities, were on display. Many of these items were trophies collected by soldiers, priests, teachers, and government bureaucrats which had once belonged to our ancestors. Native Americans felt profoundly disconnected from those sources of power. Repatriation became the process through which we sought to reconnect with the ideals represented in those objects and reclaim authority over them.

Like many young Indians in the 1970s, I was able to learn of the significance of these objects from two sources: the scholarly literature produced by non-Natives and the stories that were still known by the old people in our communities. As the Iroquois pushed an agenda of cultural and political renewal, museums, anthropologists, educators, and movie-makers were targeted as obstacles to Iroquois progress. My own search for information lead me to the campus of the State University of New York at Buffalo, where I now teach, and the place where I first met the leading proponent of repatriation, Oren Lyons, an Onondaga artist, college professor, and representative on the Onondaga Council of Chiefs. It was a meeting that changed my life.

Lyons and several other chiefs, together with the New York State Council on the Arts, had convinced the State of New York to pass legislation to return the major belts from the State Museum to the Iroquois Confederacy. However, an aggressive campaign to block that move was launched by the Committee on Anthroplogical Research in Museums under the aegis of the American Anthroplogical Association (Sturtevant et al. 1970). The scholars on this committee were able to convince then–Governor Nelson Rockefeller to veto the proposed legislation. The "Iroquoianists" subsequently became embroiled in a very public controversy with the traditional Iroquois chiefs over the primacy of cultural and religious rights versus scientific and academic rights (e.g., Henry 1970). The wampum case set the general tone for negotiations over repatriation that eventually would affect all museums with Indian materials in their collections. In many ways, the issues raised in New York are still at the forefront of the debate over repatriation.

During this battle, the Iroquois used the media effectively to create public sympathy for their cause and public opinion came to favor the return of the wampums. In addition, the Iroquois challenged the anthropologists and historians at every turn. Essays written by scholars were critiqued by the Native press. Confrontations with scholars became standard operating procedure. Academic conferences could no longer just be about Native Americans; they had to include Native Americans.

Relationships between the Iroquois and scholars reached an all-time low in 1976 as America turned its attention to the celebration of its two hundredth birthday. To the Iroquois, the dispute over the wampum was symbolic of racist policies that continued to subject Native peoples to cultural oppression. The Iroquois argued that the belts were illegally removed without the consent of the traditional chiefs, and that they were essential to the cultural and spiritual continuity of the Iroquois. They argued that for one culture group to assert that its scientific interests took precedence over the religious rights of another was itself evidence of how deeply entrenched racial bias was in the social sciences.

The scholars responded that museums "owned" the sacred objects and that these items were essential for future studies of the Iroquois. They felt that by studying Native people, American society at large could learn more about human cultures in general. Their position hinged on the argument that the public had a right to know the cultural heritage of their homeland and a right to view and enjoy these objects. To the scholars, it was an issue of academic freedom, which, for them, entailed the right to study anything, secular or religious, in the pursuit of truth. They might have won more support if they had stuck to that argument.

Instead they turned to character assassination and this lost support for their cause among many museum professionals. The anthropologists argued that the contemporary Iroquois were acculturated and no longer understood their own traditions. The scholars reasoned that they knew more about Iroquois traditions than the Iroquois themselves and that the wampums would be best left in the care of the non-Native professionals (Fenton 1971; Sturtevant et al. 1970). They tried to discredit the Iroquois by labelling them as "Red Power militants." In a letter written in 1970 to the Governor, the scholars argued that "state property should not be legislated away lightly in the illusion of religiosity or as capital in the civil rights movement" (Sturtevant et al. 1970:14).

Not to be outdone, the Iroquois painted the scholars as egomaniacal racists who were more concerned with their research, grants, and publications than the cultural preservation of their "subjects." They made it difficult for archaeologists to continue excavating Native American grave sites without publicly justifying their actions. They also forced museums to address the issue of repatriation and obliged them to publicly refute accusations of racism and political sabotage. The situation reached a boiling point in 1979 when the New York State Senate, for the ninth year in a row, failed to amend the Indian Law relating to the custody of the wampums. The scholars thought they had defeated the Iroquois once and for all, but this was not to be the end.

THE FUNCTION OF WAMPUM

Wampum undergirds the entire cultural worldview of the Iroquois. It is sacred by virtue of the shell from which it is made and because it was chosen by the Creator as the medium through which the Iroquois would retain and transmit information from generation to generation (c.f., Hewitt 1892; Noon 1948; Tooker 1978). This is why the Iroquois felt so strongly about the need to have the wampum returned. Turmoil had become a way of life in the 13 Iroquois communities spread across New York, Ontario and Quebec. Elective governments had replaced the traditional systems in all but three of the communities. Most of the Iroquois people, who now attended Christian churches, no longer visited the longhouses where traditional ceremonies took place. The legendary Grand Council, once respected and feared by Dutch, French, English and colonial American leaders, was but a shadow of its former self. The Great Law was suffering and the hope was that it could be revitalized with the return of the wampum belts, the repositories of the original messages.

The term "wampum" refers to the small, tubular beads that are drilled through their long axis and range in color from white to blue to purple (Abrams 1994; Beauchamp 1901). The word derives from the Algonquian "wampumpeag" which, during the fur trade era, came to refer to any type of shell bead and took on specifically monetary connotations. But originally, among Native American cultures of the Northeast, wampum had numerous meanings, functioning, as it did, within the social, cultural, political, and spiritual realms of the Iroquois, Huron, Ojibwa and Algonquian nations (Hewitt 1912). In the Iroquoian language, the word for wampum is *gatgoa*, while the word for a string of wampum is *sgad-goad*. Each different wampum belt originally would have had its own specific name. For instance, the wampum belt used in the Iroquois condolence ceremony was called *henodosetha gatgoa*.

Wampum had been used in many ways in the past. Wampum beads could be offered to a grieving family to atone for the death of a loved one. They could be used to ransom a captive relative. In 1622, for instance, a Dutch trader received 140 six foot-long strings of wampum in exchange for a Chief who he was holding hostage. Wampum strings were given to Chiefs and Clan Mothers as confirmation of their title and oath of office, the strands of tiny shell beads representing their pledge to uphold the Great Law. Wampum strings with notched sticks attached were used to announce upcoming council meetings, the wampum serving both as the credentials for the messenger and to prove that the delegates attending would be the official representatives of their community. The symbolic designs woven into wampum belts recorded the terms of treaties between nations. Wampum strings also recorded the order of ceremonial speeches. As an item of ritual exchange between different groups, wampum served to confirm agreements or requests. It was, for instance, the appropriate gift to offer a bride's family, and newly married couples were given wampum to verify their marriage oath. The beads also functioned as articles of personal adornment among the Iroquois and were worn as headbands, necklaces, armbands, belts, shoulder sashes, earrings, chokers, cuffs, or kilts (Abrams 1994; Tooker 1978).

The importance of wampum among Native American nations was quickly recognized by Euroamerican officials and settlers. In one account of a Native conference in Montreal in 1756, the significance of the shell beads is reported as follows:

> These belts and strings of wampum are a universal agent among Indians, serving as money, jewelry, ornaments, annals, and registers; [they are] the bond of nations and individuals, [recognized as] an inviolable and sacred pledge which guarantees messages, promises and treaties. As writing is not in use among them [the Indians], they make a local memoir by means of these belts, each of which signifies a particular affair or circumstance of affairs. The chiefs of the village are the depositories of [these belts], and communicate them to the young people, who thus learn the history and engagements of their nation (O'Callaghan 1968 [1756]:556).

It is also interesting to note how quickly wampum came to figure in intercultural protocols. Both the French and the English adopted aspects of the Native system to convince the Iroquois of the earnestness of their intentions. The French, who referred to wampum as "porcelain collars," recognized its importance as an element of ritual protocol early on. In 1636, for example, Father Le Jeune noted that ". . . as the Porcelain that takes the place of gold and silver in this country is all-powerful, I presented in this Assembly a collar of twelve hundred beads of Porcelain, telling them [the Iroquois] that it was given to smooth the difficulties of the road to Paradise." George Washington, as a military officer and later as president, used wampum both to petition the Iroquois and to confirm agreements made between his government and the Iroquois Confederacy. Wampum was regularly exchanged at treaty councils and nearly every other official function.

THE LOSS OF THE WAMPUM

Once Native Americans were no longer considered a military threat, the era of treaty making was over. Iroquois were isolated on small reservations, and wampum lost its political significance. But the belts, which verified the original treaties, remained a visible and problematic reminder of promises unkept as the Federal government attempted to discontinue its relations with the Confederacy. As the Iroquois became objects of study in the emerging field of ethnology in the mid-nineteenth century, scholars began to report on the cultural and spiritual significance of wampum in the past tense. While some wampum remained actively in use within the internal spheres of Iroquoian life, many belts began to slip away.

By the late nineteenth-century, the Iroquois were embroiled in great debates about modernization. Reformers wanted the Iroquois to give up their old ways, including the Council of Chiefs. As a result of these conflicts, the Onondaga came to have two political bodies, the traditional chiefs who sat in council in the longhouse and a dissident government that had been elected under the terms of the

Bureau of Indian Affairs. The old wampums, descended from the time of the founding of the Iroquois Confederacy, symbolized the ongoing power of the Council of Chiefs. Many modern-day Iroquois believe that the removal of the wampum that ensued was an attempt to destroy the traditional form of government.

In 1891, Onondaga Chief Thomas Webster, a member of the rival BIA-backed government, sold all the wampums in his possession to Major Carrington, a U.S. Indian Census Agent (Carrington 1892). Webster may have felt that by dislocating the wampums, the traditional chiefs would lose their source of power and authority. But many Iroquois leaders of today believe that he was coerced into selling the belts. It was well known among members of Iroquoian society that no individual had the authority to give, trade, or sell the wampum belts. These items were only held in trust by the Onondaga for the member nations of the Confederacy. The belts were understood to belong to all Iroquois people and were recognized as part of the cultural patrimony of the Iroquois Nation. It is this idea of shared communal property that lies behind much of the repatriation movement. If a collector or a museum were to have purchased wampum from individuals without the sanction of the collective, the sale would, by definition, be invalid.

Between 1900 and 1940, many of the old wampums were obtained by scholars (Fenton 1989). It is hard to understand why some Iroquois, many of them traditionalists, gave up the wampum to anthropologists, but the results were devastating. Some Iroquois feel that the scholars tricked the people into giving up their sacred materials. Some say that times were hard financially and ritualists sold the only possessions they had in order to feed their families. Other say that some longhouse people truly believed that their traditions were coming to an end and wanted museums to preserve the sacred wampums. Whatever the motivation, the modern generation of Iroquois wanted their wampum back.

THE FIRST WAMPUM COMES HOME

In 1963, a wampum belt in the collections of the Buffalo Historical Society turned up missing after becoming a primary object of interest in a lawsuit. This wampum belt had been given by the Tuscarora nation to the Holland Land company in 1799 to document the transfer of one-square mile of land to the Tuscarora people. This land today constitutes the core of the Tuscarora reservation. This particular wampum belt subsequently became the focus of a legal battle between the Tuscarora Nation and the New York State Power Authority, which was seeking to condemn part of the Tuscarora reservation to build a giant hydro-electric plant at Niagara Falls. The belt was removed from the Historical Society and supposedly sent to a laboratory for authentication. It disappeared at this point and was never seen again. Many Iroquois suspected foul play on the part of the State. The Tuscarora lost their case and one-third of their reservation (cf., Landy 1978:523–524).

In 1975, as a research assistant at the Buffalo and Erie County Historical Society, I helped to arrange the return of several thousand wampum beads to the Onondaga Nation. It was an important occasion because the traditional leaders had to develop unified statements on cultural patrimony and the way in which the repatriation of the sacred objects was to proceed. They were also meeting to negotiate the display and handling of human remains with the museum officials. Dr. Walter Dunn, then-director of the Historical Society, was open-minded and committed to a respectful resolution of the Iroquois' concerns. He and I subsequently travelled to the Onondaga reservation to return the wampum beads. For the first time in nearly a century, wampum flowed back into Iroquois hands.

The Iroquois who resided on the Canadian side of the border were also pursuing wampum missing from their territory. Their story is similar to that of the Onondaga. One of their longhouse leaders, unbeknownst to the Council of Chiefs, had sold several belts to a collector. In 1975, the Council officially declared that the belts, which were now housed in the Heye Foundation's Museum of the American Indian in New York City, had been improperly sold. The Chiefs hired Paul Williams, a young lawyer and the Director of Treaty Research for the Union of Ontario Indians, to pursue their case in 1977. The Onondaga on the American side also put pressure on the Museum. But the Museum's Board of Trustees, which included both William Fenton and William Sturtevant, two scholars who had strenuously fought the repatriation of the wampum in the New York State Museum, resisted the Onondaga claims.

The Iroquois consequently changed their tactics. Rather than pressing the Heye Foundation to respect the religious rights of the traditional people, they sought to show that the wampums had been illegally removed and that the Museum was in the possession of stolen property. Museum records clearly show that George Heye, the founder of the Museum of the American Indian, was aware of the questionable legal status of these items, and that one of the trustees actually suggested the Museum sell the wampums before the Iroquois could recover them.

In the end, the Iroquois lawyers and the traditional chiefs were able to convince then-President of the Board of Trustees, Barber Conable, of the integrity of their position, and the Trustees subsequently moved to return the belts that could be shown to have been illegally removed. In 1988, the Museum of the American Indian returned eleven wampum belts to the Council of Chiefs at the Grand River Reserve near Brantford, Ontario. It was one of the first examples of the repatriation of sacred objects from an American institution to a Native nation in Canada. The return involved only the belts that could be shown to have been unethically acquired, however. There are still a number of sacred wampums that remain part of the Museum's collections.

THE ONONDAGA WAMPUM REPATRIATION

On the American side of the border, a similar effort was underway to recover the wampum belts of the Onondaga Nation, by the traditional "Wampum Keepers" of the Iroquois Confederacy. Late in the nineteenth-century, Onondaga Chief Thomas Webster had sold four of these belts to Henry B. Carrington, U.S. Indian Census Agent, for $75. Carrington subsequently offered them to a Dr. Oliver Crane, who sold them in 1893 to the mayor of Albany, John B. Thatcher, for $500. Thatcher wanted the belts to be displayed as unique cultural treasures of great antiquity. In 1893, they were shown at the World's Columbian Exposition in Chicago where they were included in a larger display on 'American Indians.' The following year the belts were loaned to the Onondaga Historical Association for display during the Onondaga County Centennial celebration. People displayed a genuine respect for what the wampum belts represented, but they were construed as relics of the glorious Iroquoian past. The Iroquois themselves were generally understood to be a 'vanishing race' with little hope of surviving through the next century.

Chief Webster was removed from office in 1897 by the traditional chiefs for his actions. The Iroquois wanted their wampums back even then, but the collectors, who had a bill of sale, ignored the Chiefs. To strengthen their position, the Chiefs sought the assistance of anthropologists. The scholars convinced them that they needed the State University of New York to help them recover the wampum from the private collectors. In one of the strangest events in Iroquois history, the Regents of the State University of New York were appointed the Keepers of the Wampum in 1898 by a group of Onondaga. In the past, a traditional Onondaga Chief had always been the holder of that title. The University, with the implied endorsement of the Onondaga, began to acquire most of the remaining wampums in order to make a case for the cultural integrity of the belts.

Section 27 of the New York State Indian Law, passed in 1899, conferred the title of Wampum Keeper upon the University of the State of New York. The State then took possession of several wampums they had acquired from private collectors on behalf of the Iroquois. The University held that by virtue of its title of Wampum Keeper, all wampums fell under its authority. In 1900, the Onondaga Nation and the University of the State of New York combined forces to file suit against John Thatcher, the "owner" of the wampums sold by Chief Webster, seeking their return. In this important early legal case for repatriation, the Iroquois lost. Judge Frank Hiscock ruled that the wampums "are curiosities and relics of time, a condition, and a confederation that has ceased to exist," and that the Onondaga claim could not be upheld. Thatcher was allowed to keep the wampum. Ironically, the University of the State of New York later decided to bequeath the wampum it had collected to the New York State Museum, rather than return it to the Onondaga.

The Chiefs were not ready to give up. In 1907 another lawsuit was filed to obtain the return of the four wampum belts held by Thatcher. But this suit, too, was dismissed by a New York State judge who ruled, in effect, that the Confederacy no longer existed, that Thomas Webster did not hold the wampum in trust, and that he had a legal right to sell the belts. In 1909, the New York State Legislature passed another Wampum Law that bestowed upon itself the title of Wampum Keeper and claimed rights over any wampum in the possession of any Iroquois, past, present or future. Having legislated away the rights of the Iroquois, the rush was on to collect wampum with anthropologists leading the charge.

Years later, Thatcher's widow decided to end the unwanted attention that had plagued her family by donating the four wampum belts originally obtained from Chief Webster to the New York State Museum. There they rested quietly from 1927 until the 1970s when the Onondaga raised the issue of return again. Deeming repatriation one of their highest priorities, the Iroquois began to track down the museums holding wampum. They knew that the old Heye Foundation, since re-named the Museum of the American Indian, and the Smithsonian Institution had wampum in their collections, but a survey conducted between 1978 and 1982 uncovered over 200 additional wampum belts and dozens of wampum strings in numerous other museums around the country.

In the mid-1980s, Martin Sullivan, Director of the New York State Museum, and Ray Gonyea, cultural specialist for the Onondaga Nation, crafted a plan to circumvent the racist and unethical Wampum Laws of New York State. It involved transferring control of the wampum in the Museum's collection to the State Board of Regents, a body independent of the State Legislature. Previous attempts to have the wampum repatriated had been repeatedly voted down by the State Legislature. Once control over the belts was transferred to the Regents, the consent of the State Legislature was no longer required and the Regents were free to return these important items of Iroquoian cultural patrimony. The principal wampum belts in the State Museum's collection were returned to the Onondaga Nation on October 21, 1989.

WAMPUM AND THE SEVENTH GENERATION

What will the return of the wampums mean to the coming generations of Iroquois? Will the reading of the wampum affect the way the Iroquois live in the future? Will the current generation be able to interpret and transmit the messages contained in the ancient wampums? These questions remain unanswered at present. The fact is that the wampums carry a significant part of our cultural history. It remains to be seen just how much of an impact they will have on the functioning of the Great Law and in dealing with the issues faced by this generation of Iroquois. The long delay in the recovery of the wampums has taken its toll. There are only two or three people left who have enough cultural memory and linguistic fluency to interpret the meaning of these belts for the next generation. Hundreds of longhouse elders have passed away as museums and scholars argued over their rights to our heritage. With the passing of each elder, some knowledge is lost. It is as if we are burying a cultural library in the ground at each funeral.

As Iroquois, we are told to think of the seventh generation to come when we deliberate on our future. In making our decisions and choosing our paths, we are to consider not our needs or the needs of our own children but the welfare of the generations to come. If Thomas Webster and the other Iroquois who sold the wampum entrusted to them had thought about the seventh generation, we might not be in the mess we find ourselves in today.

Many of my museum colleagues question the sincerity of the repatriation requests coming from Native tribes. They ask whether Native Americans might not simply turn around and resell the objects that they are recovering from the museums. I cannot speak for other Native nations, but the Iroquois have learned an expensive lesson. It has taken us one hundred years to undo a cultural crime committed against our people. As long as we remember our cultural mandate, to consider the seventh generation to come, those wampums will never leave our possession again. Our very future as a people rests within those tiny shell beads.

But if the promise of repatriation is to be achieved, all museums need to cooperate. We need to recover all the wampum, as well as our other sacred objects. Museums need to consider new kinds of partnerships with Natives, ones that go beyond the object. Museums can help insure that cultural and religious beliefs continue and thrive. They can share their archival information, their photographs, and their recordings. They can play an important role in the Native American future. Repatriation is not an end, it is, in many ways, a new beginning. Through the processes and relations it engenders, museums will come to understand that cultural preservation is not only about keeping objects from decaying but also about keeping ideas, values, and beliefs viable for the many generations to come.

REFERENCES CITED

Abrams, George. 1994. "The case for wampum: Repatriation from the Museum of the American Indian to the Six Nations Confederacy, Brantford, Ontario." In *Museums and the Making of "Ourselves,"* edited by F. Kaplan, pp. 351–384. London: Leicester University Press.
Beauchamp, William. 1901. "Wampum and shell articles used by the New York Indians." *New York State Museum Bulletin* 41:321–480.
Carrington, Henry. 1892. "Report on the condition of the Six Nations of New York." In *Extra Census Bulletin: Indians.* edited by T. Donaldson, pp. 19–83. Washington, D.C.: Bureau of the Census.
Fenton, William. 1971. "The New York State wampum collection: The case for the integrity of cultural treasures." *Proceedings of the American Philosophical Society* 115(6):437–461.
——— 1989. "Return of eleven wampum belts to the Six Nations Iroquois Confederacy on Grand River, Canada." *Ethnohistory* 36(4):392–410.
Henry, Jeannette. 1970. "A rebuttal to the five anthropologists on the issue of the wampum belts." *Indian Historian* 3(2):15–17.
Hewitt, John. 1892. "Legend of the founding of the Iroquois League." *American Anthropologist* 5:131–148.
——— 1912. "Wampum." *Handbook of American Indians North of Mexico.* edited by E. W. Hodge, 2:904–909.
Landy, David. 1978. "Tuscarora among the Iroquois." *Handbook of North American Indians: Northeast,* edited by W. Sturtevant, pp. 518–534. Washington, D.C.: Smithsonian Institution Press.
Noon, John. 1949. *Law and Government of the Grand River Iroquois.* Viking Fund Publications in Anthropology, No. 12. New York.
O'Callaghan, E. B. 1968. "Historical Manuscripts in the Office of the Secretary of State, Albany, State of New York, 1664–1776." Ridgewood, New Jersey: Gregg Press.
Sturtevant, William, et al. 1970. "An 'illusion of religiosity'." *Indian Historian* 3(2):13–14.
Tooker, Elizabeth. 1978. "The League of Iroquois: Its history, politics and ritual." *Handbook of North American Indians: Northeast,* edited by W. Sturtevant, pp. 418–441. Washington, D.C.: Smithsonian Institution Press.

CHAPTER TEN

Medicine Bundles
An Indigenous Approach to Curation

PHILLIP E. CASH CASH

In recent years, Native communities and museums have reached an unprecedented level of interaction. The nature and import of this interaction is beginning to transform the way anthropologists and museum professionals view and
treat Native American material culture, particularly as it relates to the enduring
cultural status of the objects in their care. Clearly, the present situation is quite different from what was around the turn of the century when the intellectual interests of anthropological science and museums merged in a concerted effort to "salvage" remnant Native cultures.

While these early efforts helped to establish and foster a distinctly American
social science based on fieldwork and the acquisition of ethnographic information, human remains, and artifacts, the one-way transfer of intellectual and
cultural property that ensued has had a lasting and profound effect on Native
communities. No matter how benign or socially responsive the anthropological
project has since become, its cumulative impact across time and space has been
significant. Even so, Native communities today, through their collective efforts,
are beginning to transcend this history and are now attempting to reconcile the
past with the future through self-determined strategies of cultural renewal and
preservation.

NATIVE MATERIAL CULTURE AND MUSEUMS

The vast inventory of Native material culture now housed in Western repositories
is eloquent testimony to the larger historical realities and colonial processes
through which Native lifeways were suppressed and cultures disenfranchised. It
must be acknowledged, however, that museums have also made important and
timely contributions to the revitalization of Native cultures. Museums have been
instrumental in preserving material culture in the onslaught of change, building
unique collaborative partnerships in the presentation and display of objects,
ensuring access to sacred materials, and even repatriating objects to tribes well
before the enactment of the Native American Graves Protection and Repatriation
Act (NAGPRA) in 1990.

While these two aspects of museums may appear to be in opposition, it is the combined force of these historical contradictions that informs much of the current discussion on Native material culture and museums. As Native communities and museums begin to establish cooperative and responsive relationships, there is a mutual recognition of opportunities for the exchange of ideas and information on the nature and meaning of cultural objects. This exchange has led many museum curators to re-examine the nature of curation as a primary method of preservation. Many Native communities have begun to assert alternative methods of preservation and treatment, ideas which are herein referred to as "indigenous curation practices".

In this article, I examine the social aspects of Native material culture within the context of contemporary Native/museum relations. My primary objective is to illustrate the contrastive meanings commonly associated with the term *curation* as it is used in museum and Native cultural practice, and to encourage a reassessment of its usage relative to Native material culture. The focus for this discussion necessarily centers on material culture that Native communities and museums have often deemed "sensitive," for example sacred objects and objects of cultural patrimony. My hope is that a heightened sensitivity towards curation practices will lead to the development of a true and meaningful dialogue that recognizes the fundamental cultural differences embedded in the way Native communities view and treat objects.

The selection of medicine bundles as the focus of study is appropriate on at least two levels. First, as discrete classes of objects, medicine bundles are imbued with elaborate beliefs pertaining to usage and practice that are both corporeal and incorporeal in nature. Second, the interjection of the customary beliefs associated with medicine bundles into the museological domain clearly reflects an assertion of rights as originating cultures seek to define and re-establish control over their cultural heritage.

CURATION AS CONCEPT

The term curation derives from the Latin word *curare*, "to take care of." By extension, when we reference the term curation in speaking of museum collections, we intuitively mean "to take care of objects," and we refer to those who care for museum objects as "curators." Murdoch (1992:18–19), who offers a more recent definition, suggests that curation embodies two main principles, these being *documentation* and *care and access*. As important as these principles are in clarifying the essential elements of curation, the meaning of the term and its broader application are of limited utility in attempts to offer a cross-cultural explanation of why we do the things we do when we care for objects.

While I do not presume to offer a definitive statement on curation, I do wish to "bridge the gap," so to speak, by presenting an alternative perspective based on the idea that our relationships with objects are ultimately social ones. In light of this, I offer the following definition: *curation is a social practice predicated on the principle of a fixed relation between material objects and the human environment.*[1] By putting forward this definition, I attempt to liberate the concept of curation from its supposed neutrality in the institution and situate it within a specific cultural and historical context.

The most important aspect of curation, for the present discussion, is the role of culture in the perception and treatment of objects. In terms of the definition offered, "the principle of a fixed relation" refers to those conditions that are socially constructed and reproduced as strategic cultural orientations vis-à-vis material objects. Within this context, the curation of objects can be described as an asymmetrical assertion of power whose function is to stabilize, legitimate, and sanction the continuity of objects in space. Of particular interest here is the specific forms these cultural orientations have taken with respect to the curatorial project and its ordering of the material world.

The relationships that have existed between Native communities and museums have been described by some as a kind of "symbiosis" (Lurie 1988). Further consideration of the specifics of these relationships, however, is beginning to reveal something far more complex and enduring than previously imagined. Understandably, these relationships have been largely determined by the transfer and possession of cultural objects as property and as resource. Hinsley (1993:15) aptly describes the transformative nature of possession and the trajectory it has assumed:

> First, the exercise of extraction from the originating environment places a specific kind of claim—one of familiarity and possession—on that environment/landscape, so that the collection now removed functions as a hostage for that claim: a material reminder of exercised power. Secondly . . . the collection, by its new existence, begins also to generate a representational reality of its own. The collection has become both a recurrent claim of possession, and itself the object of possession, embodied and encased .

Consequently, as Native worlds became fashioned through museum display in the public consciousness, the emergent cultural object in Western institutions quickly succumbed to new symbolic orders and attributes. While much can be said about classification and representation in museums, the common acceptance of these practices as a means to codify and authenticate material culture is principally and inherently ethnocentric. Through the processes of removal and appropriation, a reduction occurs in which culturally constructed meanings and their original connotations are neutralized and replaced with institutionally sanctioned bodies of knowledge (Nespor 1989). Thus, object identities are created and recreated both as a matter of convenience and conformity.

At sites where cultures intersect, such as museums, the mobilization of meaning and ritual expression often loom larger than life when originating cultures assert claims of authenticity and authority over objects. More often than not, these indigenous claims are counter-hegemonic since they often arise out of lived cultural realities that exist outside the boundaries of the museum. As a result, the exclusive domains of property, representation, and control that constitute the common, everyday functions of the museum are directly challenged, thus calling into question traditional museum policies and practice.

Clearly, then, as the emergent dialogue suggests, the Native community maintains a distinctive non-Western view of their material culture. It includes the perception that cultural objects have enduring symbolic qualities and attributes that are of immense importance to present day communities. It also includes the notion that certain objects are imbued with power or possess sacredness and have the capacity to mobilize community histories, ritual, and cultural institutions. Within the Native community, objects are often perceived as locales of transcendent meaning and purpose apart from the normative importance of their physicality and form.

The indigenous ontologies that inform Native material culture warrant further consideration in the context of contemporary Native community/museum relations. The interactions currently taking place between Native communities and museums supports the assertion that cultural objects are embedded in social systems of meaning that transcend time, space and the hierarchy of the institution. For example, it is quite common for Native communities to take the opportunity of unrestricted access to museum collections as an occasion for the re-establishment of "relations" with certain objects or to engage in specific traditional cultural protocols. By applying the notion of indigenous curation to these symbolic forms of behavior and the methods of treatment and care they produce, Native people's and museum interactions are rendered meaningful in new and important ways.

In discussion of indigenous curation, a useful distinction can be made between "usage claims" (that is, rights and obligations) with respect to the appropriate disposition of sacred materials, on the one hand, and claims based solely on a "cultural property" interest, on the other. The fact that usage claims are consistently articulated in Native/museum interactions implies that the tribal care and handling of sacred objects are just as important, if not more so, than their status as potential objects of repatriation. In other words, as Native communities obtain greater access to museum collections to identify sacred material, an enactment of obligations towards the objects in question will often act as a minimum threshold in the actualization of rights concerning these types of objects. In the following example, I hope to clarify this point.

CURATORIAL ASPECTS OF MEDICINE BUNDLES

To describe medicine bundles and their attendant usage beliefs and practices requires at least a cursory understanding of the medicine bundle complex as a whole. Therefore, it is necessary to summarize the ritual processes in which medicine bundles operate and elaborate on those specific conditions that contribute to their formation and continued maintenance as material and symbolic entities.

The current and most prevalent contexts in which medicine bundles originate are those associated with transcendent power. Power, commonly perceived as an all-pervasive aspect of creation, is often manifested in the human realm through a complex series of encounters between its most primal sources and the human receiver. Though it is often viewed as an innate principle, most ethnographic descriptions of power tend to suggest that it is unevenly distributed and concentrated in sources that are either unique or shared among particular tribal groups. Such sources include geographic locales, natural and celestial phenomena, certain animals and plants, and animate and inanimate objects. The most common manner in which power is accessed and manifested is through a process of power transfer that may be either direct or indirect, and which often occurs under conditions of ritual observance. According to Harrod (1987:29):

> Power is mediated by the being or beings who appear in the vision. This notion of "transfer" is of central importance in the vision experience. Without the transfer, humans would not come to share in the power that is available (Harrod 1987:29).

As it relates to the specific origins of medicine bundles and their material aspects, however, power transfer can be seen as comprising two general types referred to as primary and secondary power transfer (Harrod 1987:30). These types are introduced here as an attempt to characterize the qualitative, experiential aspects of medicine bundle usage and the ritual forms they produce. Here, the primary type wholly emphasizes the experiential domain of the power transfer itself as it is celebrated both in the originating vision of a recipient individual or in the mythic creation or heroic emergence of the collectivity. The main distinction here is that the efficacy of the power transfer is always renewed and reproduced as originally entrusted in the vision experience, regardless of whether one is dealing with an individual, group, or tribal medicine bundle.

In the secondary type, the process of power transfer can be replicated. This occurs through what is called a "bundle transfer," such as a sanctioned purchase, duplication, or inheritance, and is usually applied only in the case of individual and group medicine bundles. A successful bundle transfer is achieved when the powers inherent in the originating vision becomes active in the experience of the recipient. Despite the corporeality of medicine bundles, they were also seen to possess intangible or incorporeal aspects such as songs, speech acts, visual representations, and attendant ritualization, which form the symbolic core of the medicine bundle as a whole (Richert 1969).

The notion of primary and secondary power transfer as it is embodied in sacred material may well be viewed in the larger context of a "visionary episteme" where the mythic structures of the visionary and the world of explicit phenomena unfold in a world-revealing process (Irwin 1994). The experiential dimension this process elicits can be understood in reference to sacred objects and the social spaces they occupy. Understandably, as our attention becomes focused on the movement of ritual objects across time and space, we can begin to appreciate the fundamental human capacity to "recreate and represent the world" through the origin, arrangement, and use of these objects (Kemnitzer 1970).

Insofar as medicine bundles are common items in museum collections, the appropriateness of the discussion of power transfer is important in that it serves to establish the concept of traditional usage rights and obligations that arise from and are ritually sanctioned by the power transfer itself as opposed to the rights emanating from Western legal concepts of ownership. Traditional usage rights and obligations are those prescriptive and proscriptive actions that grant access to power and transcendent meaning. In most cases, medicine bundle usage rights and obligations are a form of sacred trust and are appropriately maintained by designated ritual specialists, commonly called *keepers*.

Because of the experiential magnitude the power transfer produces and transposes on its recipient, whether the individual or the collective, the acquisition, retention, and control of this power is of vital importance. This is especially significant given that medicine bundles, by their very nature, serve as a kind of "repository for the transfer of supernatural power" (Hanson 1980). The crucial dilemma that Native peoples face is the fact that some of these medicine bundles, as well as other sacred objects, are no longer in their possession but rather in that of museums. Such items are of great concern since they are a result of originating power transfers and in many instances remain full of power and potency. In addition, Native communities are now required to divulge sacred and esoteric forms of knowledge to substantiate their claim to these items or to ensure the appropriate disposition of such objects, often without the guarantee of the protection of that knowledge.

Without question, the removal of sacred materials from the Native community constitutes a tremendous loss because it has been intrusive into Native religious life and further limits the ability of traditional religious practitioners to maintain the necessary ritual control, maintenance and appropriate care of such objects for the benefit of Native communities. Inadvertent or unnecessary handling of sacred materials and permanent preservation are commonplace occurrences in museums. This situation is beginning to change, however. Traditional religious practitioners are now beginning to experience greater freedom to introduce and apply indigenous forms of curation within the museum. As indigenous curators, they bring to the museum a newly added dimension of human potential and experience that is testimony to the immediacy, vitality and power of objects to mediate the lived, everyday world we have now come to share.

CONCLUSION

The postmodern challenge that calls for the inclusion of indigenous curation practice in the museum world obviously strikes at the very core of the museum discipline and its curatorial enterprise. It cannot be emphasized enough, however, that the collaborative intent of this inclusion rests upon the ability of Native communities and museums to take a proactive stance in recognizing their shared responsibilities in the preservation of material culture. To a certain extent, these shared responsibilities also include negotiation and compromise. Experience is beginning to show that the mutual benefits of cross-cultural collaboration greatly enhance the working relationship between the indigenous community and museums (Herle 1993, 1994).

As I have argued, curation practice is situated within the context of social relations and is as much a political act as a cultural one. So long as curation is maintained as the privileged enterprise of the museum institution, it is reasonable to conclude that its categories and contradictions will inspire opposition. By restoring curation to a larger conceptual framework, we can begin to account for the direct experiences of individuals and cultures whose ontology is deeply embedded in the things we call "museum specimens." Most important of all, true cultural renewal is now a real possibility.

NOTES

1. This definition has been largely influenced by readings taken from Giddens (1990).

REFERENCES CITED

Giddens, Anthony. 1990. *Central Problems In Social Theory.* Los Angeles: University of California Press.

Hanson, Jeffrey R. 1980. "Structure and complexity of medicine bundle systems of selected Plains Indian tribes." *Plains Anthropologist* 25:199–216.

Harrod, Howard L. 1987. *Renewing the World, Plains Indian Religion and Morality.* Tucson: University of Arizona Press.

Herle, Anita. 1993. "Shaman insights." *Museum Journal*, December, p. 24.

——— 1994. "Museums and shamans: A cross cultural collaboration." *Anthropology Today* 10(1):2–5.

Hinsley, Curtis M. 1993. "Collecting cultures and cultures of collecting: The lure of the American Southwest, 1880–1915." *Museum Anthropology* 16(1):12–20.

Irwin, Lee. 1994. "Dreams, theory, and culture: The Plains vision quest paradigm." *American Indian Quarterly* 18(2):229–245.

Kemnitzer, Luis S. 1970. "The cultural provenience of objects used in Yuwipi: A modern Teton Dakota healing ritual." *Ethnos* 35:40–75.

Lurie, Nancy O. 1988. "Relations between Indians and anthropologists." In *Handbook of North American Indians, Vol. 4*, edited by William Sturtevant, pp.548–556. Washington, D.C.: Smithsonian Institution Press.

Murdoch, John. 1992. "Defining curation." *Museum Journal*, March, pp.18–19.

Nespor, Jan. 1989. "Strategies of discourse and knowledge use in the practice of bureaucratic research." *Human Organization* 48(4):325–332.

Richert, Bernard E. 1969. *Plains Indian Medicine Bundles.* M.A. Thesis. Austin: University of Texas.

FUTURE PROSPECTS

CHAPTER ELEVEN

On the Course of Repatriation
Process, Practice, and Progress at the National Museum of Natural History

THOMAS W. KILLION

Repatriation legislation, now ten years old, has fundamentally and forever altered the treatment of Native American remains and objects held by museums and other repositories in the United States. Initially, it was the quest for the origins of Native Americans, undertaken almost exclusively by Euro-americans, that brought institutions like the Smithsonian into being (cf. Hinsley 1981). Ironically, this quest now seems to have come full circle. Indian participation in museum studies, mainstream archaeology, and the exploration of tribal origins and history has been expanding at a rapid rate (Echo-Hawk 1997; Handsman and Richmond 1995; Hill and Hill 1994; Merrill et al. 1993; Minthorn 1997; Swidler et al. 1997; Watkins et al. 1995). This acceleration may be attributed, in large part, to the repatriation mandate.

The two principal repatriation laws, (the *National Museum of the American Indian Act*, 20 U.S.C. 80q [P.L. 101-185], and the *Native American Graves Protection and Repatriation Act*, 25 U.S.C. 3001 [P.L. 101-601]) require institutions funded by the federal government to disclose the nature and extent of their Native American collections. The laws also oblige these institutions to enter into consultation with affiliated tribes over the final disposition of remains and culturally sensitive items (see Appendices 1 and 2, this volume; Flynn and Killion 1997). The repatriation mandate is slowly but steadily changing the way that museums and anthropologists do business in this country.

Repatriation legislation was passed to address long-standing concerns of Native Americans regarding the study, public presentation, and disposition of their ancestral remains and cultural heritage. In many ways, however, this legislation seems to have created more controversy and conflict than it has resolved. Museum professionals and Native representatives alike agree that the implementation of this law has proceeded at a glacial pace. Procedures and policies are often unclear and seem to vary randomly from institution to institution, while the resources allocated to achieve the goals of repatriation are woefully inadequate.

Dire predictions for the fate of science and the freedom of inquiry heralded the passage of repatriation legislation (Meighan 1984, 1992a, 1992b; Jones and

Harris 1997; Morell 1995). Pitched battles erupted between Indians and museum anthropologists over the identity of remains and their relationship to contemporary tribes (Billeck and Urcid 1995; Bray and Killion 1994). Arguments over the right of museums and other agencies to document and determine the cultural origins of remains have landed Native and scientific disputants in court (c.f. U.S. Court for the District of Hawaii, 1996; U.S. Court for the District of Oregon, 1996). Disagreements about the sacred or patrimonial status of objects impacted by repatriation legislation have led to litigation and animosity among the parties (c.f. U.S. Court for the District of Rhode Island, 1996). While honestly seeking the benefits of partnership, dialogue, collaboration, disclosure, renewal, consent, empowerment, and engagement, one suspects that many of the institutional players in the "repatriation game" must secretly wish that the issue would just go away. Having worked in the trenches of the National Museum of Natural History's (NMNH) Repatriation Program for the last several years, I can certainly appreciate that sentiment.

But my experience to date generally teaches one simple lesson: repatriation is a process. In any given repatriation case, there is rarely a clear path from the beginning to the end of that process. What at first appears to be a formidable (if not intractable) situation inevitably yields to the commitment and persistence of the parties involved. Potential adversaries, often strangers to one another, cautiously engage in discussion. Information is shared, ground rules are laid, and time tables are established. People miscommunicate and get angry, information is generated and reviewed, decisions are reached, requests for returns are resolved, and the intent of the law is eventually fulfilled. Through this process, which includes the preparation of inventories, physical documentation of the remains and objects in question, and consultations with tribal representatives, much new data about museum collections is being generated.

The repatriation mandate has also created unprecedented levels of access to museum collections for Native people. Native American participation in the life of the Smithsonian's National Museum of Natural History, in fact, has never been greater. Over 60 tribal representatives visited the NMNH in 1997 alone to attend informational meetings, engage in consultations, oversee returns, and conduct other repatriation-related research. This represents a significant increase over past levels of Native American involvement. In fact, repatriation and its numerous collateral activities in collections management, the National Anthropological Archives, exhibits, education, outreach, and research have become one of the principal forms of communication between the Museum and Native American communities.

Repatriation cases always have their unique problems and character but the process itself, the procedures for evaluating claims, documenting remains and objects, interacting with tribal representatives, and arranging for returns or alternatives to repatriation, have become a regular activity in the life of the Museum. Part of the process of "normalizing" relations between museums and Indian peoples that has grown out of the repatriation effort has required a certain amount of coming to terms with history. It has frequently been suggested that contemporary archaeologists are not responsible for the sins of the past and that there is no moral connection between the events of former times and the burning research questions of today. Rather, it is argued that "what is important is the rationale for the proposed scientific work, the quality of the work, and its potential value to the wider human community" (Jones and Harris 1997:15).

While this statement is laudable and certainly deserving of support, it is also somewhat naïve. As anthropologists we cannot detach ourselves from history. The past carries with it a burden that must be openly acknowledged and addressed. Nor should working through the historical transgressions of the discipline be seen as the exclusive domain of repatriation. Rather, such efforts are of critical importance to the continued growth of anthropology as a whole.

Repatriation is, at times, painful and culturally challenging. This is exemplified in a number of returns undertaken by the Smithsonian that have involved human remains dating to the historic period. The Cheyenne repatriation, for instance, required tribal members and museum personnel to revisit the tragic, government-sanctioned injustices that resulted in the massacre at Sand Creek (Killion et al. 1992; Powell 1981; Svaldi 1989). Other such returns of historic period remains have involved victims of the Apache massacres in Arizona (Speaker 1993); the remains of friendly Pawnee Scouts slain in an ambush in Nebraska (Baugh and Makseyn-Kelly 1992; Riding In 1989, 1992); a Shoshone family and its patriarch, Old Mike, who were tracked down and murdered by a Nevada posse in 1911 (Bray et al. 1992); and victims of the sorrowful events of 1898 at Wounded Knee in South Dakota (Smythe 1998). These returns have required all involved to revisit and re-evaluate some of the darkest moments of American history. Reviewing the fate of these individuals and the circumstances under which their remains came to be in the possession of the Museum illuminates old history in new and often profound ways. Presumably this exercise can invigorate a reassessment of the past in much the same way that the Holocaust Museum confronts us with the genocide of World War II.

Equally important is the fact that much of the documentation required for the repatriation of these historic remains plunges us into a critical period of Native American history that is not well studied or understood by scholars. With a few notable exceptions (Svaldi 1989; Thornton 1987), the details of depopulation and survival among Native American groups are generally ignored in contemporary surveys of American history and often overlooked as a focus of problem-oriented anthropological research. This period is central to both Native and American history, however, and is clearly critical to our understanding of the repatriation movement and its present course.

In what follows, I offer a discussion of how relations among museums, Native Americans, and anthropologists are beginning to reach an equilibrium within the context of repatriation. It is a process that I have been observing for the past several years as Director of the Repatriation Office at the National Museum of Natural History. For simplicity's sake, I focus specifically on the inventory, documentation, and repatriation of human remains and funerary objects. As mandated by the *National Museum of the American Indian* (NMAI) Act of 1989, 20 U.S.C. 80q (PL 101-185) under which the Smithsonian operates, these items were to be given priority in repatriation efforts at the Museum.[1]

As an introduction to what I refer to as "the normalization process" at the National Museum of Natural History, I look first at what repatriation efforts there have accomplished to date, focusing mainly on cases already completed. To address concerns about the effect of repatriation legislation on the conduct of science and the integrity of museum resources, I examine the impact repatriation has had on the Museum's collections to this point. Next I discuss several specific repatriation cases at the NMNH. These case studies illuminate the variability inherent in the repatriation process. At the same time, they reveal the landmarks and procedures emerging through practice that are beginning to provide a framework for the normalization of the process. In conclusion, I suggest that the effects of repatriation on the conduct of science may be brighter than many commentators have heretofore suggested. While the specific course and outcomes of individual repatriation cases may be unpredictable, the process itself is inevitable and is slowly taking on the trappings of normality within the museum.

REPATRIATION AT THE NATIONAL MUSEUM OF NATURAL HISTORY

The priority in repatriation at the NMNH, thus far, has been to inventory, document, and return culturally affiliated human remains and funerary objects, beginning with those that were most readily identifiable as affiliated with contemporary tribes. This is in accordance with the repatriation provisions of the NMAI Act (1989), the first repatriation legislation passed by Congress. In addition to establishing a National Museum of the American Indian, this Act explicitly mandated that the Smithsonian Institution inventory and assess the cultural affiliation of all Indian remains and funerary objects in its possession and that culturally identifiable remains be repatriated to affiliated groups upon request.

At the time this law was passed, the National Museum of Natural History had in its possession some 18,400 sets of remains identified as Native American.[2] This represented roughly 50 percent of the total number of remains in the collections of the Physical Anthropology division of the Department of Anthropology at the NMNH. It was the intent of the legislators to have the Smithsonian deal first with this collection, the largest assemblage of Native American human remains in the country. The repatriation provisions in the NMAI Act were included in direct response to the demands of the Native American community. Native activists and spokespersons had made it clear that it was the human remains that were of paramount concern to them. The retention of such remains in institutions was a hurtful reminder of the unequal treatment accorded Native burial grounds in light of laws that had protected most non-Native cemeteries in the United States since the nineteenth-century.

The *Native American Graves Protection and Repatriation Act* (NAGPRA), 25 U.S.C. 3001 (P.L. 101-601), passed the following year in 1990. It extended protections to Native graves found on federal lands and issued a repatriation directive similar to the one governing the Smithsonian to all other federally-funded museums, universities, and organizations. NAGPRA broadened the scope of repatriation beyond human remains and funerary objects to include items considered to be culturally sensitive. The NAGPRA legislation required museums to prepare written summaries of their ethnographic holdings by the beginning of 1993. The intent of these summaries was to provide tribes with sufficient information to make preliminary determinations about the presence of sacred or patrimonial objects in different collections. The legislation also mandated that museums produce an inventory of Native American skeletal remains and funerary objects in their possession by the beginning of 1995.

The Smithsonian Institution was specifically exempted from NAGPRA because it was already bound by the repatriation provisions of a pre-existing law. The legislation under which the Smithsonian operated, however, provided no deadlines for compliance, nor did it contain any provision for the repatriation of sacred objects or items of cultural patrimony. To bring the Smithsonian more into line with NAGPRA, the NMAI Act was amended in 1996 (P.L. 104-278). Among other changes, the Amendment required the NMNH to complete NAGPRA-like summaries of all objects in its ethnographic collections by December 31, 1996. The summaries, consisting of item by item listings of all Native American objects in the Smithsonian's collections, provided a starting point for tribal identification of objects of interest. Consultations with tribal representatives to identify sacred and patrimonial objects have steadily increased since these summaries were distributed. The Amendment also required that inventories of human remains and all Native American objects in the Museum's archaeological collections be completed and distributed to federally recognized tribes by June 1, 1998.

It is important to note that although explicit deadlines were established in this Amendment, the Museum had already completed much of the inventory process. Reports, summaries, and inventories of all classes of cultural items had already been sent to over 150 tribes as part of the Museum's voluntary compliance policy with the broader repatriation legislation. In addition, the NMNH had been responding to Native requests for information and repatriating remains and objects since 1984, well before the passage of any relevant legislation (cf. Merrill et al. 1993).

The Repatriation Office at the NMNH was established in 1991 in response to the NMAI Act. While it was initially under the administration of the Museum Director's Office, the Repatriation Office was subsequently moved to the Department of Anthropology. This office works in close coordination with curatorial and collections management staff of Anthropology to produce the required inventories and summaries, document the collections affected, and conduct the actual returns.

Since its inception, the Repatriation Office has received 80 official requests for returns from Native groups. A total of 53 repatriations have been completed to date and more than 4000 sets of Native American remains and associated funerary objects have been returned for reburial to culturally affiliated tribes. Another 1,500 sets of remains are presently scheduled to be repatriated to several Plains Indian tribes. This will bring the total number of repatriated remains to more than 5,500 individuals amounting to an average return rate of 600 sets of remains per year. This figure represents approximately thirty percent of the total number of human remains potentially subject to repatriation in the NMNH.

Projections based on other cases currently in progress indicate that another 1,500 sets of remains will likely be returned over the next few years. It is also expected that the inventories distributed in 1998 will generate additional requests and may further increase the number of repatriations. Dealing with these future requests, which will include negotiations over the disposition of "culturally unidentifiable" Native American remains, will continue for some time after 2000.

The identification of sacred and patrimonial objects within the collections of the NMNH will also continue. The number of consultations and requests for the return of culturally sensitive objects have increased significantly since collections summaries were distributed to tribes in 1996. The Museum has, to date, returned sacred and patrimonial objects to the Zuni and Haudenosaunee (Iroquois) and is currently addressing the repatriation requests of another four groups from the Great Plains, the Pacific Northwest, northern Michigan, and Alaska.

REPATRIATION NATION-WIDE

Because of the funding included within the provisions of the NMAI Act, the repatriation effort has, not surprisingly, been more extensive and proceeded at a faster rate at the National Museum of Natural History than any other institution nationwide. Nonetheless, it is still important to look at how repatriation is progressing elsewhere. Unfortunately, there are no comprehensive statistics yet available on the total number of human remains returned in the United States. In fact, we may never know exactly how many human remains are actually transferred to tribes due to the size and complexity of the overall task.

The Archaeological Assistance Division of the National Park Service is responsible for the oversight and implementation of the NAGPRA legislation. It monitors information provided to tribes by museums, federal agencies, and other organizations by tracking inventory completions and publishing notifications of intent to repatriate in the *Federal Register*. NAGPRA inventories completed to date have reported on approximately 100,000 sets of remains. Of these, about 10,000 are of known cultural affiliation and thus presumably available for return to tribes upon request. At present, however, there is no mechanism in place for documenting whether any of these remains have actually been repatriated.

It also is not clear how many of these remains have been adequately identified with respect to their cultural origins. Some institutions have simply labelled large groups of remains from the southwest, for instance, as culturally "Puebloan." To which federally recognized tribe in this region would these remains be returned? Without additional study and consultations with potentially affiliated tribes, it is difficult to say. In some parts of the country, tribes have formed consortiums to take responsibility for these less specifically identified cultural groupings.

Some of the larger natural history museums with substantial collections of human remains (5,000–15,000) have requested extensions and will not be submitting inventories for another one to two years. It is impossible to predict how many culturally affiliated remains will be identified as part of this process or, once identified, how many will be returned. The Peabody Museum of Harvard University graciously agreed to share the information they have available on their inventory process and the number of returns completed to date to provide some comparative perspective.

The Peabody Museum has 12,000 sets of human remains, of which twenty-five percent have thus far been inventoried. By 1998, 211 individuals had been offered for repatriation and 178 have actually been transferred to the custody of the tribes. Museum personnel at the Peabody report that the inventory process has been complicated by the fact that their osteological collections come from numerous sites around the country. The situation at the Peabody is likely to be indicative of the way other institutions with large collections are faring under NAGPRA, where the repatriation effort must be undertaken as an unfunded mandate.

In sum, the only statistic presently available on the impact of NAGPRA legislation on museum collections nation-wide suggests that approximately ten percent of the total number of skeletal remains housed in institutions other than the Smithsonian are eligible for return. What percentage of these have actually been repatriated is not known.

Another important issue facing museums is the problem of "unidentifiable" remains. Differences between scientists and native groups on how to handle such remains will not be resolved until there is clarification on the final disposition of all aboriginal remains recovered from proveniences within the United States. Final resolution of this issue may only be possible through additional legislation. Ongoing discussions between Native, scientific, and museum constituencies involved in repatriation have yet to yield a solution acceptable to all parties. At the NMNH, we found that Plains Indian tribes were most concerned with recovering remains that date from the last 1,000 years (Billeck et al. 1995). In other regions, Native groups are claiming remains that date to much more remote time periods. Given the present polarization over the cultural identity of Kennewick Man (Chatters 1997; Slayman 1997), it would appear that we are still far from consensus on the temporal limits of NAGPRA or the methods and procedures to be utilized in assessing the cultural affiliation of human remains.

PROCESS AND PRACTICE AT THE NATIONAL MUSEUM OF NATIONAL HISTORY

Skeletal remains originally collected for the Army Medical Museum (AMM) in the nineteenth century and subsequently transferred the NMNH represent some of the most politically sensitive items in the Museum's collections. The AMM collection contained the remains of some 2000 individuals recovered by military surgeons and civilian travelers in the Western territories. Some of these remains were taken in the course of military action against Native communities; many were clandestinely removed from Native graves. These remains were collected in response to a circular distributed by the Surgeon General of the U.S. Army directing military personnel to collect remains from Indian territories (Bieder 1990, 1992). The antiquarian and racist roots of human osteological research and collection practices of the nineteenth-century have been widely discussed and well documented in various works (Bieder 1986, 1996; Trigger 1989).

Although the AMM collection at the Smithsonian was potentially invaluable for contemporary biomedical research, these remains were given priority when the repatriation effort got underway at the NMNH due to the manner in which they had been acquired and the strong emotion they evoked in descendant groups. Since 1991, returns of remains from the AMM collection have been made to the Apache, Arapaho, Cheyenne, Clallam, Paiute, Pawnee, Shoshone-Bannock, Spokane, Sioux, Yakama, and Warm Springs groups, among others. Details of the Cheyenne and Pawnee returns discussed below highlight some of the substantive results and lessons learned from the repatriation process.

THE CHEYENNE REPATRIATION: NAEVAHOO'OHTSEME ("WE ARE GOING BACK HOME")

One of the earlier repatriations at the NMNH involved the return of human remains to the northern and southern divisions of the Cheyenne. This case quickly revealed that repatriation at the NMNH was not going to be a straightforward process (Killion et al. 1992). At the same time, the Cheyenne return became a model for the kind of collaboration that can develop within the context of repatriation.

All of the Cheyenne remains in the NMNH dated to the historic period and had been collected for the AMM by Army surgeons and other government personnel stationed at forts in the central and northern Plains between 1860 and the late 1890s. These collections included victims of the Sand Creek Massacre (Svaldi 1989) and the Fort Robinson Breakout (Powell 1981), as well as a number of other less well-documented remains from different locations. The Sand Creek and Fort Robinson incidents were both seminal events in Cheyenne history and involved some of the most important political and military figures in the history of the tribe. In both incidents, the majority of the victims were women and children (Congressional Hearing, 1865). The modern descendants of the Sand Creek and Fort Robinson victims are only four or five generations removed from these individuals and the memory of the events in which these people lost their lives is still very strong.

The Smithsonian received requests for the return of the Cheyenne victims of the Sand Creek massacre immediately after passage of the NMAI Act in 1989. This request clearly required prompt action and was given high priority at the NMNH. Unfortunately, no sooner had the Repatriation Office set to work on the case than it ran into difficulties as religious and governmental authorities from both the Oklahoma and Montana divisions of the Cheyenne began to argue over which group or groups within the tribe should take responsibility for the return. This quickly evolved into a situation in which the Museum was confronted with multiple claims from different factions within the same federally recognized tribe.

The intra-tribal disagreement was exacerbated by claims pending against the U.S. government for restitution of property lost during the Sand Creek Massacre, and by an ongoing controversy between the northern and southern divisions of the tribe over religious leadership. Although different Cheyenne factions vigorously and repeatedly claimed authority to handle the repatriations, the NMNH refrained from making final arrangements for returns until religious leaders and tribal officials had resolved their internal differences. Once a unified agreement had been reached within the tribe and forwarded to the Museum, separate repatriations to both the Northern and Southern Cheyenne quickly followed.

Part of the collection offered for return to the southern Cheyenne represented the funerary objects recovered from a rare child's scaffold burial. This scaffold
burial had been located next to a Sun Dance ground raised by the Cheyenne in
the summer of 1868, during the height of one of the tribe's most violent periods
of conflict with the military and civilian population on the Central Plains. The
funerary items were initially offered for return to the Cheyenne as unassociated
funerary objects (the child's skeletal remains had long since been lost by the Army
Medical Museum). Upon viewing these objects, Cheyenne elders decided to leave
them in the care of the Museum in order to preserve them for the future. In
explaining their thinking, the elders indicated that they wanted to use these items
to teach contemporary Cheyenne youth about the value and importance their
ancestors had accorded a single child even during times of great social stress and
violence.

The tribe and the Museum subsequently signed a formal agreement officially recognizing the shared curatorship for the items and stipulating Cheyenne
involvement in all future decisions concerning their disposition (*see* Appendix 3).
The objects were moved to a separate storage area apart from other Cheyenne
ethnographic materials to avoid indiscriminate browsing that might occur during
unrelated research. The Museum is currently working with the tribe to develop a
special exhibit focusing on children and Cheyenne family life during the late
nineteenth-century that will showcase these funerary items and other ethnographic material from this time period. This exhibit will open in Oklahoma, the
present-day home of the Southern Cheyenne, and eventually travel back to
Washington, D.C. All aspects of the proposed exhibit, including fund-raising,
design, and final development, will be carried out in a collaborative manner and
on the basis of a mutually agreeable curation policy.

THE PAWNEE REPATRIATION: DISPUTE AND RESOLUTION

The process of documentation in response to requests for the return of more
ancient remains can be difficult and protracted. The consultation provisions of the
NMAI Act mandate that the Museum be able to evaluate all available sources of
information and that tribal representatives have full access to the determination
process. Adversarial positions are equally as likely to develop under such circumstances as are collaborative ones. In many cases, the documentation process
reveals the inadequacy of existing data, methods, and theory for determining cultural affiliation. At other times, the resolution of a repatriation request can
unearth new sources of information and engender wider participation in the decision-making process.

In responding to repatriation requests, the Repatriation Office at the NMNH
has completed some of the most detailed reviews to date of existing archaeological, biological, and linguistic evidence for purposes of assessing cultural affiliation. In addition, traditional knowledge and history offered by tribes has played
an important role in resolving claims that have been disputed on the basis of the
archaeological information. The final resolution of such cases has the effect of
legitimating new forms of evidence and underscores the necessity of broad consultation with all potentially affiliated groups during the repatriation process.

A request for the return of ancestral remains presented by the Pawnee Tribe of Oklahoma illustrates the importance of traditional Native histories in the resolution of disputed claims.[3] The original request from the Pawnee was based on an inventory of the NMNH skeletal collections completed by a tribal representative (Echo-Hawk 1990) and separate analysis of the remains of six Pawnee scouts prepared by a Pawnee historian (Riding In 1989). A report recommending the repatriation of the scouts and other historic period Pawnee remains was sent to the tribe in 1993 (Baugh and Makseyn-Kelly 1992). The Pawnee acknowledged the Museum's intent to repatriate these historic remains. Rather than taking possession of these immediately, however, they asserted their right to recover all northern Caddoan ancestral remains, including some 25 individuals from the Central Plains Tradition dating from about A.D. 1,000 to A.D. 1,500 (Billeck et al. 1995).

The question of Pawnee/Arikara/Wichita affiliation with the Central Plains Tradition has been debated for many years amongst Plains archaeologists. Various scholars have argued both for and against the cultural continuity of the historical tribes with the archaeologically defined cultures of the earlier time periods. Evidence from a variety of sources, including settlement pattern studies, material culture studies, linguistic data, and biological measures of population distance based on skull shape, had been marshaled in these debates (Billeck et al. 1995). Disagreements stem from the fact that a hiatus exists in the archaeological record during the latter half of the period in question. This has led some scholars to doubt that the Pawnee and their linguistic cousins are actually the descendants of the people identified with the Central Plains Tradition of Nebraska and Kansas. Repatriation documentation efforts in the Pawnee case relied on this large body of existing information. Following a legal decision in Nebraska favoring the tribes, however, the NMNH ended up agreeing with the Pawnee's assertion that the preponderance of existing evidence argued for northern Caddoan affiliation with the remains from the Central Plains Tradition.

In the process of reviewing the inventory of Central Plains materials provided by the NMNH, the Pawnee became aware of additional skeletal remains in the Museum pertaining to the coeval Steed-Kisker phase. This archaeological culture is found at the eastern edge of the Central Plains Tradition near present day Saint Joseph, Missouri. The Pawnee subsequently revised their claim to include these remains as well on the basis of their interpretation that the Steed-Kisker phase was actually a component of the Central Plains Tradition that had already been identified as ancestral northern Caddoan. Following a review of biological (craniometric) data, archaeological information, and traditional history, the Repatriation Office concluded that the available information did not indicate that the Pawnee were any more culturally affiliated with these remains than were several other potentially descendant tribes (Billeck and Urcid 1995).

Having reached an impasse on how to handle the Steed-Kisker remains, the Pawnee and the Museum subsequently agreed to put the dispute before the NMNH Repatriation Review Committee for resolution. The NMNH Repatriation Review Committee is charged with monitoring the Museum's compliance with the repatriation legislation and facilitating the resolution of disputes that may arise in the process. The Committee, which advises the Secretary of the Smithsonian on repatriation issues, was originally composed of five individuals, three of whom were nominated by federally recognized tribes.[4]

After reviewing extensive supporting documentation provided by the both tribe and the Museum, the Committee agreed with the Pawnee, based on the legislatively defined standard of preponderance of available evidence, that the Steed-Kisker remains were affiliated with the Central Plains Tradition and the northern Caddoan descendants, among whom are included the Pawnee, Arikara, and Wichita. The Committee also noted that while some of the archaeological information suggested affiliation with traditions other than the Central Plains, conventional sources of archaeological, bioanthropological, and linguistic evidence were either irrelevant or too ambiguous to aid in assessing the strength of cultural affiliation under the law. The Committee decided unanimously that oral and traditional histories presented by the tribe argued persuasively for inclusion of the Steed-Kisker materials within the Central Plains Tradition. The Committee recommended, on the basis of the Museum's earlier decision to return the Central Plains Tradition remains to the Pawnee, Arikara, and Wichita consortium, that the Steed-Kisker remains and associated funerary objects be repatriated to this group as well.

A final recommendation of the Committee in the Steed-Kisker case was that other potentially descendant tribes identified through the documentation effort be informed of the Committee's decision and permitted sufficient time to respond should they disagree with the decision to return the Steed-Kisker remains to the exclusive control of the Pawnee-led consortium. Several tribes, including the Kansa, Omaha, Otoe-Missouria, Osage, and Ponca, subsequently petitioned for time to evaluate the Committee's decision. All, with the exception of the Osage, eventually signed a cooperative agreement to take joint responsibility for the return and the remains were re-buried at a location in Missouri near the original Steed-Kisker site in the fall of 1997.

Three important precedents were affirmed as the result of Steed-Kisker case. First, the evidence of oral and traditional history was confirmed as an important and relevant source of information in the determination of cultural affiliation in repatriation cases. This case also affirmed that the tribal histories and legitimate concerns of other potentially affiliated groups must be taken into account as well. Second, although the resolution of the Pawnee request for the Steed-Kisker remains identified weaknesses in conventional sources of archaeological, biological, and linguistic evidence, it was also determined that a consideration of these forms of evidence is fundamental to the repatriation process. It also demonstrated how our understanding of cultural history can be further expanded through this process. Questions for future research, based on the problems identified by an inclusive set of interested parties, have been generated and could be pursued by anthropologists and Native communities in a collaborative fashion. Finally, a process was established for the resolution of conflicting opinions in claims for the repatriation of more distant time periods on the basis of available evidence. The acceptability of multi-tribal claims for the recovery of remains from these more distant time periods was affirmed and a process for considering all sources of information relevant to the question of ancient cultural affiliations was tested.

ALASKAN REPATRIATIONS: CONSULTATION AND CONSENT

Since 1993, the NMNH has received requests for the return of several large collections of human remains and funerary objects from Native groups in Alaska. These requests impacted more than 2,500 sets of remains and a large number of objects. Outreach to requesting groups, which typically includes numerous field consultations, provides the foundation for the task of repatriation in Alaska and elsewhere. As part of the outreach effort in this region, repatriation staff traveled to many Native Alaskan communities to discuss the Museum's policy of fully documenting the remains and objects potentially subject to repatriation and explain what the documentation procedures consist of. The NMNH documentation protocol is undertaken for purposes of determining, or sometimes confirming, cultural affiliation, and in order to create a comprehensive record of materials being deaccessioned from the Museum. During these visits, repatriation staff also tried to convey the Museum's views on the value of archaeological and physical anthropological data.

During consultations, several Native Alaskan groups expressed concerns about Museum policies regarding the physical examination of remains subject to repatriation. These concerns centered around issues of sensitivity and the expedience of the documentation procedures. Several groups challenged what the Museum saw as a legitimate need to create a permanent record of the repatriation process—one that includes an assessment of the character and condition of remains and objects returned. Native Alaskan groups stressed that the entire repatriation process should be open, consultative, and consensual among all parties involved. In response to these and other concerns, the documentation and reporting procedures employed by the NMNH have evolved to address the justifiable concerns of both the Museum and the Native groups involved, and they continue to do so.

The responses of the different Native Alaskan entities to the Museum's documentation policy illustrate both the problems and the potential of repatriation. The outcomes of these consultations vary from group to group and reflect the unique decisions of each community involved. In some cases, the Museum has been able to establish a foundation for future research collaboration. At Point Hope, for instance, Inupiaq community elders supported the policy that the full physical documentation protocol be completed at the NMNH prior to the return of remains. They also requested that additional information from both the protocol and earlier studies be provided as part of the final repatriation report (Mudar et al. 1996a). Other Native groups from the southern Seward Peninsula and Nunivak Island agreed to permit full documentation of the remains in question but wished to have the protocol completed by physical anthropologists at the University of Alaska in Fairbanks (Mudar et al. 1996b). The documentation procedures in these cases helped ascertain the cultural affiliation of remains recovered from the Inupiaq/Yupik linguistic borderland along Norton Sound. The documentation effort also created a permanent record of the re-buried remains that will benefit future generations who may someday need to access such information.

On St. Lawrence Island in the Bering Straits, though, a series of open meetings attended by repatriation staff, elected officials, elders, and interested community members resulted in a decision to curtail the physical documentation of the remains of victims of epidemics dating to the late nineteenth-century. By mutual agreement, these remains were only counted, sexed, and aged prior to their return (Mudar and Speaker 1997). Elsewhere, in Inupiaq communities along the Bering Sea coast of the northern Seward Peninsula, local leaders are still in the process of deciding how the Museum's documentation procedures can serve community interests in Native history and archaeology while at the same time respect and conform to traditional values concerning the treatment of the dead.

NATIVE AMERICAN HISTORY, SCIENCE, AND REPATRIATION: PROGRESS AND PROGNOSIS

Documentation of almost 8,000 sets of remains that will have been completed by the year 2000 in advance of repatriation has yielded a great deal of contextual information that otherwise might never have come to light. Reports and data bases generated through the repatriation process at the NMNH reveal information on cultural origins, circumstances of recovery and acquisition, and the physical condition of the remains. Many of these remains had been previously studied but at the NMNH, as at many other large museums, no systematic records have ever been created or maintained of the work completed by outside researchers. Through the process of repatriation, more data has become part of the Museum's permanent record than ever before. Repatriation has provided the first mechanism for assembling sufficient information on the skeletal remains to answer one of the most common questions of tribal representatives and the general public alike: What have you actually learned over the last 150 years?

This permanent record consists of a clear description of the remains themselves and why they were returned to which tribes. The repatriation inventories and summaries, in most cases, represent the first systematic catalogue of museum holdings ever provided to tribes. Physical observations on the remains themselves are evaluated along side other information found in catalogue and accession records, archival sources, and other locations to identify errors, confirm assumptions, and arrive at the best assessment of cultural affiliation possible. At the NMNH, for instance, we have found that about ten percent of the information contained in museum records that refers to cultural affiliation is incorrect. Other common errors found in the records includes information on age, sex, skeletal elements present, and cause of death. In addition to creating the Smithsonian's first comprehensive catalogue of Native American remains and objects, the documentation produced by the Repatriation Office at the NMNH also represents the principal source of information for future generations about how the Museum complied with the repatriation mandate. A complete listing of all of completed repatriation-related reports and activities at the NMNH can be found at the Smithsonian Institution website:
(http://www.nmnh.si.edu/anthro/repatriation/repat.html).

How has repatriation impacted bioanthropological research? It is impossible to evaluate this question in any comprehensive sense but some general observations can be made. In 1989, Ubelaker and Grant (1989:252) reviewed submissions to the *American Journal of Physical Anthropology* from the previous two years and found that 20 percent of manuscripts focused on skeletal anatomy or paleopathological topics. However, they included in this count papers that utilized data from collections not necessarily subject to NAGPRA, that is, collections from Europe, Africa, Asia, and South and Central America.

To better assess NAGPRA's impacts on physical anthropological research, another more recent study (Killion and Molloy 2000) reviewed papers published in the *American Journal of Physical Anthropology* between 1985 and 1996, to look specifically at those focusing on remains from the United States. The authors expected to see a change in the number of papers dealing with Native American remains in the years following the passage of NAGPRA. This was not the case, however. During the years between 1985 and 1989, papers dealing with Native American remains constituted six percent of the total papers published, while the number of such papers increased slightly to seven percent during the subsequent period between 1990 and 1996.

Killion and Molloy (2000: 114) offered two observations as a result of their preliminary review. First, relying on the American Journal of Physical Anthropology as a measure, they saw no quantifiable effect on publications focusing on Native American remains. Second, physical anthropological studies of Native American remains comprise a very small part of physical anthropological research as a whole. Together, these observations suggest not only that NAGPRA has not yet produced the dire consequences for research that were predicted before the passage of the act, but also that the number of studies based on Native American skeletal collections has been overestimated.

NAGPRA's potential effects on research have been of concern not only to physical anthropologists but to archaeologists as well. To gauge how NAGPRA might have affected bioarchaeological research, the same authors reviewed all papers published in *American Antiquity* between 1985 and 1996. From 1985 through 1989, only four percent of the total number of papers in this journal focused on Native American human remains; this figure climbed to seven percent between 1990 and 1996. While these percentages are small, there actually appears to have been a slight increase in the number of published studies of Native American remains in the years following NAGPRA. As in the case of the *American Journal of Physical Anthropology,* the data from *American Antiquity* suggest that bioarchaeological studies focusing exclusively on Native American human remains comprise a very small part of archaeological research overall, and that NAGPRA has yet to produce a deleterious effect on such studies.

While to date there appears to be no quantifiable affect on research in the years following the passage of NAGPRA, it is possible that this legislation has affected the kinds of research that may be conducted. Certainly destructive analyses, such as isotopic and DNA studies, must be approached more cautiously, and in many cases have been prohibited as a result of concerns over Native American sensitivities. However, the impact of such restrictions must be evaluated in terms of the importance of the data lost, and whether or not other types of information can mitigate that loss. For example, stable isotopic analysis of human bone can reveal important dietary information; but when such studies are not permitted, other methods can be used to fill in these gaps such as archaeobotanical and faunal analyses. As for DNA analysis, its utility for illuminating Native American history is sorely limited. Currently, DNA analysis is hampered by the absence of definable population specific genetic markers, i.e., it cannot be used to assign membership to a population; the difficulty of deriving DNA from skeletal remains; problems of laboratory contamination; and the prohibitive expense of the technique (Carlson et al. 1997). In sum, while destructive analyses have been curtailed due to NAGPRA, the data lost are either of questionable utility or can be supplemented through other types of analytical processes.

Many, but not all, tribes are strongly opposed to destructive testing. In 1993, a researcher from the University of Wisconsin approached the Repatriation Office at the NMNH with a request to take samples of bone collagen from individuals being readied for return to the Chugach Eskimos of Prince William Sound, Alaska. We recommended that the researcher contact the tribe directly, explain the importance of the research, and ask permission to take the samples. The point of the proposed study was to evaluate the impact of dietary changes on the health of Pacific Eskimo groups. After discussing the nature of her work with Chugach representatives, the researcher quickly received approval to take the necessary samples. Specific osteological studies of Alaskan collections have also been facilitated by the Repatriation Office in collaboration with the affiliated Native communities (Mudar et al. 1996b). In the Plains states, physical anthropologists have recently been given permission by tribes to study pathological conditions in skeletal remains in order to evaluate general health conditions before and after contact (Miller 1995). One suspects there are many more such examples and that there is much potential for collaborative research in the context of repatriation. This kind of engagement is an important way to begin building a solid foundation for community-supported archaeology and physical anthropology in the future.

CONCLUSION

In this paper I have attempted to evaluate the course of repatriation since the passage of legislation in 1989 and 1990. Much progress has been made since that point but much remains to be done. Repatriation has yet to shed its negative associations within museums and the discipline of anthropology. Equally, it has yet to live up to the expectations of Native Americans. To be sure, there is still much confusion and misunderstanding involved on all sides and some basic questions about implementation that remain unanswered.

One of the most pressing of these is the question of how far back in time is repatriation to extend? If that question is to be evaluated in terms of cultural affiliation with contemporary Native groups, what philosophy will guide that determination? What methods or procedures will be implemented to aid in these decisions? Ethnic identity, group boundaries, nationhood, sovereignty and other issues implicated in repatriation are important questions in contemporary anthropology and other disciplines. Trying to tackle these issues within the context of the archaeology alone, however, pushes the theoretical and methodological limits of the discipline. A legal framework for resolving these issues is still outstanding and clearly at odds with the sort of answers possible in the context of open-ended anthropological inquiry.

Final answers to the unresolved issues of repatriation may have to be solved in the political arena if the differences between the poles of pro- and anti-repatriation sentiments cannot be finally resolved through compromise. Some of the most difficult questions in repatriation, such as the fate of the "culturally unidentifiable," that were left unanswered when the repatriation laws were passed in 1989 and 1990 still haunt the implementation of this legislation and have, to date, defied compromise or regulatory solution.

At the same time, the repatriation process seems to be increasingly seen as an accepted and regular practice. In museums such as the Smithsonian, the inevitable result of ten years of documentation, consultations, and returns has brought a measure of normalcy to the process. The borders between repatriation, outreach, and research have begun to blur. New information and resources are available to Native and non-Native researchers alike and the opportunity and potential for collaborative, community-based projects with the Museum in exhibits, history, and archaeology are increasingly enhanced by the processes that repatriation has set in motion. Repatriation's threat to the scientific status quo is still very real but in terms of the amount of knowledge and data produced, growth actually seems to be somewhat enhanced.

Ironically, more information has been generated or made more accessible on Native American human biology, archaeology, history, and material culture as a result of repatriation efforts. Native involvement in the life of the Museum is at an all time high. While serious differences and misunderstandings have emerged in the course of the repatriation, the Museum's contacts with the tribes have also experienced something of a renaissance. The time is fast approaching when the process of repatriation may become fully normalized within the evolving structures of museums themselves. Perhaps the "R" word will be replaced with some more socially acceptable moniker such as "community-based research" or the "collaborative anthropology program." This heightened level of interaction with Native communities facilitated by the repatriation effort is an opportunity for museum anthropology to renew its commitment to understanding and presenting the cultures of Native America and their diverse histories and origins. Time will only tell if this unusual opportunity can be fully realized.

NOTES

1.   With the 1996 amendment of the NMAI Act, the legislation pertaining to the Smithsonian now also refers explicitly to the repatriation of sacred and patrimonial objects, making the NMAI Act virtually identical to NAGPRA in terms of the repatriation process.

2.   The total number of Native American human remains held by the NMNH can be divided into four groups: (1) the Army Medical Museum remains from collections made by

military personnel in the western territories in the latter half of the 19th century; (2) remains collected by physical anthropologists, archaeologists, and other individuals working for the Smithsonian in Alaska during the late 19th and early 20th centuries; (3) remains from burials recovered during the River Basin Survey archaeological projects managed by the Smithsonian from about 1940 to 1970; and (4) the remainder of the collections which include both ancient and more recent remains recovered primarily from the Northwest, the Southwest, and the Southeast.

3.   The Pawnee request later became a group repatriation request when the Wichita of Oklahoma and the Arikara of North Dakota, signed on for purposes of creating a unified northern Caddoan block.

4.   The 1996 Amendment to the NMAI Act increased the number of persons on the Committee to seven and required that the two additional members be Native American religious leaders.

REFERENCES CITED

Baugh, Timothy and Stephanie Makseyn-Kelly. 1992. "People of the Stars: Pawnee Heritage and the Smithsonian Institution." Report on file, Repatriation Office, National Museum of Natural History, Smithsonian Institution, Washington, D. C.

Bieder, Robert E. 1986. *Science Encounters the Indian: A Study of the Early Years of American Ethnology, 1820–1880*. Norman, Oklahoma: University of Oklahoma Press.

—— 1990. "A brief historical survey of the expropriation of American Indian remains." Manuscript on file, Native American Rights Fund, Boulder, Colorado.

—— 1992. "The collecting of bones for anthropological narratives." *American Indian Culture and Research Journal* 16(2): 21–33.

—— 1996. "The representations of Indian bodies in nineteenth-century American anthropology." *American Indian Quarterly* 20(2):165–179.

Billeck, William and Javier Urcid. 1995. "Assessment of the Cultural Affiliation of the Steed-Kisker Phase for Evaluation of the National Museum of Natural History Native American Repatriation Review Committee." Report on file, Repatriation Office, National Museum of Natural History, Smithsonian Institution, Washington, D. C.

Billeck, W. T., E. B. Jones, S. A. Makseyn-Kelly, and J. Verano. 1995. "Inventory and Assessment of Human Remains and Associated Funerary Objects Potentially Affiliated with the Pawnee in the National Museum of Natural History." Report on file, Repatriation Office, National Museum of Natural History, Smithsonian Institution, Washington D. C.

Bray, Tamara L. and Thomas W. Killion editors. 1994. *Reckoning With The Dead: The Larsen Bay Repatriation and the Smithsonian Institution*. Washington, D. C.: Smithsonian Institution Press.

Bray, Tamara L., Javier Urcid, and Gary Aronsen. 1992. "Inventory and Assessment of Native American Human Remains from the Western Great Basin, Nevada Sector in the National Museum of Natural History." Report on file, Repatriation Office, National Museum of Natural History, Smithsonian Institution, Washington, D. C.

Carlson, Kerri M., Paula Molloy and Thomas W. Killion. 1997. "Determining the Biological Affiliation of Human Remains: An Assessment of Available Techniques." Report on file, Repatriation Office, National Museum of Natural History, Smithsonian Institution, Washington, D. C.

Chatters, James. 1997. "Encounter with an ancestor." *Anthropology Newsletter*, January, pp. 9–11.

Echo Hawk, Roger 1990. "Census Report on Human Remains Ancestral to the Pawnee Tribe at the Smithsonian Institution." Report on file, Native American Rights Foundation, Boulder, Colorado.

—— 1997. "Forging a new ancient history for Native America." In *Native Americans and Archaeologists: Stepping Stones to Common Ground*, edited by N. Swidler et al., pp. 88–102. Walnut Creek, California: Alta Mira Press.

Flynn, Gillian and Thomas W. Killion. 1997. "NMNH Repatriation Policy Statement: Guidelines for Repatriation, National Museum of Natural History, Smithsonian Institution." Document on file, National Museum of Natural History, Smithsonian Institution, Washington, D. C.

Handsman, Russell and Trudy Lamb Richmond. 1995. "Confronting colonialism: The Mahican and Schaghticoke peoples and us." In *Making Alternative Histories*, edited by P. Schmidt and T. Patterson, pp. 87–118. Santa Fe: School of American Research Press.

Hill, Tom and Richard W. Hill, Sr. 1994. *Creation's Journey: Native American Identity and Belief*. Washington, D. C.: Smithsonian Institution Press.

Hinsley, Curtis. 1981. *Savages and Scientists: The Smithsonian and Development of American Anthropology.* Washington, D. C.: Smithsonian Institution Press.

Joint Committee on the Conduct of War. 1865. *Report of the Joint Committee on the Conduct of the War, at the Second Session of the Thirty-Eighth Congress of the United States, 1865.* (Massacre of Cheyenne Indians). 38th Cong., 2d sess., 1865. Government Printing Office, Washington, D. C.

Jones, D. G. and R. J. Harris. 1997. "Contending for the dead." *Nature* 386:15–16.

Killion, Thomas W., Scott Brown and J. Stuart Speaker. 1992. "Naevahoo'ohtseme: The Cheyenne Repatriation." Report on file, Repatriation Office, National Museum of Natural History, Smithsonian Institution, Washington, D. C.

Killion, Thomas W. and Paula Molloy. 2000. "Repatriation's silver lining." In *Working Together: Native Americans and Archaeologists.* edited by Kurt E. Dongoske, Mark Aldenderfer, and Karen Doehner. pp. 111–118. Society for American Archaeology, Washington, D.C.

Meighan, Clement. 1984. "Archaeology, Science or Sacrilege." In *Ethics and Values in Archaeology,* edited by E. L. Green, pp. 208–223. New York: Free Press.

———— 1992a. "Some scholar's views on reburial." *American Antiquity* 57(4): 704–710.

———— 1992b. "Another view on repatriation: Lost to the public, lost to history." *The Public Historian* 14(3):39–50.

Merrill, William, Edmund Ladd and T. J. Ferguson. 1993. "Return of the Ahayu:da: Lessons for repatriation from Zuni Pueblo and the Smithsonian Institution." *Current Anthropology* 34(5):523–568.

Miller, Elizabeth A. 1995. "Refuse to be Ill: European Contact and Aboriginal Health in Northeastern Nebraska." Ph.D. Dissertation, Department of Anthropology, Arizona State University, Tucson, Arizona.

Minthorn, Phillip E. 1997. "Archaeology of the dammed: Native people and the River Basin Survey." *Common Ground* 2(1):34–39.

Morell, Virginia. 1995. "Who owns the past?" *Science* 268: 1424–1246.

Mudar, Karen, J. Stuart Speaker and Erica Bubniak. 1996a. "Inventory and Assessment of Human Remains and Funerary Remains from Point Hope, Arctic Slope Native Corporation in the National Museum of Natural History." Report on file, Repatriation Office, National Museum of Natural History, Smithsonian Institution, Washington, D. C.

Mudar, Karen, Katherine Nelson, J. Stuart Speaker, Richard Scott, Steven Street and Elizabeth Miller. 1996b. "Inventory and Assessment of Human Remains and Associated Funerary Objects from Northeast Norton Sound, Bering Straits Native Corporation, AK, in the National Museum of Natural History." Report on file, Repatriation Office, National Museum of Natural History, Smithsonian Institution, Washington, D. C.

Mudar, Karen and J. Stuart Speaker. 1997. "Inventory and Assessment of Human Remains from St. Lawrence Island, AK in the National Museum of Natural History." Report on file, Repatriation Office, National Museum of Natural History, Smithsonian Institution, Washington, D. C.

Powell, Peter J. 1981. *People of the Sacred Mountain: A History of the Northern Cheyenne Chiefs and Warrior Societies, 1830–1879.* New York: Harper and Row.

Riding In, James 1989. "Report verifying the identity of six crania now at the Smithsonian Institution and the National Museum of Health and Medicine as belonging to former Pawnee scouts killed in 1869." Manuscript on file, Native American Rights Foundation, Boulder, Colorado.

———— 1992. "Six Pawnee crania: Historical and contemporary issues associated with the massacre and decapitation of Pawnee Indians in 1869." *American Indian Culture and Research Journal* 16(2):101–119.

Slayman, Andrew. 1997. "A battle over bones." *Archaeology Magazine* 50(1):16–23.

Smythe, Charles. 1998. "Wounded Knee Memorandum." Report on file, Repatriation Office, National Museum of Natural History, Smithsonian Institution, Washington D. C.

Speaker, J. Stuart. 1993. "Inventory and Assessment of the Apache Human Remains in the National Museum of Natural History." Report on file, Repatriation Office of the National Museum of Natural History, Smithsonian Institution, Washington, D.C.

Svaldi, D. 1989. *Sand Creek and the Rhetoric of Extermination: A Case Study in Indian-White Relations*. Lanham, Maryland: University Press of America.

Swidler, N., K. Dongoske, R. Anyon, and A. Downer. 1997. *Native Americans and Archaeologists: Stepping Stones to Common Ground*. Walnut Creek, California: Altamira Press.

Thornton, Russell. 1987. *American Indian Holocaust and Survival: A Population History Since 1492*. Norman, Oklahoma: University of Oklahoma Press.

Trigger, Bruce. 1989. *A History of Archaeological Thought*. Cambridge: Cambridge University Press.

Ubelaker, Douglas H. and Lauryn G. Grant. 1989. "Human skeletal remains: Preservation or reburial?" *Yearbook of Physical Anthropology* 32:249–287.

U.S. Court for the District of Hawaii. 1996. In the United States Court for the District of Hawaii. Order Granting Federal Defendants Motions for Summary Judgement. *Na Iwi O Na Kupuna O Mopaku, Heleloa, Ulupa`u A Me Kuwa`a`ohe by and through their Guardians , Hui Malama I Na Kupuna O Hawaii Nei vs. John Dalton, Secretary of the Navy and the Bernice Pauahi Bishop Museum*. Civil No. 94-00445 DAE.

U.S. Court for the District of Oregon. 1996. In the United States Court for the District of Oregon. Complaint for Judicial Review. *R. Bonnichsen, C. Loring Brace, G.W. Will, C. Vance Haynes, Jr., R.L. Jantz, D.W. Owsley, D. Stanford and D. G. Stelle vs. the United States Department of the Army, Corps of Engineers, E. J. Harrel, and Curtis L. Turner*. Civil No. 96-1481 JE.

U.S. Court for the District of Rhode Island. 1996. In the United States Court for the District of Rhode Island. *City of Providence vs. Bruce Babbit, Secretary for the United States Department of the Interior; Hui Malama I Na Kupuna Hawai`I Nei, and the State of Hawaii Office of Hawaiian Affairs*. CA '96-668.

Watkins, J., L. Goldstein, K. Vitelli, and L. Jenkins. 1995. "Accountability: Responsibilities of archaeologists and other interest groups." In *Ethics in American Archaeology: Challenges for the 1990s*, edited by M. Lynott and A. Wylie, pp. 33–37. Special Publication of the Society for American Archaeology, Washington, D. C.

CHAPTER TWELVE

Usurping Native American Voice

LARRY J. ZIMMERMAN

Scientific colonialism is defined as the process whereby the center of gravity for acquisition of knowledge about a people is located elsewhere than with the people themselves (Hymes 1974:49). According to Galtung (1967), scientific colonialism includes claiming the right of access to unlimited data from other countries. It entails exporting data from the country of origin to one's own country for "processing" into books and articles. The most important, most creative, most entrepreneurial, most rewarding and most difficult aspects of "creating" knowledge take place away from the source of information.

Reflecting upon recent critiques of American archeology (e.g. McGuire 1992, 1997), it is difficult to see the historical relationship between archaeologists and Native Americans as anything but scientific colonialism. Certainly archaeology's claim that a Native past is a public heritage is similar to a claim to rights of unlimited access to data from another country. But do archaeologists export the data and move the creative processes and their results away from Native American nations? The answer is unequivocally yes. American archaeology is an edifice of scientific colonialism, and this has crippled its relationships with Native Americans. The crucible of the repatriation and reburial issues has made it painfully clear that archaeological interactions with Indians often have been inept and torturous. Many Native Americans go so far as to call archaeology irrelevant or inaccurate.

One reason for archaeology's lack of effective response to Native concerns is that archaeology has not been ready epistemologically to understand and address what might be called "Native American voice." In fact, Native American voice provides an epistemological foundation for American archaeology. Indeed, on one level, it provides the authority from which archaeologists speak and write about the past. In usurping Native American voice, many archaeological practitioners go so far as to claim that they "speak" for the people of the past and are the only ones truly capable of doing so.

Native people challenge the legitimacy of archaeological use of Native American voice and thereby challenge the very authority of archaeological knowledge about the past. This paper examines the notion of Native American voice, how archaeologists come to know and use it, and why this has exaggerated already difficult relationships. I suggest that an ethnocritical approach to the past may be useful in alleviating the problem, but that it will profoundly change archaeological epistemology.

EPISTEMOLOGICAL READINESS AND DIFFERENT WAYS OF KNOWING THE PAST

Epistemology is the study of the nature and grounds of knowledge with reference to its limits and validity, or as defined by Watson, LeBlanc and Redman (1971:3): ". . . how we know and how we know we know." The key elements of epistemology include: knowledge of the world and limits to it; defining and understanding "truth;" and methods of explaining "reality". Within academic disciplines epistemological issues, although sometimes debated, are relatively stable, allowing scholars to function in their exploratory, analytical, and explanatory capacities. But the very definition of epistemology implies that there are limits or boundaries to knowledge. When confronted by ways of knowing or apparent "truths" that are beyond these boundaries, archaeologists must reject them until such a time, if ever, that the discipline's epistemology can be shifted to incorporate them.

Native American peoples have confronted archaeology with different ways of knowing the past, and archaeology has had profound difficulty incorporating these approaches into its epistemology (see, for example, Clark 1996 and Mason 1997). Comparing archaeological and Native American views about the past is instructive.

Archaeological Views of Past

Archaeological time is fundamentally a Euroamerican, literalist approach that may be described as rationalist and empiricist (Littlejohn 1983). Crucial to this view are archaeological divisions of time into a past, a present, and a future. Leone (1978:28) suggests that the construction of time apart from the present moment stems from the construction of a dual world. This duality consists of the present, which is direct and immediate, and of another realm that is not, but is well articulated and distinct from the here-and-now. This "not-present" is segmented into a past and future. Processual archaeology, in particular, placed an emphasis on discovering an eternal reality with a goal of making law-like statements about reality that transcend all time, events, and cultures; in other words, it seeks to be ahistorical. In an odd way, this is not so very dissimilar from a Native view that is ahistorical, accepting natural, God-given law (Zimmerman 1989:65). However, for archaeology this goal is pursued by analyzing components of a phenomenon or event and seeking causal, mechanistic explanations for observed relationships between them. The act of seeking causes means that some condition(s) must exist before some other event can happen. This results in the past, present, and future being segmented into linear time.

For archaeologists, the present is the least significant of the three temporal realms. They assume they "know" the present by virtue of the fact that it is lived experience, and because it is only momentary, it is merely a link between past and future. Thus, past and future are valued more than the present as is amply demonstrated, for example, in the Society for American Archaeology's anti-looting campaign slogan "Save the past for the future."

Some might point out that archaeologists consider the concept of "ethnographic present," but that notion also emphasizes the importance of the past over the present. Sometimes defined as the moment at which a group was first studied, archaeologists use the ethnographic present as a baseline, a moment frozen in time. Subsequent culture change is seen as the result of "contamination" by outsiders and excluded from consideration. Such an understanding of the ethnographic present has the effect of locking Native culture into the past and may even subtly push archaeologists toward an acceptance of the usually mistaken idea that the cultures they study are extinct (see Meighan quote below) rather than as cultures that adapted and survived.

Much the same critique applies to ethnoarchaeology. Often associated with the origins of New Archaeology (c.f. Anderson 1969; Binford 1962, 1967), ethnoarchaeology focuses on the context of material practices of contemporary cultural groups who are seen as analogues of prehistoric groups for the purpose of ascertaining what happened in the past. Modern cultural practices are of incidental interest. The focus is on the past, and the aim is to develop general statements about human behavior that transcend time and individual cultures. In point of fact, the archaeological uses of ethnoarchaeology have been limited primarily to contemporary hunting and gathering groups like the !Kung (Yellen 1977) or Nunamiut (Binford 1981) and rarely applied to others.

For archaeologists, the future is unknown and yet to be formed, though it is thought the past can influence the future in some unspecified way if it can be mediated properly through the present. This idea is summarized in the aphorism: "Those who are ignorant of the past are bound to repeat it." The past, on the other hand, can be known because it has already happened. To know the past, however, requires it to be discovered or modeled, largely through written sources and archaeological exploration and interpretation. From the past, one may learn or discern what actions should be taken in the present to obtain the desired effects in the future. What happened in the past is interpreted through the hindsight of the present and becomes an "artifact of the present" (Lowenthal 1985:xvi). When archaeologists write the past, it becomes "a fixed, unalterable, indelibly recorded" entity unto itself.

Archaeologists know of no other way to write this past than through excavating, analyzing, temporally ordering objects or events, and interpreting meaning from them. This view is typified by Meighan (1985:20):

> The archaeologist is defining the culture of an extinct group and in presenting his research he is writing a chapter of human history that cannot be written except from archaeological investigation. If archaeology is not done, the ancient people remain without a history and without a record of their existence.

In this common archaeological view of time and the past, past and present are related in a linear fashion, with historical retrospection and "periods," "phases," and "traditions" serving as conceptual and linguistic partitions. Cultural developments begin and end, while events in between follow in linear fashion. The approach is analytical and rational, rather than emotional, with the past revealed in the study of remains recovered by excavation and analysis (Watson, Zimmerman, and Peterson 1989).

NATIVE AMERICAN VIEWS OF PAST

Although over-generalization is certainly a risk, Native American views of the past appear to have some common themes. American Indians in particular have directly challenged archaeological views of the past. To them the idea that discovery is the only way to know the past is absurd. For a Native American oriented toward traditional practice and belief, conceptually and pragmatically the past lives in the present, with the present viewed as the only "real" temporal realm. Past events provide exemplars for present action, but as human nature does not change, the situation is only different as to its observable factors such as people involved or locations. The past, therefore, *is* the present (cf. Lowenthal 1985:xv).[1] Indians know the past because it is spiritually and ritually a part of daily existence and relevant only as it exists in the present. A specific future is unknown and of little immediate concern except that for a future to occur, time must be renewed by proper ritual adherence to natural law. The past and present are not separate but are in a continuous process of becoming. The past is a unifying spiritual "knowledge" that is not and cannot be constrained by any versions of time made by humans (Eliade 1985:112).

   This is not to say that Native Americans have no view of chronology or try to avoid its use, but "lacking a sense of rigid chronology, most tribal religions did not base their validity on a specific event dividing man's time experience in a before and after" (Deloria 1973:113). The crucial issue is that "truth" was revealed in mythical times, specifically at creation, given by the gods, and effectively became natural law. Time is eternal, cyclical and endlessly repetitive (Eliade 1985:112). As Viola Hatch, a Southern Cheyenne, stated at the Peacekeeper reburial conference (USAF 1985:58):

> We do not have a set of guidelines written on a piece of paper to show us how to live. We got it from the Great Spirit. He told us one time, we learned it, followed it to this day.

   These approaches are supported by primary orality, the nearly complete emphasis on the spoken word by traditional cultures. In most traditional Native American cultures, "learning or knowing means achieving close, empathetic, communal identification with the known" (Ong 1982:45). "Word meanings come continuously out of the present, though past meanings of course have shaped the present meaning in many and varied ways [that are] no longer recognized" (Ong 1982:101). Though the past is recognized as important, its relevance to the present is determined by what is happening now. The mechanism for knowing the past is oral tradition, which recounts the mythic and makes the past and the present the same. Oral tradition therefore takes precedence over any other kind of knowledge about the past/present, including that generated by Euroamerican historical or archaeological techniques.

Esther Stutzman, a Coos Bay woman, phrases the differences in approaches to knowing the past as follows: "The past is obvious to the Indian people, it does not appear to be obvious to the White man" (Ross and Stutzman 1985:6). In other words, a present past is part of daily life and experience and does not have to be sought. Cecil Antone (quoted in Quick 1986:103) of the Gila River tribes elaborates:

> My ancestors, relatives, grandmother, and so on down the line, they tell you about the history of our people and it's passed on and basically, what I'm trying to say, I guess, is that archaeology don't mean nothing. We just accept it, not accept archaeology, but accept the way our past has been established and just keep on trying to live the same style, however old it is.

Gordon Pullar (1994:19), a Native Alaskan, recounts a statement made by a middle-aged woman at a 1991 planning meeting for the National Museum of the American Indian:

> You people keep talking about preserving the past. Can't you see there is no past? Can't you see that the past is today and the past is tomorrow? It's all the same! Can't you see that?

Finally the attitude toward discovery of the past is well summarized by Athabascan Ernie Turner (quoted in Anderson et al. 1983:28) who says:

> Human bones are not able to talk to the scientists and leave them information. Culture talks to us and gives us messages from the past. Spiritual communication is not a theory, it is a fact. I am not sure what the bones tell [the archaeologists] of the spiritual beliefs of my people. Even if the bones do communicate, I'm not sure what they tell you is true.

Simply stated, the past and the present are essentially the same in content and meaning, though details may differ. As a tradition-oriented Native American, if you know the oral history of your people, you need no other mechanisms for "discovering" your people's past.

ARCHAEOLOGICAL AND NATIVE AMERICAN USES OF
THE NATIVE AMERICAN VOICE

These Native American ways to knowing the past are nearly anathema to an archaeology that is empirically based or processual in approach. Yet even processualist archaeology uses Native American voice. The notion of voice is borrowed from literary criticism. In essence, it suggests that there is a voice beyond the voices that speak in a work, "a sense of a pervasive presence, a determinate intelligence and moral sensibility, which has selected, ordered, rendered, and expressed" (Abrams 1988:136) these materials in a certain way. Though critics argue over the precise meaning of voice, they agree that the purpose of authorial voice and presence is to persuade the reader to "yield to the work that unstinting imaginative consent without which a [work] would remain no more than an elab-

orate verbal game" (Abrams 1988:137). Voice contains and uses the author's values, beliefs, and moral vision as implicit controlling forces.

The use of voice is often not a matter of conscious choice for those who write
fiction, and those who write scholarly materials are most often not at all aware of
its use. Archaeologists ask that the reader accept that they have the authority to
speak for the human beings under archaeological investigation, or, that they have
some understanding that is accessible only through archaeological reconstruction. In other words, because archaeology is purported to be the only way that
information about the past can be obtained, the archaeologist may knowingly or
unknowingly claim the Native American voice and asks others to yield to that
authority. One might say that a "scientific" voice becomes equated with Native
American voice.

This is clear, for example, in the quotation from Meighan above, that the
ancient peoples remain without a past unless archaeologists write it. As physical
anthropologist Douglas Owsley (quoted in Anderson, Zieglowsky and Schermer
1983:11) noted:

> My objective is simply to note that limitations exist in other forms of evidence
> including historic records or oral tradition. Without archaeology and skeletal
> biology research, Indian history would extend no further into the past than per-
> mitted by their own oral tradition. It is at this point that the scientific communi-
> ty can provide insight into that period of time long forgotten by oral tradition.

A more recent, and stunningly clear example appeared in a recent issue of *Archaeology*. Archaeologist John Whittaker (1992:56-58) discusses the archaeology of the
Sinagua, a prehistoric complex of the American Southwest that is either Hakataya
or Anasazi. The first sentence immediately sets the voice: "Few of us would both-
er with archaeology if we weren't emotionally involved with the past. We don't
dig for dry bones and dusty potsherds, but for people" (Whittaker 1992:56). In
that sentence he has instantly sought to say that he is not "objectifying" the past,
but rather he is personalizing it. His last paragraph solidly reifies the voice; he is
speaking for the people of the past:

> It pains me to learn that the Sinagua were probably not as happy as I would like
> them to have been, although I know that is irrational. I still admire their skills and
> knowledge, even though they probably didn't bathe and had rotten teeth that
> stank. I'm sure like the rest of us they could be mean and stupid, loving and kind.
> And I am certain that I would like to meet them and talk to them, touch their bat-
> tered, calloused hand. God forbid that I should ever have to live their life, but the
> Sinagua are real people to me, and I care about them and *want to tell their story*.
> [emphasis added]

Whittaker sincerely expresses the feelings of many who are in archaeology. The
issue is not, however, a question of sincerity, but of use of Native American voice.
What Whittaker does in the emphasized line is to ask the reader to submit to his
authority, implying that he has a right and the ability to tell the story: this was the
life of the Sinagua people.

Again, do not misunderstand: for an archaeologist to use Native American
voice is legitimate, but it has ramifications for our dealings with Indian people.
The basis for archaeological authority in using Native American voice derives

from two sources. The first comes from an appeal to the universality of the human experience. Whittaker, for example, makes himself coeval with the Sinagua and other archaeologists often do this as well, to the point of claiming the archaeological past as a common human heritage.[2] The second comes from archaeological use of the scientific method, which can provide valid and important insights into prehistoric life, but remains a voice that derives from material evidence. As a result, scientific voice is often seen as "dry" and depersonalizing, failing to provide real meaning about the lives of people.[3] This is a fundamental complaint of Native American people.

Native peoples might agree with Miller and Tilley (1984:3) who recognize that "archaeology may be held to tend toward 'fetishism' [in which] . . . relationships between people may be represented as though they were relationships between objects." This 'fetishism' is a nearly exact opposite of a traditional Native American treatment of objects as sentient or animate. This is one of the keys to understanding Indian rejection of an archaeological past. Such extreme differences would seem to allow little compromise (c.f. Fagan 1991:189–190).

In a critique of Euroamerican approaches to history, Vine Deloria, Jr. (1977) says that history and archaeology are a theoretical house of cards built on an evolutionary theory in which objects or events, but not people, are put into chronological frameworks from which meaning is somehow derived. He contends that Natives focus on people and how they experienced their lives: they know what their lives mean. This is what Cecil Antone meant in the earlier quotation when he said: "archaeology don't mean nothing."

Indigenous people cannot accept archaeological use of Native American voice as reasonable because it is a matter of cultural survival. The past lives in the present for Native American people and does not exist as a separate entity. When archaeologists state that the past is gone, extinct, or lost unless archaeology is done, they send a strong message that Native American people themselves are extinct. Acceptance of the past as archaeologists view it would actually destroy the Native American present. Taken further, if the past is the present, excavated human remains are in a sense, still alive and have "personality." They must be respected as a living person should be. If Native American people were to accept archaeological views of time and the past, Native American people, to paraphrase Ong (1982:15), would have to die to continue living. This is what Deloria (1973:49) means in his book *God Is Red* when he states, "[t]he tragedy of America's Indians . . . is that they no longer exist, except in the pages of books."

J. Jefferson Reid's editorial "Recent Findings on North American Prehistory" in a 1992 issue of *American Antiquity* in one sense says it all. Reid recounts attending the Third Southwest Symposium at which an all-Native panel discussed their thoughts on archaeology and archaeologists. Reid (1992:195) comments that he was surprised "to have departed that session with the new and rather startling realization" that Native Americans feel threatened by archaeologists:

> . . . archaeological accounts of the past, especially the past of a particular Native American people, are perceived by them to present a threat to traditional, Native American accounts of that same past. The perceived threat is that the archaeological account eventually would replace the traditionally constructed past and erode, once again, another piece of their culture.

Because Reid normally used Native American voice in his archaeological writing, he assumed that Native American and archaeological views of the past were much the same, but came to recognize that there can be a traditionally constructed past that is different.

He was also surprised to hear the Native Americans declare, after two days of listening to academic papers, that the archaeology of the Southwest had no relevance for southwestern Indians. In their view "archaeology was only relevant to other archaeologists" (Reid 1992:196). Reid notes that, "[a] North American prehistory irrelevant to North American Indians would seem to be in jeopardy, or, minimally, in serious need of epistemological adjustment" (ibid.). He concludes with the following questions (ibid.):

> Should prehistory be relevant to Native Americans? And if so, how is this relevance to be achieved? Who is to judge? Do Native American oral histories and scientific accounts of prehistory complement one another, like traditional and modern medicine, or is one destined to be subsumed by the other?

Reid's opinion is amazing because he is so absolutely correct on one level, while at the same time showing a complete lack of understanding of core epistemological issues. His observations are not particularly new. That Native Americans, and indeed most indigenous peoples, mistrust archaeology and question its relevance is at the very heart of the repatriation and reburial issues. Fifteen years ago, for example, Valarie Talmage (1982:45) noted that archaeologists are "often frustrated by modern Indian groups' disinterest and disbelief in the results of archaeological study." Reid's observations are intriguing in that they seem to be the first hint in American mainstream archaeological literature that something is really wrong with archaeology, but his professed wonderment that some group might consider archaeology as irrelevant borders on the farcical. What Reid is involved with is an agile, though unintentional, effort to call for a new epistemology.

NATIVE AMERICAN VOICE, SHARED TIME AND ETHNOCRITICISM

Archaeologists worldwide have been slow to recognize that epistemological shifts must be made if archaeology is to have any relevance at all to anyone besides archaeologists. Some indigenous people have openly declared the issue to be a matter of control over the past. As Rosalind Langford stated at the 1982 meeting of the Australian Archaeological Association (quoted in Lovell-Jones 1991:1):

> The issue is control. You seek to say that as scientists you have a right to obtain and study information of our culture. You seek to say that because you are Australians you have a right to study and explore our heritage because it is a heritage to be shared by all Australians. . . . We say that it is our past, our culture and heritage, and forms part of our present life. As such it is ours to control and it is ours to share on our terms.

Langford's sentiment is an Australian Aboriginal's reflection on the scientific colonialism of archaeological epistemology. Indigenous ways of knowing the past are as rigid as those of archaeology, and when the issue becomes politicized, the matter can easily dissolve into an overt battle for control of the past. But this is not the only possible outcome.

Again, for archaeology the problem is epistemological. Because the past must be examined scientifically, it becomes rigidly objectified. Fabian (1983) carries the notion of objectification much further in a way that provides considerable insight. He contends that anthropologists must distance themselves spatially and temporally from the Other in order to create an object of study. Time is a carrier of significance, a way in which anthropology defines the content of relations between itself and the Other (Fabian 1983:ix). Labeling plays an essential role in creating that temporal distance. Labels, which may or may not have explicitly temporal references, can connote temporal distance. In archaeology, commonly used linguistic partitions such as "phase", "tradition", or "period" are examples. Terms like mythical, which many prehistorians use to describe oral tradition, "connote temporal distancing as a way of creating the objects or referents of anthropological discourse" (ibid.:30). Fabian suggests that anthropologists tend to deny "coevalness," which he defines as a "persistent and systematic tendency to place the referent(s) of anthropology in a time other than the present of the producer of anthropological discourse" (ibid:31). Archaeological "objectivity" can thus be seen as linked to the temporal distancing between archaeologists and Native American people. "To use an extreme formulation, temporal distance is objectivity in the minds of many practitioners" (ibid:30). Echoing Leone (1978), Fabian (1983:ix-x) notes that "Time may give form to relations of power and inequality...." Thus, the construction of anthropology's object through temporal concepts and devices "is a political act; there is a 'Politics of Time'" (ibid.).

Hill (1988) amplifies this point in his introduction to a volume analyzing Native South American perspectives on the past. He debunks what might be considered the "archaeological" viewpoint in which the past becomes an entity somehow distinct from both the researcher and contemporary Native Americans. Objectivity in historical research is a product of "bracketing out" the individual researcher in a sort of non-participatory, detached observation of historical "others" in which the researcher acts as a mirror reflecting spatially and temporally remote events (Hill 1988:3). History, Hill contends, should entail a critical, reflexive awareness of social and historical research as a personally mediated, historically situated activity.

Hill (1988:3) also challenges the belief that historical interpretations based on written documents (or archaeological research?) are necessarily more objective, reliable or accurate than those embodied in oral tradition or non-verbal kinds of activity:

> [a]lthough oral and non-verbal formulations cannot be literally read as direct accounts of historical processes, they can show how indigenous societies have experienced history and the ongoing means by which they struggle to make sense out of complex, contradictory historical processes.

In the end, he concludes that history is never reducible to "what really happened." History always includes all the processes through which individuals "experience, interpret, and create changes within social orders" (ibid.). Both individuals and social groups actively participate in changing the objective conditions around them, and thus, in the construction of history. This suggests that the past, the medium within which archaeologists work, is fluid, as is objectivity itself. Accepting this notion is essential if   archaeological epistemology is to accommodate Native American use of the Native American voice.

When one considers the critique of archaeological approaches to the past as part of the dominant culture's power structure and as a political act, it is easy to mistake the critique for moral condemnation. As Fabian (1983:32) observes, ". . . bad intentions alone do not invalidate knowledge. For that to happen, it takes bad epistemology which advances cognitive interests without regard for their ideological presuppositions." Fabian's discussion of the issue is complex, but it boils down to archaeologists having a right to their own views of the pasts they construct, but only so long as they recognize the fundamental paradox of their genesis. Archaeologists seek   to describe and explain peoples' lives, but largely exclude these people from direct involvement in the project. At the same time that archaeologists seek to communicate with Native American people, they are engaged in temporally distancing them. As Fabian (1983:31) contends, however, "[c]ommunication is ultimately about creating shared Time."

Archaeologists, for example, cannot continue to maintain that the past is lost with reburial. The idea that anyone can "save" the past is a false notion. As Lowenthal (1985:410) notes, preservation itself reveals that permanence is an illusion:

> The more we save, the more we become aware that such remains are continually altered and reinterpreted. We suspend their erosion only to transform them in other ways. And saviors of the past change it no less than iconoclasts bent on its destruction.

This realization leads, of course, to the doorstep of postmodern approaches which if taken to their logical extreme leave us with an empty feeling that all pasts are equally valid, when intuitively we understand otherwise. This is where many postmodern approaches fail.

ETHNOCRITICAL ARCHAEOLOGY

Some have suggested that compromise positions could accommodate problems raised in this paper (Renfrew and Bahn 1991:484; Thomas 1991:46). However, compromise in the usual sense of the word is not possible when the uses of Native American voice are anathema and politically loaded. Ethnocritical archaeology, in which archaeologists and indigenous people share construction of the past, might be more beneficial. This notion of an ethnocritical archaeology derives from the work of Arnold Krupat (1992) and his definition of ethnocriticism.

Krupat writes from the perspective of literary criticism, with a focus on Native American literature. Following Wilden (1972), he is suspicious of any scientific theory or position that looks like a metaphor for the dominant society's ideology or that might be construed as contributing to the alienation of any class or group (Krupat 1992:27). Thus when it is suggested that a compromise between archaeological and Native views be attempted, he would suspect that any such settlement would be constructed from the position of the dominant group and that it would likely be ineffective and potentially alienating. Compromises still reflect the positions of those who are party to them. For archaeology this would mean that by seeking compromise, we would just be trying to find another way of telling "our" own story, of "turning 'their' incoherent jabber into an eloquence of use only to ourselves" (Krupat 1992:6).

If epistemology is about the limits of knowledge, ethnocriticism suggests that scholars work at those limits, in other words, that we work at the boundaries of our ways of knowing. As Krupat (1992:15) suggests, this is a frontier orientation,

> . . . where oppositional sets like West/Rest, Us/Them, anthropological/biological, historical/mythical, and so on, often tend to break down. On the one hand, cultural contact can indeed produce mutual rejections, the reification of differences, and defensive retreats into celebrations of what each group regards as distinctly is own. . . . On the other hand, it may also frequently be the case that interaction leads to interchange . . . and transculturalization.

For Krupat the oppositional view serves no useful purpose. Just as dichotomized binary reasoning once served as justification for imperial domination, it serves today to justify postcolonial revisionist "victimist history." One can acknowledge that some people have been hurt by others in the colonial context, but where does that lead except to rhetoric? In ethnocriticism the concern is with differences rather than oppositions, and an effort is made to replace oppositional with dialogical models. Claims to accuracy, systematicity, and knowledge would reside in their capacity to take more into context (Krupat 1992:27). There is no master narrative, just one position among many (ibid.):

> Given its frontier condition of liminality or between-ness, ethnocriticism by its very nature must test any appeals to 'reason,' 'science,' 'knowledge,' or 'truth' it would make in relation to Other or non-Western constructions of these categories, or . . . to any categories Others may propose.

The result is a relative truth, but not in the sense of a full-blown, epistemological relativism. Ethnocriticism seeks a position between objectivism and relativism; it does have rules. We can still be scientific in ways that are meaningful, by specifying the methods and procedures followed and by indicating the empirical and logical components of arguments. "No one can doubt that such a science will be more modest and very different from what science has heretofore been in the West. . . ." (Krupat 1992:77).

ETHNOCRITICISM IN PRACTICE

Of course, the problem for ethnocriticism and its application in archaeology is that archaeologists understand so little about the Native American use of Native American voice, or for that matter, Native American epistemology. For an ethnocritical approach to work, archaeologists need to make an effort to understand Native American concepts of the past and how the past is known. This takes the discipline to the ethnocritical frontier but does not allow it to work there. Epistemology without methodology will fail. A good start toward building an appropriate methodology might be simply to turn the tools of archaeology, which tend to focus on the analysis of material culture, over to Native American peoples to apply to their own "research" questions.[4] The archaeologist becomes a facilitator. Efforts to try to operationalize such an approach have been rare, but are becoming more common. The initial results of such collaborative ventures are fascinating.

In Australia, for example, Colin Pardoe, an osteologist studying Aboriginal remains, provides a possible model for how a "shared time," to use Fabian's phrase, can be created. Pardoe does no excavation or analysis without intensive community involvement. He asks permission to work on remains even if he suspects that they are not related to groups now occupying the area in which bones are found. He asks people their opinion of the research problems he is addressing. He tells them why he needs to do certain tests, and if they are out of the ordinary (such as in destructive techniques), he asks permission. Reading one of Pardoe's (e.g. Pardoe 1988) community reports might be very instructive for many North American archaeologists. With these reports, he not only educates about what physical anthropologists do, but he provides a mechanism for community involvement in construction of the past. He maintains that he usually has little difficulty doing whatever research he needs and that he learns a great deal more about his topics by *sharing* his study with Aboriginals. He admits that it limits his kind of science but recognizes it as a cost of his research (Pardoe 1991).

In the United States an accidental ethnocritical study emerged out of reburial efforts in Nebraska. As part of preparation for a court case to force repatriation of human remains under a new Nebraska state law, the Pawnee hired an archaeologist to summarize the known archaeological record of their tribe. At the same time a Pawnee tribal historian gathered previously recorded oral history and other material pertaining to Pawnee origins and movements. The archaeological work and the oral history were then compared for concordance (Zimmerman and Echo-Hawk 1990). The Pawnee historian subsequently re-analyzed this material under a separate contract with the Denver Airport and published it as part of a final report (Echo-Hawk 1992; 1993). The report is fascinating for the way in which it takes the archaeological evidence and uses it to bolster Pawnee oral history. There is certainly not complete concordance and conflicting data are simply set aside and noted as being a different type of information (sometimes with negative comments about archaeology). From an archaeological point of view, it shows that there is historicity to oral tradition, though the time frame differs as does the meaning assigned to history.[5]

In my experience, I have found Native American peoples to be extraordinarily patient in their dealings with archaeologists. They recognize that some parts of archaeology may be useful to them if applied using their "rules" and their epistemologies. Perhaps this is because their epistemologies are less rigid than those of archaeology. What archaeologists must face is a "past" that is peculiar to their discipline and that the pasts they construct potentially have an impact on Native peoples. To communicate effectively with Native American people, archaeologists will need to learn how to share both "time" and control of the past. Anthropologists must accept that their own "faith" in positivist-based science enjoys no privileged status over the various mythic views of history as expressed by Native American people.

There is a place for Native American voice used by archaeologists, but it is not the only Native American voice possible. Indeed, working at the frontiers between archaeological and Native American epistemologies presents both archaeology and Native American peoples with seemingly infinite potential.

ACKNOWLEDGEMENTS

This paper has benefited from discussions with several people including Roger Echo-Hawk, Elizabeth Prine, Alison Wylie, Tristine Smart, Rich Fox, Tom Patterson, Mark Leone, Charles Orser, Vine Deloria, Jr., Leonard Bruguier, Jonathan Hill, Jeremy Sabloff and Randy McGuire. Their assistance should not necessarily be construed as agreement with my positions. Errors in the interpretation of their remarks are certainly my own. Deward Walker, Karen Zimmerman, and Christine Lovell-Jones assisted by providing material.

NOTES

1.   This appears to describe Australian Aborigine's understanding of time, as well. See Lovell-Jones (1991:4) for a discussion.

2.   For Native Americans we tend to devise an image that is congruent with the needs of the dominant society. This has been treated well in Trigger (1980), McGuire (1997), and a recent BBC *Horizon* program entitled "The Myth of The Noble Savage" (Hawkes 1992).

3.   An exception is a recent best-selling series of novels about prehistoric Native Americans by W. Michael Gear and Kathleen O'Neal Gear (*People of the Wolf* [1990,] *People of the Fire* [1991], *People of the Earth* [1992], and *People of the River* [1992], with others forthcoming). The authors are archaeologists. Their novels are based on solid archaeological research, and a material culture emphasis is obvious throughout. Still, the novels' popularity, in part, derives from the authors' use of what I would call archaeological voice to tell an indigenous story in a personal way that emphasizes emotion and meaning in life.

4.   Archaeologists might wish to expand the scope of their inquiry to include research about how people process and understand the past. Elliot Oring (1995:10), in commenting on one of my articles (Zimmerman 1994), suggests that this is folklore, not archaeology. He also suggests that archaeology holds *no* version of the past. On the latter point he is profoundly mistaken. On the former he makes an interesting point, but this narrow view of archaeology is precisely what makes it of no use to Native people.

5.   A number of other such projects have been tried. The University of South Dakota's work with the Northern Cheyenne (McDonald et al. 1990), and Bielawski (1989) and Loring's (n.d., and this volume) work with the Inuit are but a few examples. Many other similar projects are currently in progress. The Pawnee are continuing their work in a collaborative effort between Roger Echo-Hawk and archaeologist Steve Holen. Further work by Echo-Hawk (1994) can be seen in his Masters Thesis at the University of Colorado. Recent sessions at both the American Anthropological Association and the Society for American Archaeology meetings have addressed successful attempts to create shared time.

REFERENCES CITED

Abrams, M. H. 1988. *A Glossary of Literary Terms*. New York: Holt, Rinehart and Winston.

Anderson, Duane, D. Zieglowsky and Shirley Schermer. 1983. "The Study of Ancient Skeletal Material in Iowa: A Symposium." Manuscript on file at the Office of the State Archaeologist, Iowa City, Iowa.

Anderson, K. M. 1969. "Ethnographic analogy and archaeological interpretation." *Science* 163: 133–138.

Bielawski, Ellen. 1989. "Dual perceptions of the past." In *Conflict in the Archaeology of Living Traditions*, ed. R. Layton, pp. 228–236. London: Unwin Hyman.

Binford, Lewis R. 1962. "Archaeology as anthropology." *American Antiquity* 28:217–225.

——— 1967. "Smudge pits and hide smoking: The use of analogy in archaeological reasoning." *American Antiquity* 32:1–12.

——— 1981. *Bones: Ancient Men and Modern Myths*. New York: Academic Press.

Clark, G. A. 1996. "NAGPRA and the demon-haunted world." *Society for American Archaeology Bulletin* 14(5):3.

Deloria, Vine, Jr. 1973. *God is Red*. New York: Delta Books.

——— 1977. "A Conversation with Vine Deloria, Jr." *Words and Places*, Program 8. New York: Clearwater.

Echo-Hawk, Roger. 1992. "Discovering Ancient Worlds: Final Report of the Archaeological Monitor for the New Denver Airport Office." Manuscript on file with the Department of Public Works, Denver Colorado.

——— 1993. "Working together: Exploring ancient worlds." *Society for American Archaeology Bulletin* 11(4):5–6.

——— 1994 "Kara Katit Pakutu: Exploring the Origins of Native America in Anthropology and Oral Traditions." Masters Thesis, Department of History, University of Colorado, Boulder.

Eliade, Mircea. 1985. *Cosmos and History: The Myth of the Eternal Return*. New York: Garland.

Fabian, Johannes. 1983. *Time and the Other: How Anthropology Makes Its Object*. New York: Columbia University Press.

Fagan, Brian. 1991. Editorial. *Antiquity* 65(247):186–191.

Galtung, Johann. 1967. After Camelot. In *The Rise and Fall of Project Camelot: Studies in the Relationship between the Social Sciences and Practical Politics*, ed. I. Horowitz, pp. 281–312. Cambridge: MIT Press.

Hawkes, Nigel. 1992. "Myth of the noble savage." *World* 57:36–38.

Hill, Jonathan D. 1988. "Introduction: Myth and history." In *Rethinking Myth and History: Indigenous South American Perspectives on the Past*, ed. J. Hill, pp. 1–17. Urbana, Illinois: University of Illinois Press.

Hymes, Dell. 1974. "The use of anthropology." In *Reinventing Anthropology*, ed. D. Hymes, pp. 3–82. New York: Vintage Books.

Krupat, Arnold. 1992. *Ethnocriticism: Ethnography, History, and Literature*. Berkeley: University of California Press.

Leone, Mark P. 1978. "Time in American archaeology." In *Social Archaeology: Beyond Subsistence and Dating*, edited by C. Redman et al., pp. 25–36. New York: Academic Press.

Littlejohn, S. W. 1983. *Theories of Human Communication*. Belmont, California: Wadsworth Publishing Co.

Loring, Stephen. n.d. "Labrador Inuit interpretations: Heathen camps and Christian communities." Paper presented at the Annual Meeting of the Society for Historical Archaeology, Kingston, Jamaica, 1991.

Lovell-Jones, Christine. 1991. "Observer and Observed: A Predicament of Australian Archaeology." B.A. Honours Thesis, Department of Archaeology and Palaeoanthropology, University of New England, Armidale.

Lowenthal, David. 1985. *The Past is a Foreign Country*. Cambridge: Cambridge University Press.

McGuire, Randall. 1992. "Archaeology and the First Americans." *American Anthropologist* 94(4):816–836.

——— 1997. "Why do archaeologists think the real Indians are dead and what should we do about it." In *Indians and Anthropologists in Post-Colonial America*, ed. T. Biolsi and L. Zimmerman, pp. 63–91. Tucson: University of Arizona Press.

Meighan, Clement W. 1985. "Archaeology and anthropological ethics." *Anthropology Newsletter* 26(9):20.

Miller, D. and C. Tilley. 1984. "Ideology, power and prehistory: An introduction." In *Ideology, Power, and Prehistory*, ed. D. Miller and C. Tilley, pp. 1–15. Cambridge: Cambridge University Press.

Ong, Walter J. 1982. *Orality and Literacy: the Technologizing of the World*. London: Methuen.

Oring, Elliot. 1995. "Viewpoint rebuttals." *Archaeology* 48(2):10–11.

Pardoe, Colin. 1988. *Ancient Aboriginal burials at Cowra, NSW: A report on the study of two skeletons spanning 7,000 years*. Canberra: Australian Institute of Aboriginal Studies.

——— 1991. "Farewell to the Murray Black Australian Aboriginal skeletal collection." *World Archaeological Bulletin* 5:119–121.

Pullar, Gordon. 1994. "The Qikertarmiut and the scientist." In *Reckoning with the Dead: The Larsen Bay Repatriation and the Smithsonian Institution*, ed. T. Bray and T. Killion, pp. 15–25. Washington, D.C.: Smithsonian Institution Press.

Quick, Polly McW. 1986. *Proceedings: Conference on Reburial Issues, Newberry Library, Chicago, June 14–15, 1985*. Society for American Archaeology, Washington, D.C.

Reid, J. Jefferson. 1992. "Recent findings on North American prehistory." *American Antiquity* 57(2):195–196.

Renfrew, Colin and Paul Bahn. 1991. *Archaeology: Theories, Methods and Practice*. London: Thames and Hudson.

Ross, Richard and Esther Stutzman. 1985. "Two views of archaeology." *American Society for Conservation Archaeology Report* 12:2–13.

Talmage, Valarie A. 1982. "The violation of sepulture: Is it legal to excavate human remains?" *Archaeology* 35(6):44–49.

Thomas, David Hurst. 1991. *Archaeology: Down to Earth*. New York: Holt, Rinehart and Winston, Inc.

Trigger, Bruce. 1980. "Archaeology and the image of the American Indian." *American Antiquity* 45:662–676.

Watson, Norman, Larry J. Zimmerman, and P.M. Peterson. 1989. "The present past: An examination of archaeological and Native American thinking." In *Thinking Across Cultures*, ed. D. Topping, pp. 33–42. Hillsdale, New Jersey: Lawrence Erlbaum.

Watson, Patty Jo, Steven LeBlanc and Charles Redman. 1971. *Explanation in Archaeology: An Explicitly Scientific Approach*. New York: Columbia University Press.

Whittaker, John. 1992. "Hard times at Lizard Man." *Archaeology* 45(4): 56–58.

Wilden, Anthony. 1972. *System and Structure: Studies in Communication and Exchange*. London: Tavistock.

Yellen, John E. 1977. *Archaeological Approaches to the Present: Models for Reconstructing the Past*. New York: Academic Press.

Zimmerman, Larry J. 1989. "Human bones as symbols of power." In *Conflict in the Archaeology of Living Traditions*, ed. Robert Layton, pp. 211–216. London: Unwin Hyman.

——— 1994. "Sharing control of the past." *Archaeology Magazine* 6: 65–68.

Zimmerman, Larry J. and Roger Echo-Hawk. 1990. "Ancient History of the Pawnee Nation: A Summary of Archaeological and Traditional Evidence for Pawnee Ancestry in the Central Great Plains." Manuscript on file at the Native American Rights Fund, Boulder, Colorado and the Tribal Office of the Pawnee Tribe of Oklahoma, Pawnee City, Oklahoma.

CHAPTER THIRTEEN

Repatriation and Community Anthropology
The Smithsonian Institution's Arctic Studies Center[1]

STEPHEN LORING

COMMUNITY ANTHROPOLOGY AT THE SMITHSONIAN

As a museum anthropologist with the Smithsonian's Arctic Studies Center (ASC) I have been humbled by the collecting zeal of the nineteenth-century anthropologists who ranged the world to fill their respective institutions with the curiosities and trash from distant lands and distant epochs. Such things were once daily household objects but have, through the alchemy of time and the miracle of preservation, become the treasures of today. Much of the world's patrimony that hasn't been scattered and shorn of its history and provenance has found shelter in museums. Once the purview of a few scholars and a small cadre of museum professionals charged with the curation and care of these collections, the museum world has been transformed within the last decade or so by the enthusiasm and interest of Native groups, artists, and scholars who have, and are in the process of, rediscovering their cultural patrimony.

In part this awareness has emerged as a consequence of the passage of the Native American Graves Protection and Repatriation Act (NAGPRA) that finds museums throughout the United States and Canada reconsidering their roles vis-à-vis Native Americans. Concurrently, many Native communities are experiencing a burgeoning awareness of their cultural heritage as evidenced by the construction of local and regional cultural centers and by the growth of initiatives like Keepers of the Treasure. These new laws, new concerns, and new initiatives have the potential of realigning relations between Native Americans, museum professionals, and others concerned with the preservation of the physical patrimony and intellectual heritage of Native American and First Nations peoples.

As an anthropologist (archaeologist, ethnohistorian, ethnographer) working in the North (Labrador, Alaska, the Aleutian Islands), it has been my privilege to experience something of the drama, intensity, and integrity of community life in Arctic villages. In the North, many Native villages still retain a strong community identity based on hunting and fishing subsistence economies and an ideology that includes a special reverence for elders who retain their cultures' traditional ecological knowledge and spiritual reverence for the land and for the animals on

which life depends. These shared sentiments are leading communities throughout the Canadian Arctic and Alaska to develop cultural preservation programs
that include an appreciation of archaeological and ethnological collections, many
of which now reside in museums throughout the world.

Yet in the North today the distinction between past and present—and the
dichotomy between archaeology and ethnography—is frequently blurred. For
Native American and Inuit families, the cyclical nature of subsistence resources
and the strong inter-generational bonds instill a profound recognition of cultural
continuity and land tenure that is pervasive, spiritual, ideological and often at
variance with the perceptions of archaeologists and other non-Native interpreters
of culture. Northerners fear the loss of their culture, land, and language, and they
recognize that knowledge of the past is critical for determining group identity
and land tenure. Partly because of the Smithsonian's long involvement in the
North (and the resulting outstanding collections and archives), and partly
because my colleagues and I recognize a responsibility to facilitate and nurture an
awareness and appreciation for museum collections (as well as for archaeological
and historical research) we have made a commitment to what we have taken to
calling "community anthropology".

As part of the Arctic Studies Center mandate, we have sought to develop programs that combine the knowledge and experience of program personnel, the
archival resources and objects in the Smithsonian's collections, and the needs,
interests, and expertise of Northern communities. The goals of the community
anthropology initiatives at the Smithsonian include 1) providing training for
Native land managers and community cultural affairs administrators who are
able to articulate community needs with governmental bureaucracies and administration; 2) providing an opportunity for community scholars, artisans, elders,
and young people to discuss the use and significance of museum collections; and
3) instilling in young people knowledge about the accomplishments of their
ancestors. The integration of museum professionals' knowledge of archaeological, ethnographic, and photographic collections housed in the museum with the
knowledge, wisdom, and skills of participating community representatives and
elders is arguably among the most interesting developments in the field of Northern anthropology today.

What I refer to as "community archaeology" differs from institutional academic initiatives primarily because of its commitment to addressing community
agendas, interests, and needs. The approach combines the expertise and training
of professional archaeologists with the insight and knowledge of community
leaders and educators. The principal goal of community archaeology is to provide
experiences and training for Indian and Inuit young people. The participation of
and reliance on elders is a critical component of such endeavors. Throughout the
North, communities revere and honor their elders recognizing them as the principal authority on matters of history and heritage. Elders provide interpretations
of archaeological features and assemblages, while the knowledge and beliefs they
convey in interviews and stories reaffirm community values and testify to the
validity and significance of traditional knowledge. Community archaeology
hopes to stimulate and empower cultural, historical and community values. In

addition to the products of traditional archaeology, that is, publications, community archaeology projects often result in local exhibits and school programs. In some cases, the collections resulting from the collaborative endeavors remain in the North.

Such initiatives start with the recognition that the goals and interests of Native communities may not coincide *exactly* with those of the academy and the museum. This is especially apparent in matters of archaeology where the distant past, so dear to archaeologists, carries considerably less allure for Northerners than the stories and trails of more recent ancestors with whom the bonds of land, kinship, and animals are more tangible and more meaningful.

THE SMITHSONIAN INSTITUTION IN LABRADOR

The Smithsonian Institution's grandest passion has always been its collections. Under the inspired leadership of Secretary Spencer Baird, mid-nineteenth century naturalists scoured the continent for specimens shipping boxcars full of rocks, minerals, fossils, bird eggs, plants, shells, mammals, bones, antiquities, curiosities, and ethnographic objects back to the nation's capital. These collections provided tangible evidence of the wealth and breadth of the North American continent and offered scientific vindication of the idea of manifest destiny as the United States took its place as a world power. This acquisitive fervor was especially prevalent within the young discipline of anthropology whose practitioners were driven by the assumption that Native American cultures were rapidly disappearing and might soon be gone altogether. Anticipating by less than a decade the subsequent "rush" to acquire traditional Native materials, Smithsonian collectors made the first large, systematic ethnographic collections. In this pursuit, literally thousands of objects were acquired, from the mundane to the sacred, from Florida to British Columbia, and Alaska to Labrador.

Smithsonian collectors were especially successful in the North, where Western economic and religious systems had not yet made severe inroads. These intrepid pioneer naturalist-ethnographers included James Swan, George Gibbs, T. D. Bolles, and F. M. Ring, among others on the Northwest Coast; P. Henry Ray and John Murdoch at Point Barrow, Alaska; Edward Nelson along the Bering Straits; and Lucien Turner in northern Quebec and Labrador. Together these men and their contemporaries constructed what is now one of the world's most important repositories of traditional material culture pertaining to Northern Native peoples.

The Smithsonian's interest and research in Labrador dates back to the winters of 1882–1884 when the Museum representatives, together with the U.S. Signal Corps, participated in the First International Polar Year in which more than a dozen expeditions were sent to remote northern stations across the Arctic (Barr 1985). The Smithsonian participated in two of these expeditions, one to Point Barrow, Alaska, and a second to the Hudson's Bay Company post at Fort Chimo (Kuujjuaq) in northern Quebec. In charge of the northern Quebec station was Lucien M. Turner, a trained meteorologist and one of America's most gifted field naturalists. While his atmospheric observations kept him close to his instruments at the Hudson's Bay Company post, Turner nevertheless was able to assemble impressive collections of birds, mammals, plants, crustacea, mollusca and fish for the Smithsonian. During Turner's stay at Ft. Chimo, he cultivated the friendship of the Innu and Inuit families who visited the HBC post and camped nearby. This association enabled him to assemble the earliest and most complete collection of ethnographic material from northern Quebec and adjacent Labrador ever made (Turner 1890). When the collection was finally shipped to the Smithsonian in 1884, it contained well over 500 objects (fig. 13-1).

While a tiny portion of the Turner collection has long been on display in the North American Indian Hall at the Smithsonian's National Museum of Natural History, there have been few opportunities for Innu, Quebec Inuit, or Labrador Inuit community members to examine the collection and little discussion on how it might be used to address contemporary Native issues and concerns. With a burgeoning interest in and knowledge of museum collections, material culture studies, and cultural patrimony, Native people in Labrador, as throughout the North, have begun to show considerably more interest in the Turner collection. At a very basic level, nineteenth-century material culture provides a tangible link with the past, with community traditions, and with one's own cultural identity.

Figure 13-1. Innu coat collected by Lucien Turner in Kuujjuaq (Ft. Chimo), northern Quebec, 1883, (cat no. E74457). The painted design was the symbolic rendition of an individual hunter's quest for game. *Photograph courtesy of the National Anthropological Archives, Smithsonian Institution/SI 74457.*

In addition to its collections of Innu and Inuit material culture, the Smithsonian also houses four very important archival collections pertinent to Labrador Native history. These include (1) Lucien Turner's photographs of Innu and Inuit people and camps in the vicinity of Ft. Chimo (1883–1884); (2) William Brooks Cabot's collection of photographs, journals, and maps pertaining to his extensive travels with the Innu between 1899 and 1923 (Loring 1986/1987, 1987); (3) the notebooks and journals of William Duncan Strong from the winter of 1927–1928, when he camped with the Innu near Davis Inlet and Nain (Leacock and Rothschild 1994); and (4) the photographs, journals, and notes of E. Pep Wheeler (Morse 1977), the pioneering geologist who worked in Labrador from 1927 to 1974.

Although some incidental archaeological research had been conducted in Labrador prior to about 1950 (Bird 1945, Leechman 1943, Strong 1930), it wasn't until William Fitzhugh began his sustained archaeological and paleoecological research in Hamilton Inlet and later along the central and northern Labrador coasts that the prehistoric cultural sequence of the region was revealed (Fitzhugh 1972, 1976a, 1976b, 1978a, 1978b, 1980). After more than two decades of sustained archaeological and ethnohistorical research in Labrador by Fitzhugh and his colleagues and students (e.g. Kaplan 1983, Jordan 1978, Nagle 1978, 1984; Cox 1977, 1978; and Loring 1988, 1992), the Smithsonian has become indelibly associated with studies and interpretations of Labrador prehistory and paleoecology.

One of the attractions of archaeological research in Labrador for me was the opportunity it provided to meet and travel with members of the region's three indigenous communities: the Inuit, Innu and Settler. Local hunters and fishermen invariably provided hospitality and information about resources, settlement and subsistence strategies, weather, and game-related phenomena. They often conveyed this information in stories, weaving a rich tapestry of history and experience. Family members would occasionally guide us to archaeological sites, and over the years a number of young people worked with us as crew members. For all intents and purposes, however, archaeology in Labrador prior to 1990 was largely conducted as an independent enterprise with little community involvement or participation.

By the early 1990s, the framework of Labrador's fascinating prehistory had been well established. Archaeologists had revealed nearly 8,000 years of alternating and sometimes overlapping Indian and Inuit cultures. I myself had devoted nearly a decade to working out the late prehistoric sequence of Indian cultures in Labrador ancestral to the Innu (Loring 1992). While this research mainly addressed academically-minded questions about the boundedness of hunter-gatherer societies and the emergence and maintenance of ethnic identities, I was mindful of its political ramifications. In other words, I recognized that the demonstration of cultural continuity and past land-use had implications for on-going land-claim negotiations. Through community visits and slide presentations, I endeavored to convey something of my research results to the Innu. While my images of familiar landscapes and stone projectile points were reviewed with little comment, the slides I had made of the Smithsonian's collection of nineteenth and early twentieth-century photographs of Innu people fascinated the modern residents as they had no idea that such archival materials existed. Slide shows in Utshimassit, a small Innu village on the central coast of Labrador, would last long into the night. Having surrendered control over the projector to one of the village elders, animated conversation—in Inueimun—greeted each image. The projector's light shining through a nearly opaque cloud of cigarette smoke, was like a time machine carrying everyone present back to the past.

Such experiences convinced me that while native Labradorians might appreciate knowledge of the far-past it was the near-past, which included the landscape of myth and memory, that appealed most to them. Archaeologists in Labrador, as throughout much of the North, had designed research programs, for the most part, without input or participation of host community members. It is not surprising that this resulted in the alienation of Native communities and the hardening of their attitudes toward archaeology. At the least archaeologists were guilty of benign neglect, at the worst their actions amounted to a blatant continuation of postcolonial scientific attitudes that divorced research from any form of community (social) interaction and obligation. In effect, the past in Labrador had become dichotomized. Scientific practitioners had their materialist view of the past based on radiocarbon dates, artifacts, and old sites while local community members held title to a past that was based on oral traditions, place names, myths, genealogy and stories.

With the completion of my dissertation (Loring 1992), I was eager to initiate new research conducted in a cooperative mode with the Native communities of Labrador. As envisioned, it would be research that sought not so much a concordance of the past as a means of empowering people with the relevance and authority that is conveyed by control over the past.

COMMUNITY ARCHAEOLOGY WITH THE INNU IN LABRADOR: PATHWAYS

The Pathways Project emerged as a cooperative initiative of the Innu Nation, the Innu Resource Centre and the Smithsonian's Arctic Studies Center. It sought to address the interests and needs of the Innu community and their notions of the past while exploring their ancient tenure of the land. It also sought to empower Innu youth with another perception of their history and heritage. In light of the usurpation of Innu control of their land by a government that first flooded their rivers then used the land as a military training ground, and finally implemented massive mineral development projects, this project seemed particularly poignant.

An essential feature of the Pathways Project was the integration of my training in archaeology and familiarity with Innu prehistory with the knowledge, wisdom and skills of participating elders. During the fall of 1993, Innu students from the community of Sheshatshit, a Native community on Lake Melville, participated in two weeks of classroom training and community interviewing followed by a month in the country to learn the methods and techniques of archaeological practice. The field site was located at Amitshuakant. This was the beginning point of an Innu portage route that led from Seal Lake to the now flooded Lake Michikamau; from there it ran north to Ungava, west to Hudson's Bay, and then south to the Quebec North Shore. Although unmarked in any printed atlas, Amitshuakant was a major crossroads for the Innu in the eighteenth and nineteenth century, the point from which families departed to the furthermost corners of Nitassinan (the Quebec-Labrador peninsula).

The Innu participants, selected by community leaders for their interest in heritage issues, included students, hunters and homemakers (fig. 13-2). The excavation of late nineteenth-century and early twentieth-century tent-rings at the beginning of the portage trail revealed an array of artifacts including hunting and fishing paraphernalia, tobacco related products, knives, cookware, medicinal containers, molasses jugs, combs, beads and coins. But our time in the country was much more than an exercise in how archaeologists practice their profession. It was an opportunity to incorporate Innu values and perspectives into a construction of history and a chance to expose Innu youth to life in the bush.

Figure 13-2. Kathleen Penashue and Edwina Jack working on field notes for their excavation unit at Amitshuakant (FiCf-1) on the Naskapi river, Labrador.
Photograph courtesy of Stephen Loring.

We were accompanied into the country and into our inspections of the past by an elder couple, Louie and Mary-Adell Penashue and their infant grandson. After a day of excavating, students had the opportunity to accompany the Penashues and attend to nets and snares, hunt moose and bear, and prepare food. Later, as the autumn nights lengthened, everyone gathered in tents to listen to stories about the old days, about times of starvation and extraordinary journeys by snowshoe and canoe. At the conclusion of the field-season, we returned to She-shatshit where the students prepared the results of the project for presentation to the community.

Pathways is an example of the growing commitment and concern shown by archaeologists in addressing the needs and interests of Northern community members. In the Canadian Arctic there has been a marked increased in Inuit participation and interest in archaeology that has led a number of archaeologists to instigate fieldwork specifically aimed at addressing local interests in archaeology and providing training and fieldwork experience for young people (Bielawski 1984, Rowley 1991, Stenton and Rigby 1995). With the increased opportunities for research and fieldwork, and through the implementation of training programs designed for Northern Native students (Bertulli 1985), it is clear that the future of archaeology in the Eastern Arctic will include ever more Northerners.

A cooperative archaeology in the North combining the training of archaeologists, historians, and museum specialists with the insight and knowledge of community elders holds the promise of creating a radically different and exciting new form of archaeology with potentially revolutionary impacts on the practice and perception of the past. For one thing, Native archaeologists would bring language skills and an awareness of community values to the practice of archaeology. A Native archaeology would have considerably freer access to community elders with their erudition and wisdom, and traditional ecological or indigenous knowledge (Berkes 1993; Brooke n.d.; Cruikshank 1981, 1984; Freeman and Carbyn 1988, Saunders 1992, Stevenson 1996). Such intimate knowledge of the distribution and availability of resources, as well as of Arctic ecology, together with a historical perception of the relationships between human beings and their environments, will go far to humanize the wilderness of Northern prehistory.

Initiatives like the Pathways Project promise an exciting future for archaeology by (1) liberating it from the exclusive confines of the academy, (2) producing a product that has meaning to both anthropologists and to the communities from which collections and information is derived, and (3) celebrating a multi-vocal past that addresses social and political agendas, and embraces both humanist and scientific perspectives.

OUTREACH AND COOPERATION: NUNIVAK ISLAND, ALASKA

A second example of the practice of community anthropology at the Smithsonian's Arctic Studies Center is an undertaking centered on the village of Mekoryuk on Alaska's Nunivak Island in the Bering Sea. Surrounded by shallow seas, Nunivak escaped much of the social disruption that came in the wake of whaling, gold prospecting, and other industries, as well as Euro-american missionary and governmental interventions experienced by Native Alaskans in the nineteenth-century. Nunivak has long been of interest to anthropologists since it was believed that the Chu'pik inhabitants of the island were relatively untouched by Western concepts and economy. This belief prevailed well into the beginning of this century.

In 1874 Alaska's premier naturalist, William H. Dall, made a brief visit to Nunivak and acquired a number of objects for the Smithsonian. A few years later the Smithsonian's peripatetic Edward Nelson whose Yupik name, "the man who bought good-for-nothing things" was indicative of his inexhaustible collecting enthusiasm, purchased a number of objects from Nunivak that were carried to the mainland near Cape Vancouver.

During the summer of 1927, the Smithsonian's Ales Hrdlicka sent two young anthropologists, Henry B. Collins and T. Dale Stewart, to Nunivak. Hrdlicka had been foiled in his attempts to find Pleistocene-age sites in the interior of Alaska and hoped they would have better luck on the shores of the Bering Sea. While the chimera of "Early Man" eluded them, Stewart and Collins had a fairly productive summer conducting archaeological, ethnographic, and anthropometric research at villages along the north and east coast of the island. In the course of their stay they acquired a large number of objects for the National Museum.

The Stewart-Collins' collection from Nunivak includes approximately 700 specimens, everything from masks and painted wooden bowls to doll's clothing, harpoons, ancient ceramic vessels, and lamps. Women's artifacts included many pieces of jewelry, labrets and earrings, as well as ulu knives and sewing tools. Men's artifacts included a wide assortment of tools used in hunting and fishing. These materials were derived from several distinct contexts, including collections made in house ruins in recently abandoned villages, purchases from Nunivak craftspeople, and excavations in ancient middens. In competition with Edward Curtis (the famous photgrapher of Native Americans), a University of Alaska field party led by Otto Giest, and sailors from the U.S. Coast Guard Cutter *Algonquian*, scavenged artifacts and offerings from old burial scaffolds. Some of these items also ended up in the Smithsonian's Nunivak collection.

While objects from Nunivak have appeared in different exhibitions over the years, the collection had never been studied systematically. Since a large portion of the collection is expected to be repatriated, I was prompted to make inquiries to the community about their interest in participating in a cooperative project that would result in a complete description and analysis of the Smithsonian's Nunivak collections. A preliminary visit to discuss this proposal was made to Mekoryuk in September 1995. I was accompanied to Nunivak by Bureau of Indian Affairs; anthropologist Ken Pratt, who, along with Robert Drouza, had been working with Mekoryuk community leaders and elders to create an extraordinarily detailed gazetteer of Nunivak Island. Although a stranger to Nunivak, I brought an unusual gift: a set of nearly 70 photographs that Henry Collins had taken during his 1927 visit. Ken's introductions and the photographs provided a wonderful entreé into the Mekoryuk community.

Visits to homes throughout the village quickly transformed and personalized Collins' limited notations ("Eskimo woman and daughter," "Eskimo man in kayak") into specific individuals. The photographs evoked spirited discussions of

Nunivak genealogy, subsistence strategies, personal histories, and changes in local settlements. Copies of the prints were distributed and plans were made to incorporate them into the school curriculum.

With support from the National Museum of Natural History's Repatriation Office and a Smithsonian collections enhancement grant, I invited a party of three elders (Walter Amos, and George and Elsie Williams) and two community scholars (Howard Amos and Ike Kiokun) from Nunivak to come to the Smithsonian in February 1996. The purpose of the visit was to examine the artifacts collected on Nunivak over the years and decide upon a course of action for the objects that fell within the scope of the repatriation mandate. We hoped to use the visit to begin a research initiative that would lead to the publication of a book featuring the Collins' photographs, the narratives the photographs evoked, and an analysis and discussion of material culture and art from the island (fig. 13-3).

Figure 13-3. George Williams from Mekoryuk, Alaska, explaining details of Nunivak kayak construction. *Photograph courtesy of Stephen Loring.*

Between the notes made by Collins and others, and the knowledge of the Mekoryuk elders, a detailed history and analysis of the Nunivak collections was produced. The elders were able to provide Chu'pik names for artifacts, many of which had not been manufactured in their lifetime. One ivory wrench-like artifact that Edward Nelson had collected over a century before and which had been cataloged as an "unknown ancient ivory object", was revealed to be a *qaluarun*, a seal-intestine stretcher (figures 13-4a and 13-4b). Together we spent an intense week analyzing and discussing all the objects in the collections: masks, bowls, hunting equipment, and clothing. The elders felt an incredible responsibility to provide an accurate and detailed explanation of each object as they recognized that they were now the bearers of their community's culture history. The younger men, who had been selected by community leaders to make the trip to Washington partially because of their work in preparing a Chu'pik dictionary, were continually surprised at the words that emerged from the elders' discussions. Often these words had dropped out of the vocabulary of modern village life. After one discussion that lasted more than 40 minutes, Walter Amos apologized to me in English for not being able to find their word for a small ivory toggle: "we know what it is, and we remember hearing our fathers talk about it, but we just can't remember the word. I am sorry." My assurances that the knowledge, insight, and explanations that they provided had more than compensated for the few things they were unable to interpret did not seem to assuage the stark recognition that some part of Nunivak heritage was irretrievably lost.

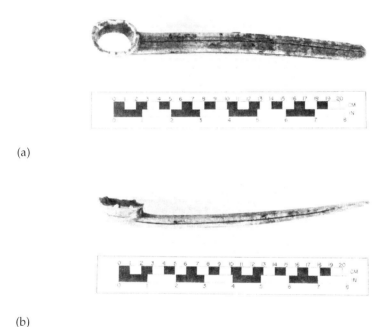

(a)

(b)

Figures 13-4a and 13-4b. *Qaluarun* (SI Cat. No. 43753), also known as "unknown ancient ivory object" in the catalogue records. *Photograph courtesy of Stephen Loring.*

Henry Collins' field notes proved a wonderful foil to the knowledge of the elders since they were based on information derived from informants whose knowledge and memory extended well back into the mid-nineteenth century. Some of the old objects removed from burial scaffolds had fallen out of common usage long before George, Elsie and Walter were born. Yet, with the hints and descriptions provided by Collins, these elders were able to greatly expand our understanding of the function and significance of many of the objects in the collections.

Midway through the visit, after we had finished reviewing the Smithsonian's entire holdings from Nunivak, George turned to me and inquired, "where is the ivory pole?"

"What ivory pole?", I asked.

George related a description of an astonishing funereal monument erected beside a burial scaffold that had consisted of a wooden pole to which a dozen or so walrus ivory tusks had been attached perpendicularly, like a ladder. The tusks, unworked at the bottom, became increasingly more elaborately decorated the higher up the pole they were placed. The theft of the ivory monument was first noticed sometime after the summer of 1927, the year in which the Smithsonian Institution, the University of Alaska, and Coast Guard personnel had overrun Nunivak Island buying curiosities, handicrafts, and clothing, and rooting around the old abandoned villages and cemeteries. We never located any references to what must have been an extremely prominent feature in either Collins' or Stewart's journals or field notes; nor did George's description match any objects in the Smithsonian collection.

The story of the ivory pole, however, brought home another realization about how much of the island's patrimony and heritage had been lost. I don't believe I ever detected any resentment or hostility from the people in Mekoryuk, or from the delegation visiting Washington, about this state of affairs. This was, in part, a reflection of their extraordinary generosity and kindness. But it also involved a shared realization about the transient nature of material objects and the extraordinary circumstances that only sometimes favor preservation.

The Nunivak delegation that visited Washington in the spring of 1996 bore a heavy responsibility. They realized that the combination of a Smithsonian collecting expedition in 1927 and the passage of NAGPRA in 1990 offered them a unique opportunity to recover materials salvaged from the mists of time and memory. Excitement at the possibility of returning Nunivak heritage to the island so that young people could learn something of their history and take pride in the accomplishments of the ancestors was tempered by the realization of the responsibilities that ownership entailed.

The contingencies of a subsistence lifestyle with seasonal movements between camps and villages was never conducive to the preservation of material culture. By their very nature, tools, clothing, and ceremonial paraphernalia were meant to be used and through use wear out and eventually be discarded. It is not surprising, then, that the community has no store of antiquities, although a few old things have survived to be passed down from generation to generation. Still, it isn't likely that there is another cultural windfall comparable to the Stewart-Collins' collection lurking in a museum vault somewhere. This collection likely represents a significant portion of the historical materials available to the community. These thoughts and observations were very much on the minds of the Nunivak delegation. They were eager to assess the significance of the collection and discuss its potential to address community concerns.

In anticipation of the return of the Stewart-Collins' collection, the community of Mekoryuk has sanctioned a complete analysis and formal publication of the collection as a collaborative venture between Smithsonian researchers and com-

munity elders. While some portion of the collection will certainly return to Mekoryuk, the fate of a portion of it—including archaeological specimens, broken
objects, and objects too fragile to be displayed, remains unresolved. Certainly the
community will gain title to the material but whether they elect to leave the
objects at the Smithsonian, bring them to Mekoryuk, or place them in an Alaskan
repository remains a matter for future deliberation.

I would add as a postscript that the human remains taken from Nunivak in
1927 were returned to the community and reburied with due ceremony outside
of the village of Mekoryuk in October 1996 (Mudar et al. 1996; Phillips 1996).

A MUSEUM WITHOUT WALLS

My experience with the Innu, and museum consultation and research conducted
with the elders from Nunivak, epitomize the intensely social component of the
production of knowledge that makes Northern research so fascinating. Through
community archaeology, the reticence of stone tools and ethnographic objects is
replaced by a richly textured layering of history, stories and knowledge. The passage of NAGPRA and the establishment of a new National Museum of the American Indian have been instrumental in expanding the awareness of museum collections in Native American communities throughout North America. As more
and more Native American researchers, scholars and educators gain access to
museum collections, the sense of shared responsibility toward the care and maintenance of collections is intensified. Collections form a unique and tangible link
to the past, a past that has begun to be liberated from the exclusive purview of
academic researchers and museum curators. However, the time machine of the
museum is extraordinarily expensive to operate. Museum collections have for the
most part insured that some objects were rescued from the inroads of time, but at
the price of being imprisoned behind cabinets, computer-generated catalogs, and
the bureaucracy of conservators and curators whose allegiance has traditionally
been to the objects themselves rather than the descendants of the people who produced them.

One exciting development in the museum world is the emergence of the world
wide web as a facility for disseminating information about collections. The museum world has aggressively embraced web technology as a means to greatly
expand its audience and increase access to museum holdings. While digitized
images will never replace hands-on observations, they still provide users with
detailed inventories that can expedite and help structure research. Given the
rapid development and global adoption of web technology, it seems apparent
that the future of education will come to reside more and more in web-like outlets. Eventually, the major collections in museums will be digitized and accessible
via computer communications. Inevitably museums will have to come to grips
with changing perspectives on their proprietary rights and control over objects
and information.

The National Museum of Natural History holds its collections in trust for the
citizens of the United States (and in a broader, more practical sense, for all people). As such it has an institutional philosophy that encourages access to and use
of its collections. With its main constituency far removed in northern climes, the
Arctic Studies Center envisions its homepage as a vehicle to help disseminate

information about the Smithsonian collections to schools and communities across the Arctic.[2] One example of such outreach initiatives has been the development of a detailed inventory and visual catalogue of the Lucien Turner collection from northern Quebec and Labrador. Making this collection internet accessible was done at the request of the Innu Nation and the Labrador Inuit Association who saw the educational and heritage potential of the material if it could be made available to students in Labrador.

As for the future of anthropology in the circumpolar North, it will have to take into account the fact that Native groups are increasingly empowered with the means to control research conducted on their land. Many Northern peoples are interested in their past, yet their concerns are for the present as well, for alleviating the tragically high rates of unemployment, alcoholism, and suicide that plague some Native communities. The archaeology of the academy needs to be replaced by an archaeology of the community. Museum studies must address the needs and concerns of the Native communities whose material pasts they have so long held in trust. Similarly, as indigenous peoples continue to confront the political and economic issues facing them, there is a concurrent revitalization of culturally distinct arts, rituals, and ceremonies. These developments, not just in the North but world-wide, pose a great challenge to museums in the next century: to evolve beyond their perceived role as giant repositories of scientific specimens derived from colonial excesses, anthropological avarice, and acquisitiveness, into institutions that increase awareness of diversity through celebration, repatriation, and revitalization.

NOTES

1.   A portion this paper formerly appeared in the American Anthropological Association's *Anthropology Newsletter* in October 1996.

2.   The homepage address for the Arctic Studies center is: http://www.nmnh.si.edu/arctic

REFERENCES CITED

Barr, William. 1985. "The expeditions of the First International Polar Year, 1882–83." *The Arctic Institute of North America Technical Paper*, No. 29. Calgary.

Berkes, F. 1993. "Traditional ecological knowledge in perspective." In *Traditional Ecological Knowledge: Concepts and Cases*, ed. J. T. Inglis, pp. 1–9. Ottawa: Canadian Museum of Nature.

Bertulli, Margaret. 1985. "Northern heritage research project." *Inuktitut* 62:51–54.

Bielawski, E. 1984. "Anthropological observations on science in the North: The role of the scientist in human development in the Northwest Territories." *Arctic* 37(1):1–6.

Bird, Junius B. 1945. "Archaeology of the Hopedale Area, Labrador." *Anthropological Papers of the American Museum of Natural History* 39(2).

Brooke, Lorraine F. n.d. "The participation of indigenous peoples and the application of their environmental and ecological knowledge in the Arctic Environmental Protection Strategy." Paper presented at the Inuit Circumpolar Conference, Ottawa, 1993.

Cox, Steven. 1977. "Prehistoric settlement and culture change at Okak, Labrador." Unpublished Ph.D. dissertation, Department of Anthropology, Harvard University, Cambridge, Massachusetts. University Microfilms, Ann Arbor, Michigan.

——— 1978. "Paleo-Eskimo occupations of the north Labrador coast." *Arctic Anthropology* 15(2):96–118.

Cruikshank, Julie. 1981. "Legend and landscape: Convergence of oral and scientific traditions in the Yukon territory." *Arctic Anthropology* 18(2):67–93.

——— 1984. "Oral tradition and scientific research: Approaches to knowledge in the North." In *Social Science in the North: Communicating Northern Values*. Occasional Publication No. 9, Association of Canadian Universities for Northern Studies, Ottawa.

Fitzhugh, William. 1972. "Environmental archaeology and cultural systems in Hamilton Inlet, Labrador." *Smithsonian Contributions to Anthropology, No. 16.*

——— 1976a. "A preliminary culture history of Nain, Labrador: Smithsonian fieldwork, 1975." *Journal of Field Archaeology* 3:123–142.

——— 1976b. "Paleoeskimo occupations of the Labrador Coast." In *Eastern Arctic Prehistory: Paleoeskimo Problems*, ed. M. Maxwell, pp.103–118. *Memoirs of the Society for American Archaeology*, No. 31.

——— 1978a. "Winter Cove 4 and the Point Revenge occupation of the central Labrador coast." *Arctic Anthropology* 15(2):146–174.

——— 1978b. "Maritime Archaic cultures of the central and northern Labrador coast." *Arctic Anthropology* 15 (2) :61–95.

——— 1980. "Preliminary report on the Torngat Archaeological Project." *Arctic* 33(3):585–606.

Freeman, M. M. R and L. N. Carbyn (editors). 1988. *Traditional Knowledge and Renewable Resource Management in Northern Regions*. Boreal Institute for Northern Studies, Occasional Publication 23, University of Alberta, Edmonton.

Jordan, Richard. 1978. "Archaeological investigations of the Hamilton Inlet Labrador Eskimo: Social and economic responses to European contact." *Arctic Anthropology* 15(2): 175–185.

Kaplan, Susan. 1983. "Economic and social change in Labrador Neo-Eskimo culture." Ph.D. dissertation, Department of Anthropology, Bryn Mawr College, Bryn Mawr, Pennsylvania. University Microfilms, Ann Arbor, Michigan.

Leacock, Eleanor B. and Nan Rothschild (editors). 1994. *Labrador Winter: the Ethnographic Journals of William Duncan Strong*. Washington, D.C.: Smithsonian Institution Press.

Leechman, Douglas. 1943. "Two new Cape Dorset sites." *American Antiquity* 8(4):363–375.

Loring, Stephen. 1986/1987. "O Darkly Bright." *Appalachia* 46(2):60–73.

⸺ 1987. "Arctic profiles: William Brooks Cabot (1858–1949)." *Arctic* 40(2):168–169.

⸺ 1988. "Keeping things whole: Nearly two thousand years of Indian (Innu) occupation in northern Labrador." In *Boreal Forest and Sub–Arctic Archaeology*, edited by C. S. Paddy Reid. *Occasional Publication of the London Chapter*, Ontario Archaeological Society 6:157–182.

⸺ 1992. "Princes and Princesses of Ragged Fame: Innu Archaeology and Ethnohistory in Labrador." Ph.D. dissertation, Department of Anthropology, University of Massachusetts, Amherst. University Microfilms, Ann Arbor, Michigan.

Morse, Sterns. 1977. "Memorial to Everett Pepperrell Wheeler II, 1900–1974." *Geological Society of America Memorials*, pp. 1–8.

Nagle, Christopher. 1978. "Indian occupations of the Intermediate Period on the central Labrador coast." *Arctic Anthropology* 15(2):119–145.

⸺ 1984. "Lithic raw materials procurement and exchange in Dorset culture along the Labrador coast." Ph.D. Dissertation, Department of Anthropology, Brandeis University. University Microfilms, Ann Arbor, Michigan.

Phillips, Natalie. 1996. "The Bones". *Anchorage Daily News* 51(292), October 20, 1996, pp. 1, 6–7.

Rowley, Susan. n.d."'Ungaluyat:'" On the interface between archaeology and history." Paper presented at the 24th Annual Meeting of the Canadian Archaeological Association, St. John's, Newfoundland, 1991.

Saunders, A. 1992. "Indigenous knowledge." *Northern Perspectives* 20(1).

Stenton, Douglas R. and Bruce G. Rigby. 1995. "Community-based heritage education, training and research: Preliminary report on the Tungatsivvik Archaeological Project." *Arctic* 48(1):47–56.

Stevenson, Marc G. 1996. "Indigenous knowledge in environmental assessment." *Arctic* 49(3):278–291.

Strong, William Duncan. 1930. "A stone culture from northern Labrador and its relation to the Eskimo-like cultures of the Northeast." *American Anthropologist* 32:126–144.

Turner, Lucien. 1890. "Ethnology of the Ungava District." In *the Eleventh Annual report of the Bureau of Ethnology*, pp.167–350. Washington D.C.: Smithsonian Institution.

CHAPTER FOURTEEN

Reflections on *Inyan Ceyaka Atonwan* (Village at the Rapids)
A Nineteenth Century Wahpeton Dakota Summer Planting Village[1]

JANET D. SPECTOR

I began doing archaeological fieldwork in 1964 as an undergraduate at the University of Wisconsin. It was more than two decades later that I had the first experience of my professional career working with Native Americans at *Inyan Ceyaka Atonwan* (Village at the Rapids; also known as Little Rapids), a nineteenth-century Wahpeton Dakota village, located in what is now south-central Minnesota. The work was undertaken in the context of a University field program and before the passage of the Native American Graves Protection and Repatriation Act (NAGPRA) in 1990, though the project was certainly influenced by the political issues and struggles underlying this landmark legislation (see Bray 1996).

The Wahpeton were one of four council fires or divisions of the Dakota Confederacy in the region at the time of initial European penetration. In the early decades of the nineteenth-century, they relied on the rich array of resources available on a seasonal basis and on corn horticulture. They were active participants in the fur trade. Written sources place the Wahpeton at Little Rapids from the early 1800s until 1851 when they ceded their lands to the U.S. government. Our excavations uncovered traces of a summer planting village occupied from the 1830s to 1840s, a time of rapid colonial expansion and escalating conflicts between Native Americans and Euroamerican colonists which culminated in the "Dakota Conflict"of 1862. This war led to the forced incarceration and subsequent removal of Dakota people from the region and to the hanging of 38 Dakota men in Mankato, Minnesota (see Meyer 1967). This tragedy continues to taint relations between Dakota and non-Dakota people.

Figure 14-1. Archaeological field school students with Dakota project advisors Dr. Chris Cavender and Carolynn Schommer at the Wahpeton Dakota village site of Little Rapids in 1986. *Photograph courtesy of Janet Spector.*

My interaction with Dakota colleagues began late in the project, the year before our fourth and final field season. The experience was powerful and transformative. This essay is a reflection on our work together and its impact on the field program, the site analysis, and my writing about the nineteenth-century Wahpeton community (fig. 14-1). My Dakota colleagues, Dr. Chris Cavender, Professor of American Indian Studies at Southwest State University in Marshall, Minnesota, and Carolynn Schommer, a recently retired Dakota language instructor at the University of Minnesota, are direct descendants of *Mazomani*, a prominent leader at Little Rapids in the early to mid-1800s. Their family connection to the site, not legislative mandates or formal institutional relationships, provided the basis for our work together. They participated in the project because they were related to people from Little Rapids, not because of an interest in archaeology per se.

WHY DID IT TAKE SO LONG TO WORK WITH NATIVE AMERICANS?

Nothing in my graduate training at the University of Wisconsin (1967–73) predisposed or prepared me to work with Native Americans. In fact, there were many disincentives to doing so, few of them deliberate, but powerful nonetheless. My education was fairly standard for people specializing in the archaeology of the U.S. Upper Midwest. It was an apprenticeship that discouraged me from even imagining productive archaeological collaborations between Natives and non-Natives. Here are the relevant messages conveyed in my academic training:

MESSAGE 1.

Artifacts are more important than people. This message was most obvious in considering the amount of time we spent learning artifact classification schemes, sequences, and manufacturing techniques. Presumably, we were on safer scientific ground analyzing artifacts than speculating about the people who produced and used them.

MESSAGE 2.

Native people do not participate in archaeology as students, teachers, excavators, or authors. I had no models—positive or negative—of archaeologists working with Native educators, or spiritual or community leaders.

MESSAGE 3.

There is very little, if any, connection between contemporary Indian people and the archaeological materials—prehistoric or historic—we study. "Contact" with Europeans (the euphemism commonly used instead of colonization) quickly led to acculturation, dislocation, cultural disintegration, and a breakdown of cultural distinctiveness and vitality. The implication was that modern Native Americans had little knowledge about the past; too much time had elapsed and too much had been lost.

These presumed ruptures between the past and present are reinforced in the way the discipline is subdivided. Anthropology fragments knowledge about Native histories and cultures by breaking the field into cultural anthropology and archaeology, and within archaeology, into historic and prehistoric studies. Cultural anthropologists conventionally study so-called "traditional Native cultures" in the timeless, "ethnographic present;" while archaeologists study groups living "before history," that is, *pre*-historic people, known to us primarily through the archaeological record. Archaeological "cultures" are distinct from those known ethnographically and have no direct relationship to them. They are defined taxonomically on the basis of characteristic materials, and named after geographic places or time periods (e.g. Mississippian, Woodland, Archaic, Oneota) rather than as ancestral Winnebago, Dakota, or Anishnabe. The Eurocentric sub-field division between "historic" and "prehistoric" archaeology, based primarily on the presence or absence of European-authored written sources, further disrupts any sense of long term Indian cultural continuity and also obscures the dynamics of colonization.

MESSAGE 4.

Contemporary Native Americans are interested in archaeological sites and site materials for "political" reasons, not because of cultural, spiritual, or historical ties. This false dichotomization is reinforced by the absence of courses in archaeology programs about local colonial history and the lingering legacies of those distressing times, particularly from Native American perspectives. In our region, transcripts of nineteenth-century treaty negotiations document a 150-year history of Native concerns about the desecration of burial and other sacred sites. These protests predate the extensive archaeological surveys and subsequent excavations of mounds and other earthworks which laid the foundation for regional archaeology—projects done without Native consent or participation that established the "authority" of archaeologists with regard to Native sites. Students need to know the history of relations between Native Americans and archaeologists.

These messages created real barriers to establishing active, mutually beneficial, respectful relationships with Indian people. These barriers began to diminish for me after becoming involved in feminist archaeology. Since the late 1960s, feminist, Third–World, African-American, Chicano, and Native American scholars, activists, and their allies have seriously challenged many academic disciplines, including anthropology. A central focus has been to delineate the ramifications of the fact that, until fairly recently, academic knowledge has been produced almost exclusively by white, middle-class men of European descent, who were socialized in cultures that discriminate on the basis of race, sex, and class. This domination by a narrow segment of the population has shaped the content of our courses and how they are taught our research priorities and practices and what gets published, funded or otherwise rewarded, and what does not.

Across the disciplines, critics exposed pervasive androcentric and Eurocentric (less delicately put—sexist, racist, and classist) portrayals of human life past and present on the planet (see Conkey and Spector 1984 for a critique of archaeology). They have shown that who we are—our gender, cultural background, social and economic position, and personal histories—influences our work in significant though often unacknowledged ways. They have also called for more responsible academic work, recognizing that those who produce public knowledge about other people hold a powerful and privileged position.

THE LITTLE RAPIDS PROJECT

Initiated in 1980, the overall goal of the Little Rapids project was to learn about what life was like for the Wahpeton community living here in the early 1800s, a time when U.S. government officials and Protestant missionaries were pressuring Dakota people to give up their lands and their way of life. I was interested in how these pressures affected men and women; and how gender roles, relations, and beliefs shaped encounters between Dakota people and Euroamerican colonists.

I was committed to making contacts with Native Americans from the outset, but did not know how to proceed or who to consult. In the process of securing permission to excavate the site from the land owners and the State Archaeologist, I sent the project proposal to the Minnesota Indian Affairs Intertribal Board (now the Minnesota Indian Affairs Council). Within a few weeks, Donald Gurnoe, the Board's Executive Director, sent me a copy of his letter to Norman Crooks, then chairman of the Prior Lake Sioux Community, one of the four Dakota communities now resident in the state and geographically the closest to Little Rapids. Gurnoe wrote:

> Many times in the past, the scientific community has run afoul of Indian people through failure to communicate and their insensitive approach to the concerns of the community. This, apparently, is not the case in respect to this project, as Pro-

fessor Spector has made every effort to enlist the support of Indian people through our offices (D. Gurnoe to N. Crooks, April 7, 1980).

Gurnoe's response encouraged me to pursue more direct contacts with Dakota people. Dr. Chris Cavender was referred to me as an educator willing to consult with non-Dakota people. He was unavailable at the time and, having no further leads, we began the first season of fieldwork without any Dakota involvement. We excavated at Little Rapids during the summers of 1980–82 through the University of Minnesota's archaeological field school program, then suspended work to analyze the materials recovered up to that point. In 1984–85, while on a sabbatical, I decided I could no longer, in good conscience, continue doing Dakota archaeology without Dakota participation. As my criticisms of archaeology became increasingly pointed with respect to the treatment of women in the discipline and as subjects of study, I became acutely aware of the exclusion of Native people from archaeology and from the creation of archaeological knowledge. Five years into the project, I was determined to involve Dakota people in the work or stop it.

I tried again, this time successfully, to reach Chris Cavender. Our initial conversation was awkward for me. It seemed late to be consulting him about a project designed several years earlier without any Dakota input. Chris had never heard of Little Rapids, and although he was cordial, he was also distant and, I felt, suspicious. Candid about his views of "anthros" as he calls us, Chris was openly cynical about the motives of most academics, including me.

During this initial conversation, I mentioned that nineteenth-century written records consistently named *Mazomani* as an important leader at Little Rapids (fig. 14-2). Chris said nothing at the time, but telephoned later to ask if we could visit the site together. It turned out that he was related to *Mazomani*, through his mother, Elsie Cavender (who died February 1, 1993), a well known oral historian. Elsie was raised by her grandmother, *Mazaokiyewin* (Isabel Roberts), the daughter of *Mazomani* and *Hazawin* (Blueberry Woman).

Over the next few months, Chris and I made several trips to Little Rapids, often with other members of his family. We had long conversations about the tensions between archaeologists and Native Americans and I learned a good deal about his family history. Being at the site with people linked to it by kinship was a profoundly moving experience for me. We shared a deep respect for the place that, unlike many Native sites in our area, had been shielded from modern plowing though not from local artifact collectors who were drawn to Little Rapids by the burial mounds and nineteenth-century fur trade goods. They had been digging there for decades, and signs of their activity were permanently etched into the landscape. Though our Native visitors knew we were not digging in the cemetery, it was excruciating for me to walk with them near the scarred, sacred mounds.

Figure14-2. Circa 1858 portrait of the Dakota chief, Mazomani, an important leader who resided at the Little Rapids village site in the nineteenth-century. *Photograph courtesy of National Anthropological Archives, The Smithsonian Institution/43,205-A.*

During the next school year, Chris and I planned the 1986 summer field school program. We secured University funding and recruited other instructors. Chris's aunt, Carolynn (Carrie) Schommer, introduced crew members to the Dakota language, tailoring her lessons to the work we were doing. Ed Cushing, a University ecologist, led students on environmental and natural history field trips in the area. He, Chris, and Carrie compared Dakota and non-Dakota names for the plants near Little Rapids. Sara Evans, a history professor, helped us critically evaluate nineteenth-century written records and Chris shared what he knew from Dakota sources about the people and events described in those documents.

Chris and I tried to recruit Native American students for the field school by visiting Native Studies classes, showing slides, and discussing the project. Even though we had secured tuition scholarships from the University as an incentive, we were not able to attract Indian students to the program. One student's response encapsulated the situation. After our slide presentation, a young woman approached us. She was clearly interested in the project but, she told us, she had been raised in a community that viewed archaeologists as grave robbers. Our presentation contradicted that image. She could see how archaeology could recover unrecorded traces of her own history respectfully and without desecration, but still, she was not willing to risk alienation from her community by participating in a dig.

Despite this disappointment, in many other respects the 1986 field program felt much better than previous ones. Before we began to dig, Chris spoke briefly in Dakota, expressing our collective respect for the spirit of the place and our hopes to be guided by wisdom and sensitivity in our treatment of the people who had once lived there. Amos Owen, a Dakota elder and spiritual leader conducted a pipe ceremony with us, communicating in words that had been spoken at Little Rapids for centuries before the voices there were silenced in the 1850s.

We worked as an interdisciplinary, multicultural team. Every day Chris and Carrie talked with the crew about their family history, Dakota community and spiritual life, Dakota philosophy, place names, the Dakota Confederacy, and the Conflict of 1862 and its tragic aftermath. We also talked about racism—nineteenth-century and contemporary—including incidents that erupted periodically during the field season.

The fusion of family history and archaeology was often remarkable. Each source of knowledge amplified the other. Knowing about *Mazomani* from the documentary records made it possible for Chris and Carrie to participate in the project. They in turn introduced us to other members of *Mazomani's* immediate family: his wife, *Hazawin* (Blueberry Woman) and their daughter, *Mazaokiyewin* (Iron Talker Woman), women who were not mentioned in the documentary records. Simply being at the site with people whose relatives had lived there created powerful connections to the past, and hearing Dakota spoken at the site after more than a century's silence was extraordinary. The archaeological record was no longer anonymous. We could picture and name a family who lived there and hear words they might have spoken.

Just as the Cavender family connection to the site enriched our knowledge about the Little Rapids community, archaeology enhanced their family history. Chris, Carrie and their relatives can now trace their roots to *Inyan Ceyaka Atonwan.* Our detection of a possible Medicine Dance enclosure at the site, suggested by a feature on the landscape first mapped by an archeologist in the 1880s and resembling earlier nineteenth-century illustrations of Dakota Dance areas, led us to new biographical information about *Mazomani*. We tested the enclosure to determine when and how it might have been used. Although the archaeology was inconclusive, related literature revealed that *Mazomani* was a leader of the Wahpeton *Wakan Wacipi* (Medicine Dance Lodge)—an important social, spiritual, and healing institution. This was a piece of *Mazomani's* life story that had been lost or perhaps suppressed over time as his descendants became involved in Christianity.

Those of us with previous experience appreciated the 1986 field season even more than the novice crew members who had no basis for comparing our program with a more typical dig. The way we viewed Little Rapids was dramatically affected by working with people directly related to the place and its history; hearing Dakota spoken there after the silences of more than a century by; and by sharing the pipe with a Dakota elder. The inexperienced students could not imagine archaeology being done any other way.

In fact, it was hard not to romanticize our Dakota colleagues. Just as we some-times fantasized about finding an ideal document or artifact that would reveal elusive aspects of the past, we also hoped that Chris and Carrie would have spe-cial insights about the site or the artifacts we found. Though we learned a great deal from them, neither Chris nor Carrie was particularly interested in the archae-ology or the materials we unearthed. Moreover, this was true of most of the Native visitors to the site. Given the long and troubled history of relations between Native Americans and archaeologists, I knew that Chris and Carrie themselves had agreed to participate in the project with considerable ambiva-lence.

WRITING ABOUT LITTLE RAPIDS

In 1987, I began to write *What this Awl Means: Feminist Archaeology at a Wahpeton Dakota Village* (Spector 1993). I wanted to produce an accessible, human scale por-trayal of the community, one that would give readers an empathetic sense of those times and of the connections between *that* past and the present. I wanted to claim my own voice and authorship while at the same time introducing other voices and perspectives. For some time I was tethered by the conventions of archaeological writing—the dull, lifeless, esoteric, distanced, detached, object-centered, taxonomic rhetoric of our field—a rhetoric that objectifies and subordi-nates the people we study.

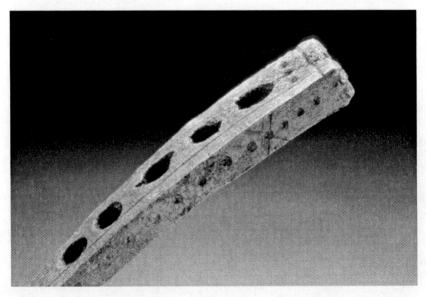

Figure 14-3. Carved antler awl handle recovered during excavations at the Little Rapids site. *Photograph courtesy of Janet Spector.*

I turned my attention to an artifact that we had discovered in 1980 in a garbage dump, a small antler awl handle, about three inches long and delicately inscribed with a series of dots and lines (fig. 14-3). The handle would have held a short, pointed, iron tip, forming a tool for perforating leather hides to be made into tipi covers, clothing, bags, and other accessories.

Inspired by this evocative find, and after discovering the meaning of the inscriptions—they were tallies women kept marking their hide-working accomplishments—I wrote a short interpretive narrative encapsulating a good deal of what we had learned about the community at Little Rapids. This story sets the scene and the tone environmentally, culturally, and historically; it introduces some of the people associated with the site; it reveals what the awl might have meant to the woman who used it and to her community; and it suggests how the awl handle might have ended up in the dump. The rest of the book unravels the narrative layer by layer, exposing what we learned through excavations, documents, and Dakota sources. I discuss   how awls are traditionally treated by archaeologists (taxonomically if at all)—illustrating androcentric and eurocentric biases—and describe the history of relationships between Dakota and non-Dakota people including fur traders, military men, missionaries, and archaeologists. *Mazomani*'s nineteenth-century family and their contemporary descendants figure prominently in the narrative and throughout the book. The book is partly a critique of archaeology, partly a professional memoir and story of the dig, and partly a community study, all presented with as little technical jargon as possible.

Consultations with Native people continued through the publication process. In addition to three archaeologists, editors at the Minnesota Historical Society Press sent the book manuscript to three Native reviewers. Not surprisingly, the Native readers' responses were quite different from the archaeologists'. They urged me to write more about the damage done at Little Rapids by artifact collectors, more about Native American criticisms of archaeology, and more about repatriation issues and laws, especially given the recent passage of NAGPRA. And I did.

One reader was especially concerned about my discussion of the possible Dakota dance enclosure and the ethics of digging in this part of the site. As it turns out, he was a member of the Minnesota Indian Affairs Council in 1988 when Randall Withrow, a graduate assistant on the project, requested permission to do more extensive excavations of the enclosure to see if he could find conclusive evidence about its use. Even though the Board member and subsequent reviewer of the book manuscript was not Dakota, he strongly objected to any further disturbance of the area. From his perspective, a Medicine Dance area was sacred. Respecting this view, Randy abandoned plans for further sub-surface testing there.

In response to this reviewer, I wrote candidly about the situation in the book (Spector 1993: 121–122), using it to describe some of the ethical dilemmas of digging, adding that however much I might wish to know more about the enclosure, I would never knowingly excavate in a sacred area. But this side skirts a broader issue: who, among the various stake holders, gets to define sacred parts of sites—what can and cannot be excavated? In this case, neither Chris nor Carrie objected to our excavations in the possible Medicine Dance area in 1986, or to Randy's later request to conduct more extensive testing there. Yet excavation plans were halted by the objections of a non-Dakota member of the Indian Affairs Council, a group officially designated to work with archaeologists on repatriation and reburial matters. In this case, his voice and authority carried more weight than those of Dakota family members.

SOME RESPONSES TO *WHAT THIS AWL MEANS*

In general, responses to the book *What this awl means* have been extremely grati-fying. It has been widely and positively reviewed in various professional and "popular" publications, featured in two recent textbooks, and sparked lively debate and discussion about writing in archaeological circles. I have been invited to talk about my work in bookstores, classrooms, museums, a tribal community centers, county historical societies, and at professional meetings in the United States and Australia. For the most part, audiences have been very receptive to the feminist dimensions of the book and the writing style, and have appreciated the importance of Dakota participation in the project.

Many non-Native people are curious about Native responses to the book. These too have been heartening though writing about this feels awkward and self-serving. Knowing their criticisms of archaeology (and basically agreeing with them), I did not write *What This Awl Means* with Native American audiences in mind. It was frankly too paralyzing to write for a potentially hostile audience. Instead I wrote for people who I thought would be receptive to my approach: anthropology and women's studies graduate and undergraduate students; sec-ondary school teachers; the general public interested in archaeology and Dakota history and culture; and professional colleagues dedicated to doing archaeology differently.

Still, I did hope that Native people would like the book and "approve" of the work. When they do, I am elated, perhaps too much so. Outside of *Mazomani*'s descendants, who were honored to see their family featured in the book, the first "outside" Native response was from Rayna Green, Director of the American Indi-an Program at the National Museum of American History. Invited by the pub-lishers to do a book jacket "blurb," she wrote: "Janet Spector has put real Indians back into Indian sites, real women back into feminist theoretical speculation, and real ethics into the practice of digging around the Indian past." I do not know of any other commentaries on the book written by Native Americans, though it is to be reviewed and listed on a world wide web site featuring sources primarily by and about Native Americans being created by an Anishnabe (Ojibway) woman in Minnesota.

Other Native American responses have been more personal. Three colleagues in American Indian Studies at the University of Minnesota have been enthusias-tic about the book and recommend it to their students. A small group from a southern Minnesota Native organization presented me with a long poem one of them had written as an expression of thanks after hearing me speak about the project.

Finally, two Native American friends have had special connections to the project though they did not participate in it. Karen Miller has expressed an affinity for the awl and for the site that has helped me understand spiritual dimensions of the work that I had not previously grasped. We made a leather case together for the awl handle and she gave me new ideas about how to care for the materials we excavate. Another friend, Kathleen Kalina, now living in Vermont, recently sent me an email message about the book:

> For months your book has been going around the tribal office for everyone to read (that in itself is a compliment to you). I kept trying to catch up with it, but couldn't until yesterday. Now those who were involved in the reburial issue have all read it. . . . Christopher . . . has loved it so much that for months he has spoken of you as a friend who will come here and see the work they've done. . . . I thought it was interesting that he was always making references to you as if he knew you and yet [had] only read the book. . . . I wonder if the . . . feminist and the peoples' living history approach that you so elegantly wrote about can be something that helps tribes during this repatriation period. It seems that just reburying all the artifacts is too simple. . . .

I cannot imagine a more gratifying response.

CONCLUDING THOUGHTS

When Dan Monroe and Walter Echo-Hawk wrote about the significance of NAGPRA, they said: "It recognizes that scientific rights of inquiry do not automatically take precedence over religious and cultural beliefs; it provides a mechanism for return of objects that were not acquired with the consent of rightful owners; and it creates an opportunity for Native Americans and . . . [scientists] to work in partnership together" (Monroe and Echo-Hawk 1991:55). One of the greatest challenges of the NAGPRA era may be to delineate the terms and conditions of such partnerships especially since these may vary widely depending on who initiates the partnerships, for what reasons, and in what contexts or settings.

Regardless of these specifics, a number of issues need to be addressed. First, potential partners need to be clear about their interests, expectations, levels of involvement and investment, and their access to resources with respect to a given project. These will be quite different for each party. Second, we need more nuanced language to describe different types of relationships between Native and non-Native people on archaeological projects. For example, seeking advice, that is, "consulting," is different from working together, that is, "collaborating." The term "collaboration" is problematic given the connotations of the word "collaborator," implying as it does "one who collaborates with the enemy" (Scribner Bantam English Dictionary 1977: 174). A partnership suggests shared control and power as opposed to simply working together on a project which could entail very unequal power relations.

A third issue that arises is who should be involved in the working relationships. In part, this depends on the purposes or goals of the project and who initiates it. In instances such as reburial and repatriation, there may be community or institutional policies governing the relationships. But in other cases it may not be clear who to contact. In the Little Rapids project, there was no established protocol to follow. By serendipity, I met people directly related to the archaeological community and because of their family connection to Little Rapids, no one publicly questioned why I was working with Chris and Carrie rather than other Dakota people. Without this connection, Dakota community politics and divisions could have affected the project in complex ways. For their part, Native people attempting to identify potential archaeologists to work with could as easily confront politics and divisions within archaeological communities.

Issues of funding and credentials may also arise in attempting to establish viable partnerships. It is very costly to support team taught or directed field programs and there are still few Native Americans with the professional qualifications typically required for staff appointments in archaeology. Similarly, Native people may find it difficult to locate archaeologists with the credentials they value such as cultural knowledge, language skills, and sensitivity to their views about the landscape, material remains, or sacred sites.

For more than two decades, critics of the field have examined the ramifications of the fact that to date, a very narrow segment of the population has controlled the production and distribution of archaeological knowledge. A truly inclusive archaeology will entail much more than simply adding the voices of so-called "others." It will transform the power dynamics and practice of archaeology and enrich the discipline. In my view, the future of the field depends on it.

ACKNOWLEDGEMENTS

Many thanks to Tamara L. Bray for suggesting revisions for this version and to Susan Geiger, for her expert editorial eye and insights.

NOTES

1.	An earlier version of this paper was presented at the 92nd Annual Meeting of the American Anthropological Association (November 1993) Plenary Session entitled "Collaborative Approaches to Understanding the Past" and subsequently published in the *Society for American Archaeology Bulletin*: 12(3):8-10.

REFERENCES CITED

Bray, Tamara L. 1996 "Repatriation, Power Relations and the Politics of the Past," *Antiquity* 20:440–444.

Conkey, Margaret and Janet Spector. 1984. "Archaeology and the Study of Gender". In *Advances and Archaeological Method and Theory*, ed. M. Schiffer, Vol. 7, pp. 1-38. New York: Academic Press, Inc.

Gurnoe, D. 1980. Letter to Norman Crooks, April 7. On file in the Department of Anthropology, University of Minnesota, Minneapolis.

Johnson, R. 1990. "The Bones of Their Fathers". *Sunday Denver Post*, Feb. 4, 1990, Contemporary Sec., 13,21.

Meyer, Roy W. 1967. *History of the Santee Sioux.* Lincoln: University of Nebraska Press.

Monroe, Dan L. and Walter Echo-Hawk. 1991. "Deft Deliberations." *Museum News* 70 (4):55–58.

Spector, Janet. 1993 *What This Awl Means: Feminist Archaeology at a Wahpeton Dakota Village.* St. Paul, Minnesota: Minnesota Historical Society Press.

Appendix One

CHAPTER 3—SMITHSONIAN INSTITUTION, NATIONAL MUSEUMS AND ART GALLERIES

SUBCHAPTER XIII—NATIONAL MUSEUM OF THE AMERICAN INDIAN

Sec. 80q. Findings

The Congress finds that—

(1) there is no national museum devoted exclusively to the history and art of cultures indigenous to the Americas;

(2) although the Smithsonian Institution sponsors extensive Native American programs, none of its 19 museums, galleries, and major research facilities is devoted exclusively to Native American history and art;

(3) the Heye Museum in New York, New York, one of the largest Native American collections in the world, has more than 1,000,000 art objects and artifacts and a library of 40,000 volumes relating to the archaeology, ethnology, and history of Native American peoples;

(4) the Heye Museum is housed in facilities with a total area of 90,000 square feet, but requires a minimum of 400,000 square feet for exhibition, storage, and scholarly research;

(5) the bringing together of the Heye Museum collection and the Native American collection of the Smithsonian Institution would—

(A) create a national institution with unrivaled capability for exhibition and research;

(B) give all Americans the opportunity to learn of the cultural legacy, historic grandeur, and contemporary culture of Native Americans;

(C) provide facilities for scholarly meetings and the performing arts;

(D) make available curatorial and other learning opportunities for Indians; and

(E) make possible traveling exhibitions to communities throughout the Nation;

(6) by order of the Surgeon General of the Army, approximately 4,000 Indian human remains from battlefields and burial sites were sent to the Army Medical Museum and were later transferred to the Smithsonian Institution;

(7) through archaeological excavations, individual donations, and museum donations, the Smithsonian Institution has acquired approximately 14,000 additional Indian human remains;

(8) the human remains referred to in paragraphs (6) and (7) have long been a matter of concern for many Indian tribes, including Alaska Native Villages, and Native Hawaiian communities which are determined to provide an appropriate resting place for their ancestors;

(9) identification of the origins of such human remains is essential to addressing that concern; and

(10) an extraordinary site on the National Mall in the District of Columbia (U.S. Government Reservation No. 6) is reserved for the use of the Smithsonian Institution and is available for construction of the National Museum of the American Indian.

(Pub. L. 101-185, Sec. 2, Nov. 28, 1989, 103 Stat. 1336.)

Short Title of 1996 Amendment

Pub. L. 104-278, Sec. 1(a), Oct. 9, 1996, 110 Stat. 3355, provided that: ``This Act [enacting section 80q-9a of this title and amending sections 80q-3, 80q-9, and 80q-10 of this title] may be cited as the `National Museum of the American Indian Act Amendments of 1996'.''

Short Title

Section 1 of Pub. L. 101-185 provided that: ``This Act [enacting this subchapter] may be cited as the `National Museum of the American Indian Act'.''

Sec. 80q-1. National Museum of the American Indian

(a) Establishment

There is established, within the Smithsonian Institution, a living memorial to Native Americans and their traditions which shall be known as the ``National Museum of the American Indian''.

(b) Purposes

The purposes of the National Museum are to—

(1) advance the study of Native Americans, including the study of language, literature, history, art, anthropology, and life;

(2) collect, preserve, and exhibit Native American objects of artistic, historical, literary, anthropological, and scientific interest;

(3) provide for Native American research and study programs; and

(4) provide for the means of carrying out paragraphs (1), (2), and (3) in the District of Columbia, the State of New York, and other appropriate locations.

(Pub. L. 101-185, Sec. 3, Nov. 28, 1989, 103 Stat. 1337.)

Section Referred to in Other Sections

This section is referred to in sections 80q-2, 80q-14 of this title.

Sec. 80q-2. Authority of Board of Regents to enter into agreement providing for transfer of Heye Foundation assets to Smithsonian Institution

The Board of Regents is authorized to enter into an agreement with the Heye Foundation, to provide for the transfer to the Smithsonian Institution of title to the Heye Foundation assets. The agreement shall—

(1) require that the use of the assets be consistent with section 80q-1(b) of this title; and

(2) be governed by, and construed in accordance with, the law of the State of New York.

The United States District Court for the Southern District of New York shall have original and exclusive jurisdiction over any cause of action arising under the agreement.

(Pub. L. 101-185, Sec. 4, Nov. 28, 1989, 103 Stat. 1337.)

Sec. 80q-3. Board of Trustees of National Museum of the American Indian

(a) In general

The National Museum shall be under a Board of Trustees with the duties, powers, and authority specified in this section.

(b) General duties and powers

The Board of Trustees shall—

(1) recommend annual operating budgets for the National Museum to the Board of Regents;

(2) advise and assist the Board of Regents on all matters relating to the administration, operation, maintenance, and preservation of the National Museum;

(3) adopt bylaws for the Board of Trustees;

(4) designate a chairman and other officers from among the members of the Board of trustees; and

(5) report annually to the Board of Regents on the acquisition, disposition, and display of Native American objects and artifacts and on other appropriate matters.

(c) Sole authority

Subject to the general policies of the Board of Regents, the Board of Trustees shall have the sole authority to—

(1) lend, exchange, sell, or otherwise dispose of any part of the collections of the National Museum, with the proceeds of such transactions to be used for additions to the collections of the National Museum or additions to the endowment of the National Museum, as the case may be;

(2) purchase, accept, borrow, or otherwise acquire artifacts and other objects for addition to the collections of the Natural Museum; and

(3) specify criteria for use of the collections of the National Museum for appropriate purposes, including research, evaluation, education, and method of display.

(d) Authority

Subject to the general policies of the Board of Regents, the Board of Trustees shall have authority to—

(1) provide for restoration, preservation, and maintenance of the collections of the National Museum;

(2) solicit funds for the National Museum and determine the purposes to which such funds shall be applied; and

(3) approve expenditures from the endowment of the National Museum for any purpose of the Museum.

(e) Initial appointments to Board of Trustees

(1) Membership

The initial membership of the Board of Trustees shall consist of—

(A) the Secretary of the Smithsonian Institution;

(B) an Assistant Secretary of the Smithsonian Institution appointed by the Board of Regents;

(C) 8 individuals appointed by the Board of Regents; and

(D) 15 individuals, each of whom shall be a member of the board of trustees of the Heye Museum, appointed by the Board of Regents from a list of nominees recommended by the board of trustees of the Heye Museum.

(2) Special rule

At least 7 of the 23 members appointed under subparagraphs (C) and (D) of paragraph (1) shall be Indians.

(3) Terms

The trustee appointed under paragraph (1)(B) shall serve at the pleasure of the Board of Regents. The terms of the trustees appointed under subparagraph (C) or (D) of paragraph (1) shall be 3 years, beginning on the date of the transfer of the Heye Foundation assets to the Smithsonian Institution.

(4) Vacancies

Any vacancy shall be filled only for the remainder of the term involved. Any vacancy appointment under paragraph (1)(D) shall not be subject to the source and recommendation requirements of that paragraph, but shall be subject to paragraph (2).

(f) Subsequent appointments to Board of Trustees

(1) Membership

Upon the expiration of the terms under subsection (e) of this section, the Board of Trustees shall consist of—

(A) the Secretary of the Smithsonian Institution;

(B) a senior official of the Smithsonian Institution appointed by the Board of Regents; and

(C) 23 individuals appointed by the Board of Regents from a list of nominees recommended by the Board of Trustees.

(2) Special rule

At least 12 of the 23 members appointed under paragraph (1)(C) shall be Indians.

(3) Terms

The trustee appointed under paragraph (1)(B) shall serve at the pleasure of the Board of Regents. Except as otherwise provided in the next sentence, the terms of members appointed under paragraph (1)(C) shall be 3 years. Of the members first appointed under paragraph (1)(C)—

(A) 7 members, 4 of whom shall be Indians, shall be appointed for a term of one year, as designated at the time of appointment; and

(B) 8 members, 4 of whom shall be Indians, shall be appointed for a term of 2 years, as designated at the time of appointment.

(4) Vacancies

Any vacancy shall be filled only for the remainder of the term involved.

(g) Quorum

A majority of the members of the Board of Trustees then in office shall constitute a quorum.

(h) Expenses

Members of the Board shall be entitled (to the same extent as provided in section 5703 of title 5 with respect to employees serving intermittently in the Government service) to per diem, travel, and transportation expenses for each day (including travel time) during which they are engaged in the performance of their duties.

(Pub. L. 101-185, Sec. 5, Nov. 28, 1989, 103 Stat. 1337; Pub. L. 104-278, Sec. 2, Oct. 9, 1996, 110 Stat. 3355.)

Amendments

1996—Subsec. (f)(1)(B). Pub. L. 104-278 substituted ``a senior official'' for ``an Assistant Secretary''.

Sec. 80q-4. Director and staff of National Museum

(a) In general

The Secretary of the Smithsonian Institution shall appoint—

(1) a Director who, subject to the policies of the Board of Trustees, shall manage the National Museum; and

(2) other employees of the National Museum, to serve under the Director.

(b) Offer of employment to Heye Foundation employees

Each employee of the Heye Museum on the day before the date of the transfer of the Heye Foundation assets to the Smithsonian Institution shall be offered employment with the Smithsonian Institution—

(1) under the usual terms of such employment; and

(2) at a rate of pay not less than the rate applicable to the employee on the day before the date of the transfer.

(c) Applicability of certain civil service laws

The Secretary may—

(1) appoint the Director, 2 employees under subsection (a)(2) of this section, and the employees under subsection (b) of this section without regard to the provisions of title 5, governing appointments in the competitive service;

(2) fix the pay of the Director and such 2 employees without regard to the provisions of chapter 51 and subchapter III of chapter 53 of such title, relating to classification and General Schedule pay rates; and

(3) fix the pay of the employees under subsection (b) of this section in accordance with the provisions of chapter 51 and subchapter III of chapter 53 of such title, relating to classification and General Schedule pay rates, subject to subsection (b)(2) of this section.

(Pub. L. 101-185, Sec. 6, Nov. 28, 1989, 103 Stat. 1339.)

References in Text

The provisions of title 5 governing appointments in the competitive service, referred to in subsec. (c)(1), are classified generally to section 3301 et seq. of Title 5, Government Organization and Employees.

Sec. 80q-5. Museum facilities

(a) National Museum mall facility

The Board of Regents shall plan, design, and construct a facility on the area bounded by Third Street, Maryland Avenue, Independence Avenue, Fourth Street, and Jefferson Drive, Southwest, in the District of Columbia to house the portion of the National Museum to be located in the District of Columbia. The Board of Regents shall pay not more than 2/3 of the total cost of planning, designing, and constructing the facility from funds appropriated to the Board of Regents. The remainder of the costs shall be paid from non-Federal sources.

(b) National Museum Heye Center facility

(1) Lease of space from GSA

(A) Terms

Notwithstanding section 490(j) of title 40, the Administrator of General Services may lease, at a nominal charge, to the Smithsonian Institution space in the Old United States Custom House at One Bowling Green, New York, New York, to house the portion of the National Museum to be located in the city of New York. The lease shall be subject to such terms as may be mutually agreed upon by the Administrator and the Secretary of the Smithsonian Institution. The term of the lease shall not be less than 99 years.

(B) Reimbursement of Federal buildings fund

The Administrator of General Services may reimburse the fund established by section 490(f) of title 40 for the difference between the amount charged to the Smithsonian Institution for leasing space under this paragraph and the commercial charge under section 490(j) of title 40 which, but for this paragraph, would apply to the leasing of such space. There are authorized to be appropriated to the Administrator such sums as may be necessary to carry out this subparagraph for fiscal years beginning after September 30, 1990.

(2) Construction

(A) Museum facility

The Board of Regents shall plan, design, and construct a significant facility for the National Museum in the space leased under paragraph (1).

(B) Auditorium and loading dock facility

The Administrator of General Services shall plan, design, and construct an auditorium and loading dock in the Old United States Custom House at One Bowling Green, New York, New York, for the shared use of all the occupants of the building, including the National Museum.

(C) Square footage

The facilities to be constructed under this paragraph shall have, in the aggregate, a total square footage of approximately 82,500 square feet.

(3) Repairs and alterations

After construction of the facility under paragraph (2)(A), repairs and alterations of the facility shall be the responsibility of the Board of Regents.

(4) Reimbursement of GSA

The Board of Regents shall reimburse the Administrator for the Smithsonian Institution's pro rata share of the cost of utilities, maintenance, cleaning, and other services incurred with respect to the space leased under paragraph (1) and the full cost of any repairs or alterations made by the General Services Administration at the request of the Smithsonian Institution with respect to the space.

(5) Cost sharing

(A) General rules

The Board of Regents shall pay \1/3\ of the costs of planning, designing, and constructing the facility under paragraph (2)(A) from funds appropriated to the Board of Regents. The remainder of the costs shall be paid from non- Federal sources.

(B) Responsibilities of New York City and State

Of the costs which are required to be paid from non-Federal sources under this paragraph, the city of New York, New York, and the State of New York have each agreed to pay $8,000,000 or an amount equal to \1/3\ of the costs of planning, designing, and constructing the facility under paragraph (2)(A), whichever is less. Such payments shall be made to the Board of Regents in accordance with a payment schedule to be agreed upon by the city and State and the Board of Regents.

(C) Limitation on obligations of Federal funds

Federal funds may not be obligated for actual construction of a facility under paragraph (2)(A) in a fiscal year until non- Federal sources have paid to the Board of Regents the non- Federal share of such costs which the Board of Regents estimates will be incurred in such year.

(6) Designation

The facility to be constructed under paragraph (2)(A) shall be known and designated as the ``George Gustav Heye Center of the National Museum of the American Indian''.

(c) Museum Support Center facility

The Board of Regents shall plan, design, and construct a facility for the conservation and storage of the collections of the National Museum at the Museum Support Center of the Smithsonian Institution.

(d) Minimum square footage

The facilities to be constructed under this section shall have, in the aggregate, a total square footage of at least 400,000 square feet.

(e) Authority to contract with GSA

The Board of Regents and the Administrator of General Services may enter into such agreements as may be necessary for planning, designing, and constructing facilities under this section (other than subsection (b)(2)(B)). Under such agreements, the Board of Regents shall transfer to the Administrator, from funds available for planning, designing, and constructing such facilities, such amounts as may be necessary for expenses of the General Services Administration with respect to planning, designing, and constructing such facilities.

(f) Limitation on obligation of Federal funds

Notwithstanding any other provision of this subchapter, funds appropriated for carrying out this section may not be obligated for actual construction of any facility under this section until the 60th day after the date on which the Board of Regents transmits to Congress a written analysis of the total estimated cost of the construction and a cost-sharing plan projecting the amount for Federal appropriations and for non-Federal contributions for the construction on a fiscal year basis.

(Pub. L. 101-185, Sec. 7, Nov. 28, 1989, 103 Stat. 1339.)

Sec. 80q-6. Custom House office space and auditorium

(a) Repairs and alterations

The Administrator of General Services shall make such repairs and alterations as may be necessary in the portion of the Old United States Custom House at One Bowling Green, New York, New York, which is not leased to the Board of Regents under section 80q-5(b) of this title and which, as of November 28, 1989, has not been altered.

(b) Authorization of appropriation

There is authorized to be appropriated to the Administrator of General Services $25,000,000 from the fund established pursuant to section 490(f) of title 40 to carry out this section and section 80q-5(b)(2)(B) of this title.

(Pub. L. 101-185, Sec. 8, Nov. 28, 1989, 103 Stat. 1341.)

Section Referred to in Other Sections

This section is referred to in section 80q-15 of this title.

Sec. 80q-7. Audubon Terrace

(a) In general

The Board of Regents shall—
(1) assure that, on the date on which a qualified successor to the Heye Foundation at Audubon Terrace first takes possession of Audubon Terrace, an

area of at least 2,000 square feet at that facility is accessible to the public and physically suitable for exhibition of museum objects and for related exhibition activities;

    (2) upon written agreement between the Board and any qualified successor, lend objects from the collections of the Smithsonian Institution to the successor for exhibition at Audubon Terrace; and

    (3) upon written agreement between the Board and any qualified successor, provide training, scholarship, technical, and other assistance (other than operating funds) with respect to the area referred to in paragraph (1) for the purposes described in that paragraph.

(b) Determination of charges

    Any charge by the Board of Regents for activities pursuant to agreements under paragraph (2) or (3) of subsection (a) of this section shall be determined according to the ability of the successor to pay.

(c) Definition

    As used in this section, the terms ``qualified successor to the Heye Foundation at Audubon Terrace'', ``qualified successor'', and,\1\ ``successor'' mean an organization described in section 501(c)(3) of title 26, and exempt from tax under section 501(a) of title 26, that, as determined by the Board of Regents—

    (1) is a successor occupant to the Heye Foundation at Audubon Terrace, 3753 Broadway, New York, New York;

    (2) is qualified to operate the area referred to in paragraph (1) for the purposes described in that paragraph; and

    (3) is committed to making a good faith effort to respond to community cultural interests in such operation.

(Pub. L. 101-185, Sec. 9, Nov. 28, 1989, 103 Stat. 1342.)

Sec. 80q-8. Board of Regents functions with respect to certain agreements and programs

(a) Priority to be given to Indian organizations with respect to certain agreements

    In entering into agreements with museums and other educational and cultural organizations to—

    (1) lend Native American artifacts and objects from any collection of the Smithsonian Institution;

    (2) sponsor or coordinate traveling exhibitions of artifacts and objects; or

    (3) provide training or technical assistance;

the Board of Regents shall give priority to agreements with Indian organizations, including Indian tribes, museums, cultural centers, educational institutions, libraries, and archives. Such agreements may provide that loans or services to such organizations may be furnished by the Smithsonian Institution at minimal or no cost.

(b) Indian programs

    The Board of Regents may establish—

    (1) programs to serve Indian tribes and communities; and

    (2) in cooperation with educational institutions, including tribally controlled community colleges (as defined in section 1801 of title 25), programs to enhance the opportunities for Indians in the areas of museum studies, management, and research.

(c) Indian Museum Management Fellowships

The Board of Regents shall establish an Indian Museum Management Fellowship program to provide stipend support to Indians for training in museum development and management.

(d) Authorization of appropriations

There is authorized to be appropriated $2,000,000 for each fiscal year, beginning with fiscal year 1991, to carry out subsections (b) and (c) of this section.

(Pub. L. 101-185, Sec. 10, Nov. 28, 1989, 103 Stat. 1342.)

Section Referred to in Other Sections

This section is referred to in section 80q-15 of this title.

Sec. 80q-9. Inventory, identification, and return of Indian human remains and Indian funerary objects in possession of Smithsonian Institution

(a) Inventory and identification

(1) The Secretary of the Smithsonian Institution, in consultation and cooperation with traditional Indian religious leaders and government officials of Indian tribes, shall—

(A) inventory the Indian human remains and Indian funerary objects in the possession or control of the Smithsonian Institution; and

(B) using the best available scientific and historical documentation, identify the origins of such remains and objects.

(2) The inventory made by the Secretary of the Smithsonian Institution under paragraph (1) shall be completed not later than June 1, 1998.

(3) For purposes of this subsection, the term ``inventory'' means a simple, itemized list that, to the extent practicable, identifies, based upon available information held by the Smithsonian Institution, the geographic and cultural affiliation of the remains and objects referred to in paragraph (1).

(b) Notice in case of identification of tribal origin

If the tribal origin of any Indian human remains or Indian funerary object is identified by a preponderance of the evidence, the Secretary shall so notify any affected Indian tribe at the earliest opportunity.

(c) Return of Indian human remains and associated Indian funerary objects

If any Indian human remains are identified by a preponderance of the evidence as those of a particular individual or as those of an individual culturally affiliated with a particular Indian tribe, the Secretary, upon the request of the descendants of such individual or of the Indian tribe shall expeditiously return such remains (together with any associated funerary objects) to the descendants or tribe, as the case may be.

(d) Return of Indian funerary objects not associated with Indian human remains

If any Indian funerary object not associated with Indian human remains is identified by a preponderance of the evidence as having been removed from a specific burial site of an individual culturally affiliated with a particular Indian tribe, the Secretary, upon the request of the Indian tribe, shall expeditiously return such object to the tribe.

(e) Interpretation

Nothing in this section shall be interpreted as—

(1) limiting the authority of the Smithsonian Institution to return or repatriate Indian human remains or Indian funerary objects to Indian tribes or individuals; or

(2) delaying actions on pending repatriation requests, denying or otherwise affecting access to the courts, or limiting any procedural or substantive rights which may otherwise be secured to Indian tribes or individuals.

(f) Authorization of appropriations

There is authorized to be appropriated $1,000,000 for fiscal year 1991 and such sums as may be necessary for succeeding fiscal years to carry out this section and section 80q-9a of this title.

(Pub. L. 101-185, Sec. 11, Nov. 28, 1989, 103 Stat. 1343; Pub. L. 104-278, Sec. 3, Oct. 9, 1996, 110 Stat. 3355.)

Amendments

1996—Subsec. (a). Pub. L. 104-278, Sec. 3(a), designated existing provisions as par. (1), added pars. (2) and (3), and redesignated former pars. (1) and (2) as subpars. (A) and (B), respectively, of par. (1).Subsec. (f). Pub. L. 104-278, Sec. 3(b), inserted ``and section 80q-9a of this title'' after ``to carry out this section''.

Section Referred to in Other Sections

This section is referred to in sections 80q-10, 80q-11, 80q-12, 80q-15 of this title.

Sec. 80q-9a. Summary and repatriation of unassociated funerary objects, sacred objects, and cultural patrimony

(a) Summary

Not later than December 31, 1996, the Secretary of the Smithsonian Institution shall provide a written summary that contains a summary of unassociated funerary objects, sacred objects, and objects of cultural patrimony (as those terms are defined in subparagraphs (B), (C), and (D), respectively, of section 3001(3) of title 25, based upon available information held by the Smithsonian Institution. The summary required under this sectionshall include, at a minimum, the information required under section 3004 of title 25.

(b) Repatriation

Where cultural affiliation of Native American unassociated funerary objects, sacred objects, and objects of cultural patrimony has been established in the summary prepared pursuant to subsection (a) of this section, or where a requesting Indian tribe or Native Hawaiian organization can show cultural affiliation by a preponderance of the evidence based upon geographical, kinship, biological, archaeological, anthropological, linguistic, folkloric, oral traditional, historical, or other relevant information or expert opinion, then the Smithsonian Institution shall expeditiously return such unassociated funerary object, sacred object, or object of cultural patrimony where—

(1) the requesting party is the direct lineal descendant of an individual who owned the unassociated funerary object or sacred object;

(2) the requesting Indian tribe or Native Hawaiian organization can show that the object was owned or controlled by the Indian tribe or Native Hawaiian organization; or

(3) the requesting Indian tribe or Native Hawaiian organization can show
that the unassociated funerary object or sacred object was owned or controlled by
a member thereof, provided that in the case where an unassociated funerary
object or sacred object was owned by a member thereof, there are no identifiable
lineal descendants of said member or the lineal descendants, upon notice, have
failed to make a claim for the object.

(c) Standard of repatriation

If a known lineal descendant or an Indian tribe or Native Hawaiian organization
requests the return of Native American unassociated funerary objects, sacred objects, or
objects of cultural patrimony pursuant to this subchapter and presents evidence which, if
standing alone before the introduction of evidence to the contrary, would support a finding that the Smithsonian Institution did not have the right of possession, then the
Smithsonian Institution shall return such objects unless it can overcome such inference
and prove that it has a right of possession to the objects.

(d) Museum obligation

Any museum of the Smithsonian Institution which repatriates any item in good faith
pursuant to this subchapter shall not be liable for claims by an aggrieved party or for
claims of fiduciary duty, public trust, or violations of applicable law that are inconsistent
with the provisions of this subchapter.

(e) Statutory construction

Nothing in this section may be construed to prevent the Secretary of the Smithsonian
Institution, with respect to any museum of the Smithsonian Institution, from making an
inventory or preparing a written summary or carrying out the repatriation of unassociated funerary objects, sacred objects, or objects of cultural patrimony in a manner that
exceeds the requirements of this subchapter.

(f) ``Native Hawaiian organization'' defined

For purposes of this section, the term ``Native Hawaiian organization'' has the meaning provided that term in section 3001(11) of title 25.

(Pub. L. 101-185, Sec. 11A, as added Pub. L. 104-278, Sec. 4, Oct. 9, 1996, 110 Stat. 3355.)

Section Referred to in Other Sections

This section is referred to in sections 80q-9, 80q-10 of this title.

**Sec. 80q-10. Special committee to review inventory, identification, and return of Indian
human remains and Indian funerary objects**

(a) Establishment; duties

Not later than 120 days after November 28, 1989, the Secretary of the Smithsonian
Institution shall appoint a special committee to monitor and review the inventory, identification, and return of Indian human remains and Indian funerary objects under section
80q-9 of this title and unassociated funerary objects, sacred objects, and objects of cultural
patrimony under section 80q-9a of this title. In carrying out its duties, the committee
shall—

(1) with respect to the inventory and identification, ensure fair and objective consideration and assessment of all relevant evidence;

(2) upon the request of any affected party or otherwise, review any finding
relating to the origin or the return of such remains or objects;

(3) facilitate the resolution of any dispute that may arise between Indian tribes with respect to the return of such remains or objects; and

(4) perform such other related functions as the Secretary may assign.

(b) Membership

The committee shall consist of 7 members, of whom—

(1) 4 members shall be appointed from among nominations submitted by Indian tribes and organizations;

(2) at least 2 members shall be traditional Indian religious leaders; and

(3) the Secretary shall designate one member as chairman.

The Secretary may not appoint to the committee any individual who is an officer or employee of the Government (including the Smithsonian Institution) or any individual who is otherwise affiliated with the Smithsonian Institution.

(c) Access

The Secretary shall ensure that the members of the committee have full and free access to the Indian human remains and Indian funerary objects subject to section 80q-9 of this title and to any related evidence, including scientific and historical documents.

(d) Pay and expenses of members

Members of the committee shall—

(1) be paid the daily equivalent of the annual rate of basic pay payable for grade GS-18 of the General schedule under section 5332 of title 5; and

(2) be entitled (to the same extent as provided in section 5703 of such title, with respect to employees serving intermittently in the Government service) to per diem, travel, and transportation expenses;

for each day (including travel time) during which they are engaged in the performance of their duties.

(e) Rules and administrative support

The Secretary shall prescribe regulations and provide administrative support for the committee.

(f) Report and termination

At the conclusion of the work of the committee, the Secretary shall so certify by report to the Congress. The committee shall cease to exist 120 days after the submission of the report.

(g) Nonapplicability of Federal Advisory Committee Act

The Federal Advisory Committee Act (5 U.S.C. App.) shall not apply to the committee.

(h) Authorization of appropriations

There is authorized to be appropriated $250,000 for fiscal year 1991 and such sums as may be necessary for succeeding fiscal years to carry out this section.

(Pub. L. 101-185, Sec. 12, Nov. 28, 1989, 103 Stat. 1344; Pub. L. 104-278, Sec. 5, Oct. 9, 1996, 110 Stat. 3357.)

References in Text

The Federal Advisory Committee Act, referred to in subsec. (g), is Pub. L. 92-463, Oct. 6, 1972, 86 Stat. 770, as amended, which is set out in the Appendix to Title 5, Government Organization and Employees.

Amendments

1996—Subsec. (a). Pub. L. 104-278, Sec. 5(1), in first sentence, inserted ``and unassociated funerary objects, sacred objects, and objects of cultural patrimony under section 80q-9a of this title'' before period.

Subsec. (b). Pub. L. 104-278, Sec. 5(2)(A), substituted ``7 members'' for ``five members'' in introductory provisions.

Subsec. (b)(1). Pub. L. 104-278, Sec. 5(2)(B), substituted ``4 members'' for ``three members'' and struck out ``and'' at end.

Subsec. (b)(2), (3). Pub. L. 104-278, Sec. 5(2)(C), (D), added par. (2) and redesignated former par. (2) as (3).

References in Other Laws to GS-16, 17, or 18 Pay Rates

References in laws to the rates of pay for GS-16, 17, or 18, or to maximum rates of pay under the General Schedule, to be considered references to rates payable under specified sections of Title 5, Government Organization and Employees, see section 529 [title I, Sec. 101(c)(1)] of Pub. L. 101-509, set out in a note under section 5376 of Title 5.

Section Referred to in Other Sections

This section is referred to in sections 80q-11, 80q-15 of this title.

Sec. 80q-11. Inventory, identification, and return of Native Hawaiian human remains and Native Hawaiian funerary objects in possession of Smithsonian Institution

(a) In general

The Secretary of the Smithsonian Institution shall—

(1) in conjunction with the inventory and identification under section 80q-9 of this title, inventory and identify the Native Hawaiian human remains and Native Hawaiian funerary objects in the possession of the Smithsonian Institution;

(2) enter into an agreement with appropriate Native Hawaiian organizations with expertise in Native Hawaiian affairs (which may include the Office of Hawaiian Affairs and the Malama I Na Kupuna O Hawai'i Nei) to provide for the return of such human remains and funerary objects; and

(3) to the greatest extent practicable, apply, with respect to such human remains and funerary objects, the principles and procedures set forth in sections 80q-9 and 80q-10 of this title with respect to the Indian human remains and Indian funerary objects in the possession of the Smithsonian Institution.

(b) Definitions

As used in this section—

(1) the term ``Malama I Na Kupuna O Hawai'i Nei'' means the nonprofit, Native Hawaiian organization, incorporated under the laws of the State of Hawaii by that name on April 17, 1989, the purpose of which is to provide guidance and expertise in decisions dealing with Native Hawaiian cultural issues, particularly burial issues; and

(2) the term ``Office of Hawaiian Affairs'' means the Office of Hawaiian Affairs established by the Constitution of the State of Hawaii.

(Pub. L. 101-185, Sec. 13, Nov. 28, 1989, 103 Stat. 1345.)

Sec. 80q-12. Grants by Secretary of the Interior to assist Indian tribes with respect to agreements for return of Indian human remains and Indian funerary objects

(a) In general

The Secretary of the Interior may make grants to Indian tribes to assist such tribes in reaching and carrying out agreements with—
(1) the Board of Regents for the return of Indian human remains and Indian funerary objects under section 80q-9 of this title; and
(2) other Federal and non-Federal entities for additional returns of Indian human remains and Indian funerary objects.

(b) Authorization of appropriations

There is authorized to be appropriated $1,000,000 for fiscal year 1991 and such sums as may be necessary for succeeding fiscal years for grants under subsection (a) of this section.

(Pub. L. 101-185, Sec. 14, Nov. 28, 1989, 103 Stat. 1345.)

Section Referred to in Other Sections

This section is referred to in section 80q-15 of this title.

Sec. 80q-13. Grants by Secretary of the Interior to assist Indian organizations with respect to renovation and repair of museum facilities and exhibit facilities

(a) Grants

The Secretary of the Interior may make grants to Indian organizations, including Indian tribes, museums, cultural centers, educational institutions, libraries, and archives, for renovation and repair of museum facilities and exhibit facilities to enable such organizations to exhibit objects and artifacts on loan from the collections of the Smithsonian Institution or from other sources. Such grants may be made only from the Tribal Museum Endowment Fund.

(b) Indian organization contribution

In making grants under subsection (a) of this section, the Secretary may require the organization receiving the grant to contribute, in cash or in kind, not more than 50 percent of the cost of the renovation or repair involved. Such contribution may be derived from any source other than the Tribal Museum Endowment Fund.

(c) Tribal Museum Endowment Fund

(1) Establishment

There is established in the Treasury a fund, to be known as the ``Tribal Museum Endowment Fund'' (hereinafter in this subsection referred to as the ``Fund'') for the purpose of making grants under subsection (a) of this section. The Fund shall consist of (A) amounts deposited and credited under paragraph (2), (B) obligations obtained under paragraph (3), and (C) amounts appropriated pursuant to authorization under paragraph (5).

(2) Deposits and credits

The Secretary of the Interior is authorized to accept contributions to the Fund from non-Federal sources and shall deposit such contributions in the Fund. The Secretary of the Treasury shall credit to the Fund the interest on, and the proceeds from sale and redemption of, obligations held in the Fund.

(3) Investments

The Secretary of the Treasury may invest any portion of the Fund in interest-bearing obligations of the United States. Such obligations may be acquired on original issue or in the open market and may be held to maturity or sold in the open market. In making investments for the Fund, the Secretary of the Treasury shall consult the Secretary of the Interior with respect to maturities, purchases, and sales, taking into consideration the balance necessary to meet current grant requirements.

(4) Expenditures and capital preservation

Subject to appropriation, amounts derived from interest shall be available for expenditure from the Fund. The capital of the Fund shall not be available for expenditure.

(5) Authorization of appropriations

There is authorized to be appropriated to the Fund $2,000,000 for each fiscal year beginning with fiscal year 1992.

(d) Annual report

Not later than January 31 of each year, the Secretary of the Interior, in consultation with the Secretary of the Treasury, shall submit to the Congress a report of activities under this section, including a statement of—
(1) the financial condition of the Fund as of the end of the preceding fiscal year, with an analysis of the Fund transactions during that fiscal year; and
(2) the projected financial condition of the Fund, with an analysis of expected Fund transactions for the six fiscal years after that fiscal year.

(Pub. L. 101-185, Sec. 15, Nov. 28, 1989, 103 Stat. 1345.)

Native American Cultural Center in Oklahoma City, Oklahoma; Feasibility Study and Report

Pub. L. 102-196, Dec. 9, 1991, 105 Stat. 1620, directed Secretary of the Interior to conduct a study and make a report to Congress on the feasibility of establishing a Native American Cultural Center in Oklahoma City, Oklahoma, and made appropriations for that purpose.

Section Referred to in Other Sections

This section is referred to in section 80q-15 of this title.

Sec. 80q-14. Definitions

As used in this subchapter—

(1) the term ``Board of Regents'' means the Board of Regents of the Smithsonian Institution;

(2) the term ``Board of Trustees'' means the Board of Trustees of the National Museum of the American Indian;

(3) the term ``burial site'' means a natural or prepared physical location, whether below, on, or above the surface of the earth, into which, as a part of a death rite or ceremony of a culture, individual human remains are deposited;

(4) the term ``funerary object'' means an object that, as part of a death rite or ceremony of a culture, is intentionally placed with individual human remains, either at the time of burial or later;

(5) the term ``Heye Foundation assets'' means the collections, endowment, and all other property of the Heye Foundation (other than the interest of the Heye Foundation in Audubon Terrace) described in the Memorandum of Understanding between the Smithsonian Institution and the Heye Foundation, dated May 8, 1989, and the schedules attached to such memorandum;

(6) the term ``Heye Museum'' means the Museum of the American Indian, Heye Foundation;

(7) the term ``Indian'' means a member of an Indian tribe;

(8) the term ``Indian tribe'' has the meaning given that term in section 450b of title 25;

(9) the term ``National Museum'' means the National Museum of the American Indian established by section 80q-1 of this title;

(10) the term ``Native American'' means an individual of a tribe, people, or culture that is indigenous to the Americas and such term includes a Native Hawaiian; and

(11) the term ``Native Hawaiian'' means a member or descendant of the aboriginal people who, before 1778, occupied and exercised sovereignty in the area that now comprises the State of Hawaii.

(Pub. L. 101-185, Sec. 16, Nov. 28, 1989, 103 Stat. 1346.)

Sec. 80q-15. Authorization of appropriations

(a) Funding

There is authorized to be appropriated to the Board of Regents to carry out this sub-chapter (other than as provided in sections 80q-5(b)(1)(B), 80q-6, 80q-8, 80q-9, 80q-10, 80q-12, and 80q-13(c)(5) of this title)—

(1) $10,000,000 for fiscal year 1990; and

(2) such sums as may be necessary for each succeeding fiscal year.

(b) Period of availability

Funds appropriated under subsection (a) of this section shall remain available without fiscal year limitation for any period prior to the availability of the facilities to be constructed under section 80q-5 of this title for administrative and planning expenses and for the care and custody of the collections of the National Museum.

(Pub. L. 101-185, Sec. 17, Nov. 28, 1989, 103 Stat. 1347.)

Appendix Two

One Hundred first Congress of the United States of America

AT THE SECOND SESSION

Begun and held at the City of Washington on Tuesday, the twenty-third day of January, one thousand nine hundred and ninety

An Act

To Provide for the protection of Native American graves, and for other purposes,

Be it enacted by the Senate and House of Represenatatives of the United States of America in Congress assembled.

SECTION 1. SHORT TITLE.

This Act may be cited as the "**Native American Grave Protection and Repatriation Act**"

SEC. 2. DEFINITIONS.

For purposes of this Act, the term

(1) **"burial site"** means any natural or prepared physical location, whether originally below, on, or above the surface of the earth, into which as a part of the death rite or ceremony of a culture, individual human remains are deposited.

(2) **"cultural affiliation"** means that there is a relationship of shared group identity which can be reasonably traced historically or prehistorically between a present day Indian tribe or Native Hawaiian organization and an identifiable earlier group.

(3) **"cultural items"** means human remains and

>   (A) **"associated funerary objects"** which shall mean objects that, as a part of the death rite or ceremony of a culture, are reasonably believed to have been placed with individual human remains either at the time of death or

later, and both the human remains and associated funerary objects are presently in the possession or control of a federal agency or museum, except that other items exclusively made for burial purposes or to contain human remains shall be considered as associated funerary objects.

(B) **"unassociated funerary objects"** which shall mean objects that, as a part of the death rite or ceremony of a culture, are reasonably believed to have been placed with individual human remains either at the time of death or later, where the remains are not in the possession or control of the Federal agency or museum and the objects can be identified by a preponderance of the evidence as related to specific individuals or families or to known human remains or, by a preponderance of the evidence, as having been removed from a specific burial site of an individual culturally affiliated with a particular Indian tribe,

(C) **"sacred objects"** which shall mean specific ceremonial objects which are needed by traditional Native American religious leaders for the practice of traditional Native American religions by their present day adherents, and

(D) **"cultural patrimony"** which shall mean an object having ongoing historical, traditional, or cultural importance central to the Native American group or culture itself, rather than property owned by an individual Native American, and which, therefore, cannot be alienated, appropriated, or conveyed by any individual regardless of whether or not the individual is a member of the Indian tribe or Native Hawaiian organization and such object shall have been considered inalienable by such Native American group at the time the object was separated from such group.

(4) **"Federal agency"** means any department, agency, or instrumentality of the United States and shall include, except as may be inconsistent with the provisions of P.L. 101-185, the Smithsonian Institution.

(5) **"Federal lands"** means any land other than tribal lands which are controlled or owned by the United States.

(6) **"Hui Malama I Na Kupuna O Hawai'i Nei"** means the nonprofit, Native Hawaiian organization incorporated under the laws of the State of Hawaii by that name on April 17, 1989, for the purpose of providing guidance and expertise in decisions dealing with Native Hawaiian cultural issues, particularly burial issues.

(7) **"Indian tribe"** shall have the meaning given such term in section 4 of the Indian Self Determination and Education Assistance Act (25 U.S.C. 450b).

(8) **"museum"** means any institution or State or local government agency (including any institution of higher learning) that receives Federal funds and has possession of, or control over, Native American cultural items, but does not include any Federal agency.

(9) **"Native American"** means of, or relating to, a tribe, people, or culture that is indigenous to the United States.

(10) **"Native Hawaiian"** means any individual who is a descendant of the aboriginal people who, prior to 1778, occupied and exercised sovereignty in the area that now constitutes the State of Hawaii.

(11) **"Native Hawaiian organization"** means any organization which

> (A) serves and represents the interests of Native Hawaiians,
>
> (B) has a primary and stated purpose the provision of services to Native Hawaiians, and
>
> (C) has expertise in Native Hawaiian Affairs, and shall include the Office of Hawaiian Affairs and Hui Malama I Na Kupuna O Hawai'i Nei.

(12) **"Office of Hawaiian Affairs"** means the Office of Hawaiian Affairs established by the constitution of the State of Hawaii.

(13) **"right of possession"** means possession obtained with the voluntary consent of an individual or group that had authority of alienation. The original acquisition of a Native American funerary object, sacred object, or object of cultural patrimony from an Indian tribe or Native Hawaiian organization with the voluntary consent of an individual or group with authority to alienate such object is deemed to give right of possession of that object. The original acquisition of Native American human remains which were excavated, exhumed, or otherwise obtained with full knowledge and consent of the next of kin or the official governing body of the appropriate culturally affiliated Indian tribe or Native Hawaiian organization is deemed to give right of possession to those remains. Nothing in this paragraph shall affect the application of relevant State law to the right of ownership of unassociated funerary objects, sacred objects, or objects of cultural patrimony.

(14) **"Secretary"** means the Secretary of the Interior.

(15) **"tribal land"** means

> (A) all lands within the exterior boundaries of any Indian reservation;
>
> (B) all dependent Indian communities;
>
> (C) lands conveyed to, or subject to an interim conveyance of, Native Corporations pursuant to the Alaska Native Claims Settlement Act; and
>
> (D) any lands administered for the benefit of Native Hawaiians pursuant to the Hawaiian Homes Commission Act, 1920, and section 4 of Public Law 86-3.

SEC. 3. OWNERSHIP.

(a) NATIVE AMERICAN HUMAN REMAINS AND OBJECTS. The ownership or control of Native American cultural items which are excavated or discovered on Federal or triballands after the date of enactment of this Act shall be (with priority given in the order listed)

(l) in the case of Native American human remains and associated funerary objects, in the lineal descendants of the Native American; or

(2) in any case in which such lineal descendants cannot be ascertained, and in the case of unassociated funerary objects, sacred objects, and objects of cultural patrimony

> (A) in the Indian tribe or Native Hawaiian organization on whose tribal land such objects or remains were discovered;
>
> (B) in the Indian tribe or Native Hawaiian organization which has the closest cultural affiliation with such remains or objects and which, upon notice, states a claim for such remains or objects; or

(C) if the cultural affiliation of the objects cannot be reasonably ascertained and if the objects were discovered on Federal land that is recognized by a final judgement of the Indian Claims Commission as the aboriginal land of some Indian tribe

> (1) in the Indian tribe that is recognized as aboriginally occupying the area in which the objects were discovered, if upon notice, such tribe states a claim for such remains or objects, or

> (2) if it can be shown by a preponderance of the evidence that a different tribe has a stronger cultural relationship with the remains or objects than the tribe or organization specified in paragraph (1), in the Indian tribe that has the strongest demonstrated relationship, if upon notice, such tribe states a claim for such remains or objects.

(b) UNCLAIMED NATIVE AMERICAN HUMAN REMAINS AND OBJECTS. Native American cultural items not claimed under subsection (b) shall be disposed of in accordance with regulations promulgated by the Secretary in consultation with the review committee established under section 8, Native American groups, representatives of museums and the scientific community.

(c) INTENTIONAL EXCAVATION AND REMOVAL OF NATIVE AMERICAN HUMAN REMAINS AND OBJECTS. The intentional removal from or excavation of Native American cultural items from Federal or tribal lands for purposes of discovery, study, or removal of such items is permitted only if

> (1) such items are excavated or removed pursuant to a permit issued under section 4 of the Archaeological Resources Protection Act of 1979 (93 Stat. 721; 16 U.S.C. 470aa et seq.) which shall be consistent with this Act;

> (2) such items are excavated or removed after consultation with or, in the case of tribal lands, consent of the appropriate (if any) Indian tribe or Native Hawaiian organization;

> (3) the ownership and right of control of the disposition of such items shall be as provided in subsections (a) and (b); and

> (4) proof of consultation or consent under paragraph (2) is shown.

(d) INADVERTENT DISCOVERY OF NATIVE AMERICAN REMAINS AND OBJECTS.

(1) Any person who knows, or has reason to know, that such person has discovered Native American cultural items on Federal or tribal lands after the date of enactment of this Act shall notify, in writing, the Secretary of the Department, or head of any other agency or instrumentality of the United States, having primary management authority with respect to Federal lands and the appropriate Indian tribe or Native Hawaiian organization with respect to tribal lands, if known or readily ascertainable. If the discovery occurred in connection with an activity, including (but not limited to) construction, mining, logging, and agriculture, the person shall cease the activity in the area of the discovery, make a reasonable effort to protect the items discovered before resuming such activity, and provide notice under this subsection. The activity may resume after a reasonable amount of time and following notification under this subsection.

(2) The disposition of and control over any cultural items excavated or removed under this subsection shall be determined as provided for in this section.

(3) If the Secretary of the Interior consents, the responsibilities (in whole or in part) under paragraphs (1) and (2) of the Secretary of any department (other than the Department of the Interior) or the head of any other agency or instrumentality may be delegated to the Secretary with respect to any land managed by such other Secretary or agency head.

(e) RELINQUISHMENT. Nothing in this section shall prevent the governing body of an Indian tribe or Native Hawaiian organization from expressly relinquishing control over any Native American human remains, or title to or control over any funerary object, or sacred object.

SEC. 4. ILLEGAL TRAFFICKING.

(a) ILLEGAL TRAFFICKING. Chapter 53 of title 18, United States Code, is amended by adding at the end thereof the following new section:

SEC. 1170. ILLEGAL TRAFFICKING IN NATIVE AMERICAN HUMAN REMAINS AND CULTURAL ITEMS

"(a) Whoever knowingly sells, purchases, uses for profit, or transports for sale or profit, the human remains of a Native American without the right of possession to those remains as provided in the Native American Graves Protection and Repatriation Act shall be fined in accordance with this title, or imprisoned not more than 12 months, or both, and in the case of a second or subsequent violation, be fined in accordance with this title, or imprisoned not more than 5 years, or both.

"(b) Whoever knowingly sells, purchases, uses for profit, or transports for sale or profit any Native American cultural items obtained in violation of the Native American Graves Protection and Repatriation Act shall be fined in accordance with this title, imprisoned not more than one year, or both, and in the case of a second or subsequent violation, be fined in accordance with this title, imprisoned not more than 5 years, or both."

(b) TABLE OF CONTENTS. The table of contents for chapter 53 of title 18, United States Code, is amended by adding at the end thereof the following new item:

"1170. Illegal Trafficking in Native American Human Remains and Cultural Items."

SECTION. 5. INVENTORY FOR HUMAN REMAINS AND ASSOCIATED FUNERARY OBJECTS.

(a) IN GENERAL. Each Federal agency and each museum which has possession or control over holdings or collections of Native American human remains and associated funerary objects shall compile an inventory of such items and, to the extent possible based on information possessed by such museum or federal agency, identify the geographical and cultural affiliation of such item.

(b) REQUIREMENTS.

(1) The inventories and identifications required under subsection (a) shall be

(A) completed in consultation with tribal government and Native Hawaiian organization officials and traditional religious leaders;

(B) completed by not later than the date that is 5 years after the date of enactment of this Act, and

(C) made available both during the time they are being conducted and afterward to a review committee established under section 8.

(2) Upon request by an Indian tribe or Native Hawaiian organization which receives or should have received notice, a museum or federal agency shall supply additional available documentation to supplement the information required by subsection (a) of this section. The term "documentation" means a summary of existing museum or Federal agency records, including inventories or catalogues, relevant studies, or other pertinent data for the limited purpose of determining the geographical origin, cultural affiliation, and basic facts surrounding acquisition and accession of Native American human remains and associated funerary objects subject to this section. Such term does not mean, and this Act shall not be construed to be an authorization for, the initiation of new scientific studies of such remains and associated funerary objects or other means of acquiring or preserving additional scientific information from such remains and objects.

(c) EXTENSION OF TIME FOR INVENTORY. Any museum which has made a good faith effort to carry out an inventory and identification under this section, but which has been unable to complete the process, may appeal to the Secretary for an extension of the time requirements set forth in subsection (b)(1)(B). The Secretary may extend such time requirements for any such museum upon a finding of good faith effort. An indication of good faith shall include the development of a plan to carry out the inventory and identification process.

(d) NOTIFICATION. (1) If the cultural affiliation of any particular Native American human remains or associated funerary objects is determined pursuant to this section, the Federal agency or museum concerned shall, not later than 6 months after the completion of the inventory, notify the affected Indian tribes or Native Hawaiian organizations.

(2) The notice required by paragraph (1) shall include information

(A) which identifies each Native Amrican human remains or associated funerary objects and the circumstances surrounding its acquisition;

(B) which lists the human remains or associated funerary objects that are clearly identifiable as to tribal origin; and

(C) which lists the Native American human remains and associated funerary objects that are not clearly identifiable as being culturally affiliated with that Indian tribe or Native Hawaiian organization, but which, given the totality of circumstances surrounding acquisition of the remains or objects, are determined by a reasonable belief to be remains or objects culturally affiliated with the Indian tribe or Native Hawaiian organization.

(3) A copy of each notice provided under paragraph (1) shall be sent to the Secretary who shall publish each notice in the Federal Register.

(e) INVENTORY. For the purposes of this section, the term "inventory" means a simple itemized list that summarizes the information called for by this section.

SEC. 6. SUMMARY FOR UNASSOCIATED FUNERARY OBJECTS, SACRED OBJECTS, AND CULTURAL PATRIMONY.

(a) IN GENERAL. Each Federal agency or museum which has possession or control over holdings or collections of Native American unassociated funerary objects, sacred objects, or objects of cultural patrimony shall provide a written summary of such objects based upon available information held by such agency or museum. The summary shall describe the scope of the collection, kinds of objects included, reference to geographical location, means and period of acquisition and cultural affiliation, where readily ascertainable.

(b) REQUIREMENTS. (1) The summary required under subsection (a) shall be

(A) in lieu of an object-by-object inventory;

(B) followed by consultation with tribal government and Native Hawaiian organization officials and traditional religious leaders; and

(C) completed by not later than the date that is 3 years after the date of enactment of this Act.

(2) Upon request, Indian tribes and Native Hawaiian organizations shall have access to records, catalogues, relevant studies or other pertinent data for the limited purposes of determining the geographic origin, cultural affiliation, and basic facts surrounding acquisition and accession of Native American objects subject to this section. Such information shall be provided in a reasonable manner to be agreed upon by all parties.

SEC. 7. REPATRIATION.

(a) REPATRIATION OF NATIVE AMERICAN HUMAN REMAINS AND OBJECTS POSSESSED OR CONTROLLED BY FEDERAL AGENCIES AND MUSEUMS. (1) If, pursuant to section 5, the cultural affiliation of Native American human remains and associated funerary objects with a particular Indian tribe or Native Hawaiian organization is established, then the Federal agency or museum, upon the request of a known lineal descendant of the Native American or of the tribe or oranization and pursuant to subsections (b) and (e) of this section, shall expeditiously return such remains and associated funerary objects.

(2) If, pursuant to section 6, the cultural affiliation with a particular Indian tribe or Native Hawaiian organization is shown with respect to unassociated funerary objects, sacred objects or objects of cultural patrimony, then the Federal agency or museum, upon the request of the Indian tribe or Native Hawaiian organization and pursuant to subsections (b), (c) and (e) of this section, shall expeditiously return such objects.

(3) The return of cultural items covered by this Act shall be in consultation with the requesting lineal descendant or tribe or organization to determine the place and manner of delivery of such items.

(4) Where cultural affiliation of Native American human remains and funerary objects has not been established in an inventory prepared pursuant to section 5 or where Native American human remains and funerary objects are not included upon any such inventory, then, upon request and pursuant to subsections (b) and (e) and, in the case of unassociated funerary objects, subsection (c), such Native American human remains and funerary objects shall be expeditiously returned where the requesting Indian tribe or Native Hawaiian organization can show cultural affiliation by a preponderance of the evidence based upon geographical, kinship, biological, archaeological, anthropological, linguistic, folkloric, oral traditional, historical, or other relevant information or expert opinion.

(5) Upon request and pursuant to subsections (b), (c) and (e), sacred objects and objects of cultural patrimony shall be expeditiously returned where

(A) the requesting party is the direct lineal descendant of an individual who owned the sacred object;

(B) the requesting Indian tribe or Native Hawaiian organization can show that the object was owned or controlled by the tribe or organization; or

(C) the requesting Indian tribe or Native Hawaiian organization can show that the sacred object was owned or controlled by a member thereof, provided that in the case where a sacred object was owned by a member thereof, there are no identifiable lineal descendants of said member or the lineal descendants, upon notice, have failed to make a claim for the object under this Act.

(b) SCIENTIFIC STUDY. If the lineal descendant, Indian tribe, or Native Hawaiian organization requests the return of culturally affiliated Native American cultural items, the Federal agency or museum shall expeditiously return such items unless such items are indispensable for completion of a specific scientific study, the outcome of which would be of major benefit to the United States. Such items shall be returned by no later than 90 days after the date on which the scientific study is completed.

(c) STANDARD OF REPATRIATION. If a known lineal descendant or an Indian tribe or Native Hawaiian organization requests the return of Native American unassociated funerary objects, sacred objects or objects of cultural patrimony pursuant to this Act and presents evidence which, if standing alone before the introduction of evidence to the contrary, would support a finding that the Federal agency or musuem did not have the right of possession, then such agency or museum shall return such objects unless it can overcome such inference and prove that it has a right of possession to the objects.

(d) SHARING OF INFORMATION BY FEDERAL AGENCIES AND MUSEUMS. Any Federal agency or museum shall share what information it does possess regarding the object in question with the known lineal descendant, Indian tribe, or Native Hawaiian organization to assist in making a claim under this section.

(e) COMPETING CLAIMS. Where there are multiple requests for repatriation of any cultural item and, after complying with the requirements of this Act, the Federal agency or museum cannot clearly determine which requesting party is the most appropriate claimant, the agency or museum may retain such item until the requesting parties agree upon its disposition or the dispute is otherwise resolved pursuant to the provisions of this Act or by a court of competent jurisdiction.

(f) MUSEUM OBLIGATION. Any museum which repatriates any item in good faith pursuant to this Act shall not be liable for claims by an aggrieved party or for claims of breach of fiduciary duty, public trust, or violations of state law that are inconsistent with the provisions of this Act.

SEC. 8 REVIEW COMMITTEE.

(a) ESTABLISHMENT. Within 120 days after the date of enactment of this Act, the Secretary shall establish a committee to monitor and review the implementation of the inventory and identification process and repatriation activities required under sections 5, 6 and 7.

(b) MEMBERSHIP.

(1) The Committee established under subsection (a) shall be composed of 7 members,

(A) 3 of whom shall be appointed by the Secretary from nominations submitted by Indian tribes, Native Hawaiian organizations, and traditional Native American religious leaders with at least 2 of such persons being traditional Indian religious leaders;

(B) 3 of whom shall be appointed by the Secretary from nominations submitted by national museum organizations and scientific organizations; and

(C) 1 who shall be appointed by the Secretary from a list of persons developed and consented to by all of the members appointed pursuant to subparagraphs (A) and (B).

(2) The Secretary may not appoint Federal officers or employees to the committee.

(3) In the event vacancies shall occur, such vacancies shall be filled by the Secretary in the same manner as the original appointment within 90 days of the occurrence of such vacancy.

(4) Members of the committee established under subsection (a) shall serve without pay but shall be reimbursed at a rate equal to the daily rate for GS-18 of the General Schedule for each day (including travel time) for which the member is actually engaged in committee business. Each member shall receive travel expenses, including per diem in lieu of subsistence, in accordance with sections 5702 and 5703 of title 5, United States Code.

(c) **RESPONSIBILITIES.** The committee established under subsection (a) shall be responsible for

(1) designating one of the members of the committee as chairman;

(2) monitoring the inventory and identification process conducted under sections 5 and 6 to ensure a fair, objective consideration and assessment of all available relevant information and evidence;

(3) reviewing upon the request of any affected party and finding relating to

      (A) the identity or cultural affiliation of cultural items, or

      (B) the return of such items;

(4) facilitating the resolution of any disputes among Indian tribes, Native Hawaiian organizations, or lineal descendants and Federal agencies or museums relating to the return of such items including convening the parties to the dispute if deemed desirable;

(5) compiling an inventory of culturally unidentifiable human remains that are in the possession or control of each Federal agency and museum and recommending specific actions for developing a process for disposition of such remains;

(6) consulting with Indian tribes and Native Hawaiian organizations and museums on matters within the scope of the work of the committee affecting such tribes or organizations;

(7) consulting with the Secretary in the development of regulations to carry out this Act;

(8) performing such other related functions as the Secretary may assign to the committee; and

(9) making recommendations, if appropriate, regarding future care of cultural items which are to be repatriated.

(d) **RECOMMENDATIONS AND REPORT.** The committee shall make the recommendations under paragraph (c)(5) in consultation with Indian tribes and Native Hawaiian organizations and appropriate scientific and museum groups.

(e) **ACCESS.** The Secretary shall ensure that the committee established under subsection (a) and the members of the committee have reasonable access to Native American cultural items under review and to associated scientific and historical documents.

(f) DUTIES OF SECRETARY. The Secretary shall

(1) establish such rules and regulations for the committee as may be necessary, and

(2) provide reasonable administrative and staff support necessary for the deliberations of the committee.

(g) ANNUAL REPORT. The committee established under subsection (a) shall submit an annual report to the Congress on the progress made, and any barriers encountered, in implementing this section during the previous year.

(h) TERMINATION. The committee established under subsection (a) shall terminate at the end of the 120-day period beginning on the day the Secretary certifies, in a report submitted to Congress, that the work of the committee has been completed.

SEC. 9. PENALTY.

(a) PENALTY. (1) Any museum that fails to comply with the requirements of this Act may be assessed a civil penalty by the Secretary of Interior pursuant to procedures established by the Secretary through regulation. No penalty may be assessed under this subsection unless such museum is given notice and opportunity for a hearing with respect to such violation. Each violation shall be a separate offense.

(2) The amount of such penalty shall be determined under regulations promulgated pursuant to this Act, taking into account, in addition to other factors

(A) the archeological, historical or commercial value of the item involved;

(B) the damages suffered, both economic and non-economic, by an aggrieved party;

(C) the number of violations that have occurred.

(3) Any museum aggrieved by an order assessing a civil penalty under this subsection may file a petition of judicial review of such order with the United States District Court for the District of Columbia or for any other district in which the museum is located. Such a petition may only be filed within the 30-day period beginning on the date the order making such assessment was issued. The court shall hear such action on the administrative record and sustain the imposition of the penalty if it is supported by substantial evidence on the record considered as a whole.

(4) If any museum fails to pay an assessment of a civil penalty after a final administrative order has been issued and not appealed or after a final judgement has been rendered, the Attorney General may institute a civil action in a district court of the United States for any district in which such museum is located to collect the penalty and such court shall have jurisdiction to hear and decide such action. In such action, the validity and amount of such penalty shall not be subject to review.

(5) Hearings held during proceedings for the assessment of civil penalties authorized by this subsection shall be conducted in accordance with section 554 of Title 5. Subpoenas may be issued for the attendance and testimony of witnesses and the production of relevant papers, books and documents. Witnesses summoned shall be paid the same fees and mileage that are paid to witnesses in the courts of the United States. In the case of contumacy or refusal to obey a subpena served upon any person pursuant to this paragraph, the district court of the United States for any district in which such person is located, resides or transacts business, upon application by the United States and after notice to such person shall have jurisdiction to issue an order requiring such person to appear and give testimony or produce documents, or both, and any failure to obey such order of the court may be punished by such court as a contempt thereof.

SEC. 10. GRANTS.

(a) INDIAN TRIBES AND NATIVE HAWAIIAN ORGANIZATIONS. The Secretary is authorized to make grants to Indian tribes and Native Hawaiian organizations for the purpose of assisting such tribes and organizations in the repatriation of Native American cultural items.

(b) MUSEUMS. The Secretary is authorized to make grants to museums for the purpose of assisting the museums in conducting the inventories and identification required under sections 5 and 6.

SEC. 11. SAVINGS PROVISIONS.

Nothing in this Act shall be construed to

(1) limit the authority of any Federal agency or museum to

> (A) return or repatriate Native American cultural items to Indian tribes, Native Hawaiian organizations, or individuals, and

> (B) enter into any other agreement with the consent of the culturally affiliated tribe or organization as to the disposition of control over items covered by this Act;

(2) delay actions on repatriation requests that are pending on the date of enactment of this Act;

(3) deny or otherwise affect access to any court;

(4) limit any procedural or substantive right which may otherwise be secured to individuals or Indian tribes or Native Hawaiian organizations; or

(5) limit the application of any State or Federal law pertaining to theft or stolen property.

SEC. 12. SPECIAL RELATIONSHIP BETWEEN THE FEDERAL GOVERNMENT AND INDIAN TRIBES.

This Act reflects the unique relationship between the Federal government and Indian tribes and Native Hawaiian organizations and should not be construed to establish a precedent with respect to any other individual, organization or foreign government.

SEC. 13. REGULATIONS.

The Secretary shall promulgate regulations to carry out this Act within 12 months of enactment.

SEC. 14. AUTHORIZATION OF APPROPRIATIONS.

There is authorized to be appropriated such sums as may be necessary to carry out this Act.

SEC. 15. ENFORCEMENT.

The United States district courts shall have jurisdiction over any action brought by any person alleging a violation of this Act and shall have the authority to issue such orders as may be necessary to enforce the provisions of this Act.

Appendix Three

This agreement is entered into this Fifth day of December, 1996, by and between the National Museum of Natural History, hereinafter NMNH, and the Cheyenne and Arapaho Tribes of Oklahoma represented by and through the designated NAGPRA Representative of the Cheyenne Tribe, hereinafter referred to as CHEYENNE, to establish certain understandings and conclusions regarding the below-specified objects in the collections of the NMNH.

Whereas the NMNH and the CHEYENNE, under the authority of and on behalf of the Cheyenne Tribe and representatives of Cheyenne men and women, have engaged in repatriation of human remains and consultations regarding Cheyenne objects in the collections of NMNH pursuant to the provisions of the National Museum of the American Indian Act (20 USC Section 80q), and

Whereas the NMNH and representatives of the Cheyenne people have jointly identified the following thirty-six (36) funerary objects of Cheyenne origin in the collection of the NMNH that are subject to repatriation as funerary objects:

E008847	Willow Frame
E008848	Piece of Tanned Buffalo Robe
E008849	Tanned Buffalo Robe (entire)
E008850	Buffalo Rawhide (entire)
E008851	Buffalo Robe (entire)
E008852	Piece of Tanned Buffalo Hide
E008853	Piece of Tanned Buffalo Robe
E008854	Piece Buffalo Rawhide
E008855	Cradle Cover Hood of Buffalo Hide
E008856	Cradle Cover Hood
E008857	Red Trade Blanket (three points)

E008858	Red Trade Blanket (three points)
E008859	Blue Trade Blanket (three points)
E008860	Blue Trade Cloth
E008861	Trade Textile sewn into bag
E008862	White Trade Blanket (two and one-half points)
E008863	Sash or Scarf of trade cloth
E008864	Woven Shawl
E008865	Child's Jacket
E008866	Child's Knit Stockings
E008867	Child's Fur Cap
E008868	Cradle Cover Hood of Buffalo Hide
E008869	Moccasins
E008870	Leather Glove
E008871	Portion of Beaded Buffalo Hide
E008872	Paint-Bag
E008873	Beaded Belt
E008874	Belt Ornamented with Beads
E008875	Hide Lariat or Lashing
E008876	Willow Rod Bed
E008877	Belt Leather
E008878	Tobacco Pouch
E008879	Rawhide Line (three lengths)
E008905	German Silver Ornament
E008906	Necklace
E008907	Small Tin Dish

Whereas it is stipulated by both parties to this agreement that said objects listed above are subject to repatriation as funerary objects under the provisions of 20 USC Section 80q, and

Whereas the NMNH and the CHEYENNE wish to maintain a cooperative and mutually-beneficial relationship,

NOW, THEREFORE, the NMNH and the CHEYENNE agree as follows:

1)   That said objects subject to repatriation shall be retained by NMNH for purposes of continued preservation of the objects, and for purposes of research and educational studies conducted by NMNH staff, Cheyenne people, and scholars.

2)   Publication of photographs or exhibition/display of said objects by the parties or other entities or persons are prohibited without the written consent and approval of the Chairman, Department of Anthropology, National Museum of Natural History, and the Cheyenne people by and through the Cheyenne NAGPRA Representative or other official tribal designee in the event that a Cheyenne NAGPRA Representative does not exist.

3)   That in order for the Cheyenne people to have the opportunity to utilize their cultural resources in the collections of the NMNH, the NMNH agrees to make these objects available to the Cheyenne people through temporary loans for exhibition and visual study to the Cheyenne Cultural Center and other local or regional institutions as may be jointly agreed upon. The terms and conditions of such loans will be mutually arranged and agreed upon by the parties to this agreement and shall be the same or similar to standard NMNH practices for loans from its collections to other museums and cultural institutions.

4)   Any special considerations for the exhibition or conservation, sampling, handling, photographing, shipping, etc., of the objects will be detailed, discussed and agreed upon by the NMNH and the Cheyenne Cultural Center, Inc., prior to the execution of the activities.

SIGNED:

_____   _____
Robert W. Fri   Gordon Yellowman, Sr.
Director   Cheyenne NAGPRA
                                         Representative
National Museum of Natural History   Cheyenne and Arapaho Tribes of
                                         Oklahoma

Index